Praise for *Millionaire Teacher, Second Edition*

"The first edition of *Millionaire Teacher* had a huge readership because Andrew Hallam writes with such passion and conviction. This new edition deserves to reach an even larger audience. Andrew brings years of wisdom to his discussion of smart saving and simple, low-cost investing. Readers who follow this teacher's advice will retire at the top of their class."

—**Dan Bortolotti,** CFP, CIM, associate portfolio manager at PWL Capital, and creator of the *Canadian Couch Potato* blog

"*Millionaire Teacher, Second Edition* is packed with humor, solid evidence, and advice. It might be the clearest and most engaging investment book that has ever been written!"

—**Sam Instone,** founder and chief executive of AES International

"While there are scads of fine books on passive investing for US residents, until Andrew Hallam came along, non–US investors were left to the tender mercies of local brokers, advisors, and investment companies that serviced their clients in the same way that John Dillinger serviced banks. If you're in that boat and you've just come across *Millionaire Teacher, Second Edition,* consider yourself lucky: read, enjoy, and fatten up your portfolio!"

—**William J. Bernstein,** author of *A Splendid Exchange* and *The Investor's Manifesto*

"Andrew Hallam's second edition of *Millionaire Teacher* is perfect for novice investors. He recommends the right kind of investment products. He also demonstrates a strong awareness of how human emotions can sabotage even the best-laid plan. Hallam does a great job showing how to avoid this trap, whether you choose to invest on your own or you hire an advisory firm to build you a portfolio of index funds."

—**Larry Swedroe,** author of *Your Complete Guide to Factor-Based Investing,* and principal and director of research, The Buckingham Family of Financial Services

"Billionaire teacher Warren Buffett and millionaire teacher Andrew Hallam offer you the same advice and guarantee: invest in low-fee and low-tax index funds on a regular basis over your lifetime, and you too will be financially independent."

—**Robert P. Miles,** Warren Buffett scholar, and author of *Warren Buffett Wealth* and *The Warren Buffett CEO*

"If investing were a religion, the second edition of *Millionaire Teacher* would be the Holy Grail. Everyone with a pulse should read this book! I'm confident your time and effort will be rewarded."

—**Sonny Wadera,** MBA financial security advisor, Kelson Financial

"This is a must-read book for any first-time investor. Andrew Hallam helps build the framework for those looking to build real wealth. Hallam's simple, yet powerful, lessons of 'start young, spend less, do your homework, and keep costs low' cannot be overstated."

—**Ryan A. Hughes,** founder and
portfolio manager, Bull Oak Capital

"This book provides some great and simple guidelines for people who are serious about building and protecting their wealth. The principles provided are an excellent roadmap to financial security and peace of mind."

—**Richard E. Reyes,** CFP, The Financial Quarterback™,
Wealth and Business Planning Group, LLC, Maitland, FL

"*Millionaire Teacher, Second Edition* is one of those must-read books for both novice and experienced investors. Through experience and humor, the author identifies an approach that's in the best interest of investors, and he provides the evidence to back it up. Understand what you spend. Save and invest monthly into a well-diversified portfolio of index funds. Ignore the investment industry 'noise,' and manage your own emotions. This book offers the reader a clear path to prosperity!"

—**Chris Turnbull,** portfolio manager, Index House

"Managing one's financial life doesn't have to be rocket science. We have been living below our means and investing simply long before it became popular. Retired almost three decades now, we have been traveling the world, taking advantage of great weather, food, culture, and lifestyle. Andrew Hallam hits upon understandable and basic points that can make you wealthy too, and uses plain English, not fancy jargon, to get his message across."

—**Billy and Akaisha Kaderli,**
RetireEarlyLifestyle.com (Free Newsletter)

"As an industry veteran of more than 20 years, I know all too well how the financial services industry exploits people. But if you read Andrew's enjoyable book and follow his straightforward suggestions, you can simplify your life and save an amazing amount of money for you and your family!"

—**Mark Zoril,** AIF, and founder of PlanVisio

"Mr. Hallam teaches what you don't learn in school—how to be rich. He built a $1 million portfolio before he was 40 years old. With his nine rules of wealth he shows how you can, too. I recommend *Millionaire Teacher, Second Edition*. Class is in session."

—**Robin Speziale,** author of *Market Masters*

"*Millionaire Teacher, Second Edition* provides such smart and simple investing advice that it should be required reading for every investor. Using analogies and humor mixed with hard data, Andrew Hallam spells out an investing strategy that will outperform the vast majority of professional money managers—and with less than an hour a year of portfolio maintenance. How brilliant is that?!"

—**Joe Snyder,** CIM®, and product analyst,
Tangerine Investments

Millionaire
Teacher

Millionaire Teacher

The Nine Rules of Wealth You Should Have Learned in School

Second Edition

ANDREW HALLAM

WILEY

For Adam, Tyler, Matthias, Anna Claire,
Niklas, Abby, and Jeremy

Contents

Acknowledgments

I want to thank Ian McGugan, who first inspired me to write this book. He and Scott Burns have been great writing coaches. Nick Wallwork, my first publisher at John Wiley & Sons, offered to publish this book's first edition back in 2011. My continued thanks, Nick.

I also want to thank my friends at Singapore American School. You guided this book's first edition, helping to ensure that it was jargon-free.

Thank you, also, to the team at Wiley. Tula Weis, you're a great publisher to work with. I hope you enjoy many adventures to some of the coolest corners of the world. Julie Kerr, thanks for the excellent edits. I'm thrilled that you appear to be an ice hockey fan.

The rest of my production team at Wiley also deserves my gratitude. And I can't forget John S. Woerth, at Vanguard, who helped me with the charts.

Finally, this book wouldn't exist without the encouragement of my wife, Pele Hallam-Young.

Introduction

"Don't Stay In School." That's the title of a rap song on YouTube. More than 11 million people have viewed it. It was created by David Brown, a young twenty-something rapper with long, dyed red hair. He walks along a path in the trees and rants about the education system. Despite the provocative title, however, he isn't against school.

When I first saw the video, I shared it on Facebook. I'm not the sort of guy who posts pictures of his food. But if I decided to post a hamburger, about a dozen of my friends would politely click "like." So what do you think happened when I posted "Don't Stay In School"? In a popularity contest among my friends, a burger would have crushed it.

You see, I'm a schoolteacher. Most of my friends are teachers. The title, "Don't Stay In School," was a fly in a glass of wine. But those who watched the video saw the wisdom of its message.

The young rapper's beef is with the absence of real-world learning. Higher-level mathematics, for example, is mandatory in most schools. Everybody also learns some Shakespeare. But learning about laws, human rights, voting procedures, mortgages, how to get a job, and how to invest aren't mandatory.

I think most schools let us down. I first started to learn about money from a wealthy mentor. From there, I read more than 400 personal finance books before I turned 35. I boiled my learning down to nine rules of wealth that I should have learned in school. By applying them, I became a debt-free millionaire in my late 30s.

No, I didn't inherit money, nor did I take big risks.

I became a high school personal finance teacher. I worked at a school that viewed the subject as important.

Kids want to know about money. So do their parents. But most people run straight into adulthood with no more knowledge about building wealth than the typical eighth grader. Money is taboo.

Yes, I can hear your Aunt Matilda. "Talking about money really isn't polite." But that kind of thinking leads to huge personal debts, financial exploitation, and leveraged lifestyles on the edge. These problems are a lot like toenail fungus. They're tough to clear up. Mr. and Mrs. Jones didn't sign up for this.

But the Jones's spend most (or all) of their income. They don't know how to invest. They hire the wrong kinds of financial planners who usually rob them blind. They're at the whim of big mortgages, credit card companies, and a consumption-based treadmill. They make such huge mistakes because, in school, nobody taught them otherwise. That's why I wrote *Millionaire Teacher: The Nine Rules of Wealth You Should Have Learned in School*. Such rules are timeless.

So why did I write a second edition?

I wanted to update my examples. The investment landscape is also changing for the better. In the past, virtually every financial adviser stuffed their clients' portfolios with actively managed mutual funds. Such products layer the pockets of advisers and their firms. But they're bad for investors. Fortunately, people have demanded something better.

Enter the firms that many call Robo Advisers. Such firms have said, "Hey, people won't be conned forever. Let's offer something better." These firms follow the rules I outline in this book. They're companies worth knowing. Unlike most banks and investment firms, they don't play their clients for fools.

Other great investment products have also come on the market for DIY investors. They're simplifying the process. Vanguard, a fabulous US-based investment firm, has also spread its wings. Today, people around the world can use their products. This book explains how.

But why should you bother with my book when hundreds of others distill similar themes? To explain, I need to tell you why I wrote *Millionaire Teacher* in the first place. I used to teach at a private school. None of us were eligible for defined benefit pensions. For that reason, our money had to hum.

When I first arrived at the school, many of my colleagues knew that I was also a personal finance writer. They asked me questions about investing, so I volunteered to give after-school seminars. They were more popular than I had imagined.

But I wanted to deliver more than a handful of seminars. I wanted to find the simplest investment books I could and gift them to my colleagues. So I did just that. I bought 80 investment books that represented 12 different titles.

The next day, I posted an "all school" e-mail. "I have free investment books in my classroom," I wrote. "Please come and take one." They got gobbled up faster than cookies in a staffroom. Then, as if I were teaching a group of English students, I met the readers in small groups to discuss what they had learned.

But there was a problem. Many of the terms used by the financial authors were as decipherable as Egyptian hieroglyphics to my colleagues. Too many financial writers don't realize that much of what they write flies over the heads of the average person.

I told Ian McGugan. At the time, he was my editor at *MoneySense* magazine. "Write your own book," he said. But I couldn't do it alone. I asked for help. More than 100 of my friends and colleagues contributed to the book. Continuing to hold free financial seminars, I probably did more questioning than lecturing to find out what the average person understood about money so I could reach the broadest possible audience.

I shared my early drafts with non-financially minded friends. They all gave feedback, which I used to eliminate jargon and make things clear.

The result is this book: written by a millionaire teacher who listened closely to his students. In it, I share the nine rules of wealth you should have learned in school. You'll learn how to spend like a millionaire and invest with the very best, while avoiding the trappings of fear, greed, and the manipulations of those who want their hands on your hard-earned money.

I followed these timeless principles and became a debt-free millionaire in my 30s. Now let me pass them on to you.

RULE 1

Spend Like You Want to Grow Rich

I wasn't rich as a 30-year-old. Yet if I wanted to, I could have leased a Porsche, borrowed loads of money for an expensive, flashy home, and taken five-star holidays around the world. I would have looked rich, but instead, I would have been living on an umbilical cord of bank loans and credit cards. Things aren't always what they appear to be.

In 2004, I was tutoring an American boy in Singapore. His mom dropped him off at my house every Saturday. She drove the latest Jaguar, which in Singapore would have cost well over $250,000 (cars in Singapore are very expensive). They lived in a huge house, and she wore an elegant Rolex watch. I thought they were rich.

After a series of tutoring sessions the woman gave me a check. Smiling, she gushed about her family's latest overseas holiday and expressed how happy she was that I was helping her son.

The check she wrote was for $150. Climbing on my bicycle after she left, I pedaled down the street and deposited the check in the bank.

But here's the thing: the check bounced—she didn't have enough money in her account. This could, of course, happen to anyone. With this family, however, it happened with as much regularity as a Kathmandu power outage. Dreading the phone calls where she would implore me to wait a week before cashing the latest check finally took its toll. I eventually told her that I wouldn't be able to tutor her son anymore.

Was this supposed to be happening? After all, this woman had to be rich. She drove a Jaguar. She lived in a massive house. She wore a Rolex. Her husband was an investment banker. He should have been doing the backstroke in the pools of money he made.

It dawned on me that she might not have been rich at all. Just because someone collects a large paycheck and lives like Persian royalty doesn't necessarily mean he or she is rich.

The Hippocratic Rule of Wealth

If we're interested in building wealth, we should all make a pledge to ourselves much like a doctor's Hippocratic oath: above all, DO NO HARM. We're living in an era of instant gratification. If we want to communicate with someone half a world away, we can do that immediately with a text message or a phone call. If we want to purchase something and have it delivered to our door, it's possible to do that with a smartphone and a credit-card number—even if we don't have the money to pay for it.

Just like that seemingly wealthy American family in Singapore, it's easy to sabotage our future by blowing money we don't even have. The story of living beyond one's means can be heard around the world.

To stay out of harm's way financially, we need to build assets, not debts. One of the surest ways to build wealth over a lifetime is to spend far less than you make and intelligently invest the difference. But too many people hurt their financial health by failing to differentiate between their "wants" and their "needs."

Many of us know people who landed great jobs right out of college and started down a path of hyperconsumption. It usually began innocently. Perhaps, with their handy credit cards they bought a new dining room table. But then their plates and cutlery didn't match so they felt the pull to upgrade.

Then there's the couch, which now doesn't jibe with the fine dining room table. Thank God for Visa—time for a sofa upgrade. It doesn't take long, however, before our friends notice that the carpet doesn't match the new couch, so they scour advertisements for a deal on a Persian beauty. Next, they're dreaming about a new entertainment system, then a home renovation, followed by the well-deserved trip to Hawaii.

Rather than living the American Dream, they're stuck in a mythological Greek nightmare. Zeus punished Sisyphus by forcing him to continually roll a boulder up a mountain. It then rolled back down every time it neared the summit. Many consumers face the same relentless treadmill with their consumption habits. When they get close to paying off their debts, they reward themselves by adding weight to their Sisyphean stone. It knocks them back to the base of their own daunting mountain.

Buying something after saving for it (instead of buying it with a credit card) is so 1950s—at least, that's how many consumers see it. As a result, the twenty-first century has brought mountains of personal debt that often gets pushed under the rug.

Before we learn to invest to build wealth, we have to learn how to save. If we want to grow rich on a middle-class salary, we can't be average. We have to sidestep the consumption habits to which so many others have fallen victim.

The US Federal Reserve compiles annual credit card debt levels. Cardhub.com publishes those results. In 2015, the average US household owed $7,879 in outstanding credit card debt.[1] In 2015, *MarketWatch* news editor Quentin Fottrell reported that 15.4 percent of US homeowners have mortgage debt that is higher than their homes are actually worth.[2] That's surprising, considering that the United States may be the fourth cheapest place to buy a home in the world.

Numbeo.com compares global home costs relative to income. In 2016, it compared 102 countries. US homes were among the four cheapest. Only those in South Africa, Oman, and Saudi Arabia cost less, relative to income.[3]

Now here's where things get interesting. You might assume it's mostly low-salaried workers who overextend themselves. But that isn't true.

The late US author and wealth researcher, Thomas Stanley, had been surveying America's affluent since 1973. He found that most US homes valued at a million dollars or more (as of 2009) were not owned by millionaires. Instead, the majority of million-dollar homes were owned by nonmillionaires with large mortgages and very expensive tastes.[4] In sharp contrast, 90 percent of millionaires lived in homes valued at less than a million dollars.[5]

If there were such a thing as a financial Hippocratic oath, self-induced malpractice would be rampant. It's fine to spend extravagantly if you're truly wealthy. But regardless of how high people's salaries are, if they can't live well without their job, then they aren't truly rich.

How Would I Define Wealth?

It's important to make the distinction between real wealth and a wealthy pretense so that you don't get sucked into a lifestyle led by the wealthy pretenders of the world. Wealth itself is always relative. But for people to be considered wealthy, they should meet the following two criteria:

1. They should have enough money to never have to work again, if that's their choice.

2. They should have investments, a pension, or a trust fund that can provide them with twice the level of their country's median household income over a lifetime.

According to the US Census Bureau, the median US household income in 2014 was $53,657.[6] Based on my definition of wealth, if an American's investments can annually generate twice that amount ($107,314 or more), then that person is rich.

Earning double the median household in your home country—without having to work—is a dream worth attaining.

How Do Investments Generate Enough Cash?

Because this book will focus on building investments using the stock and bond markets, let's use a relative example. If John builds an investment portfolio of $2.5 million, then he could feasibly sell 4 percent of that portfolio each year, equating to roughly $100,000 annually, and never run out of money. (See,

"Retiring Early Using The 4 Percent Rule.") If his investments are able to continue growing by 6 to 7 percent a year, he could likely afford, over time, to sell slightly more of his investment portfolio each year to cover the rising costs of living.

Retiring Early Using The 4 Percent Rule

Billy and Akaisha Kaderli retired when they were just 38 years old. They have been retired for more than 25 years. They live off their investments. In fact, they have pulled more money out of their investment portfolio than their portfolio was worth when they first retired.

Does that mean they're almost broke? Not even close. Compound interest worked its magic. When they retired in 1991, they had $500,000. Today, they have a lot more money. How did they do it? They live frugally, in low-cost locations. They also followed the 4 percent rule.

In 2010, Philip L. Cooley, Carl M. Hubbard and Daniel T. Walz published a research paper in the *Journal of Financial Planning*.[7] They back-tested a variety of portfolio allocations between January 1926 and December 2009. They found that if investors withdrew an inflation-adjusted 4 percent per year, their money stood an excellent chance of lasting more than 30 years.

I wanted to see how it would have worked for Billy and Akaisha. They own an S&P 500 index. That means they invest the way that I describe in this book. They withdraw less than 4 percent from their investments in a year. But let's see what would have happened if they had taken out exactly 4 percent annually.

Over the past 25 years, their money would have kept growing. So if they took out 4 percent of their portfolio every year, they would have taken a total of $1,325,394 from their initial $500,000 portfolio. Yes, you read that right. They would also have plenty left. By April 30, 2016, despite those annual withdrawals, their portfolio would be valued at $1,855,686.

Frugal living, compound interest, and the 4 percent rule are powerful combinations.[8]

If John were in this position, I would consider him wealthy. If he also owned a Ferrari and a million-dollar home, then I'd consider him extremely wealthy.

But if John had an investment portfolio of $400,000, owned a million-dollar home with the help of a large mortgage, and leased a Ferrari, then John wouldn't be rich—even if his take-home pay exceeded $600,000 a year.

I'm not suggesting that we live like misers and save every penny we earn. I've tried that already (as I'll share with you) and it's not much fun. But if we want to grow rich we need a purposeful plan. Watching what we spend, so we can invest our money, is an important first step. If wealth building were a course that everyone took and if we were graded on it every year (even after high school), do you know who would fail? Professional basketball players.

Most National Basketball Association (NBA) players make millions of dollars a year. But are they rich? Most seem to be. But it's not how much money you make that counts: it's what you do with what you make. According to a 2008 *Toronto Star* article, a NBA Players' Association representative visiting the Toronto Raptors team once warned the players to temper their spending. He reminded them that 60 percent of retired NBA players go broke five years after they stop collecting their enormous NBA paychecks.[9] How can that happen? Sadly, the average NBA basketball player has very little (if any) financial common sense. Why would he? High schools don't prepare us for the financial world.

By following the concepts of wealth in this book, you can work your way toward financial independence. With a strong commitment to the rules, you could even grow wealthy—truly wealthy. This starts by following the first of my nine wealth rules: spend like you want to be rich. By minimizing the purchases that you don't really need, you can maximize your money for investment purposes.

Of course, that's easier said than done when you see so many others purchasing things that you would like to have as well. Instead of looking where you think the grass is greener, admire your own yard, and compare it, if you must, to my father's old car. Doing so can build a foundation of wealth. Let me explain how it worked for me.

Can You See the Road When You're Driving?

Riding shotgun as a 15-year-old in my dad's 1975 Datsun, I thought we were traveling a bit fast. I leaned over to look at the speedometer and noticed that it didn't work. "Dad," I asked, "how do you know how fast you're going if your speedometer doesn't work?"

My dad asked me to lift up the floor mat beneath my feet. "Fold it back," he grinned. There was a fist-sized hole in the floor beneath my feet, and I could see the rushing road below. "Who needs a speedometer when you can get a better feel for speed by looking at the road," he told me.

The following year, I turned 16. I bought my own car with cash that I had saved from working at a supermarket. It was a six-year-old 1980 Honda Civic. The speedometer worked, and best of all, there wasn't a draft at my feet. Because it was the nicest car in the family, I always felt like I was riding in style, which leads me to one of the greatest secrets of wealth building: your perceptions dictate your spending habits.

The surest way to grow rich over time is to start by spending a lot less than you make. If you can alter your perspective to be satisfied with what you have, then you won't be as tempted to blow your earnings. You'll be able to invest money over long periods of time, and thanks to the compounding miracles of the stock market, even middle-class wage earners eventually can amass sizable investment accounts. Thanks to my dad's car (which also leaked), I felt rich because I had a road-worthy steed that didn't leak from the roof and windows when it rained. Instead of comparing my car with those that were newer, faster, and cooler, I viewed my dad's car (which you could start with a screwdriver in the ignition slot) as the comparative benchmark.

Buddhists believe that "wanting" leads to suffering. In the case of the boy I tutored in Singapore, the family's insatiable appetite for fine things will only lead to pain. Their suffering will accelerate if the head of the family loses his job or wants to retire. It reminds me of a bumper sticker I once saw, parodying the infamous line of Snow White's dwarves: "I owe, I owe, it's off to work I go."

Why the Aspiring Rich Should Drive Rich People's Cars

If you want to improve your odds of growing rich, you don't have to drive a piece of junk. Where's the fun in that? How about driving the sort of car driven by the average US millionaire? At first it might sound counterproductive to dole out many tens of thousands of dollars for a BMW, Mercedes-Benz, or Ferrari while expecting to grow rich. But most millionaires might surprise you with their taste in cars. In 2009, the median price paid for a car by US millionaires was US$31,367.[10] In 2016, they would have paid a bit more as a result of inflation. But one thing is clear. If you want to grow rich, forget about expensive European darlings such as BMW, Mercedes-Benz, and Jaguar. When Thomas Stanley polled US millionaires, the most popular brand of car was the humdrum Toyota.[11]

Many of the wanna-be rich try to outdo their peers in the car-spending department, easily parting with $40,000 and upward on a luxury vehicle. But how can you build wealth and reduce financial stress when you're paying far more for a car than an average millionaire? It's like trying to keep up with a pack of Olympic sprinters but giving them a 50-meter head start.

Image is nothing if you lose your job, can't make your car payments, or if you're stuck having to work until you're 80 years old.

If you want to keep pace with the millionaires, begin on the start line or give yourself the biggest lead you can. It doesn't make sense to spend more than most rich people do on a set of wheels.

Paying More for a Car than a Decamillionaire

In 2006, Warren Buffett, one of the three richest men in the world, bought the most expensive car he has ever owned: a $55,000 Cadillac.[12] The average decamillionaire—a person with a net worth of more than $10 million—paid $41,997 for his or her latest car.[13] If you find yourself at an upscale mall, check out the parking lot and you'll see many vehicles worth a lot more than $41,997.

Many will be worth more than Warren Buffett's car. But how many of the car owners do you think have $10 million or more? If your answer is "probably none," then you're catching on fast. Many have jeopardized their own pursuit of wealth or financial independence for the allusion of looking wealthy instead of being wealthy.

Whatever money you save on a car (not to mention the savings from interest payments if you can't buy the car outright) can go toward wealth-building investments.

Cars aren't investments. Unlike long-term assets such as real estate, stocks, and bonds, cars depreciate in value with each passing year.

One of the Savviest Guys I Ever Met—And His View on Buying Cars

When I was 20 years old, I took a summer job washing buses at a bus depot to pay for my college tuition. What I learned there from an insightful mechanic was more valuable than anything I learned at college. Russ Perry was a millionaire mechanic raising two kids as a single dad. His financial acumen was revered by the other mechanics. They told me, "Hey, if Russ ever wants to talk to you about money, make sure you listen."

We worked the night shift together, which wasn't particularly busy—especially on weekends—so we had plenty of time to talk.

My job was pretty simple. I washed buses, fueled them, and recorded their mileage at the end of the day. During my free moments at work I alternated between cringing and laughing out loud when Russ sermonized about money and people. Not everything Russ had to say was politically correct, but his crassness always had an element of truth to it.

Russ claimed he could tell how smart someone was by looking at what they drove. He couldn't figure out why anyone would pay a lot of money for something—such as a luxury car—that depreciated in value over time. And if they leased it, or borrowed money to buy it, he was really left scratching his head. Russ recommended investing in assets such as houses or stocks. They appreciate over time. But cars lose money every year.

"Andrew," he said, "If you can go through life without losing money on cars, you're going to have a huge advantage." He pointed to the guy across the parking lot. He worked in management. "You see that guy getting into that BMW?"

I had admired the car when I arrived at work that night. It was a beauty. "He bought that car two years ago, brand new," Russ said. "But he has already lost $17,000 on it from depreciation and loan-interest costs. And in about three years, he's probably going to buy another one." I wondered what the car would be worth in three years if it had already depreciated so much in just two.

"If you're truly wealthy," Russ explained, "then there's nothing wrong with blowing money you can afford to lose on the odd luxury item. But if you're trying to become wealthy," Russ said in a serious tone, "and you make those kinds of purchases, you'll never get there. Never."

Russ turned conventional wisdom on its head. Most people expect to lose money on cars. But expecting it becomes a self-fulfilling prophecy. He told me that people don't have to lose money on cars if they're careful.

I expected that from someone both financially and mechanically inclined. My biggest question at the time was whether it could work for me. Mechanically, I'm as gifted as a blind Neanderthal with two left hands.

"When you buy a car," Russ said, "think about the resale value." The bulk of the depreciation on a new vehicle occurs in the first year. Russ recommended I never buy new cars, and only buy a car if someone else had covered the bulk of the depreciation.

The best resale value, he figured, came from Japanese cars. He said I should look for low-mileage models that had been fastidiously maintained with original paint, great tires, and a great interior.

If I paid the right price for a car and the bulk of the depreciation was covered by someone else, he preached, I might be able to sell the car a year or two later for the same price I paid, if not a bit more.

A Future Millionaire's Car-Buying Strategies

Putting Russ's theory to the test, I searched for cars that wouldn't put holes in the bottom of my financial bucket.

It didn't take me long to get a feel for the market. I read a few consumer reports on reliable automobiles. One useful resource was Phil Edmonston's annually updated guide, *Lemon-Aid Used Cars.* Certain cars and models are bona fide lemons. Others can be great little workhorses. I would spend a few minutes each morning looking through the classifieds in the local paper. When I saw something interesting at a good price, I would check it out. Over the next few years, I bought several low-mileage, reliable Japanese models. I paid between $1,500 to $5,000 for each car. In most cases, I drove them for at least 12 months without putting any extra money into them. My cars were cheap, so my profits didn't amount to much, usually $800 to $1,000 a car.

Unfortunately there are too many people who aren't good with money. It's often easy to find desperate people who have overextended themselves financially. Buy from them. Generally, they want money quickly, either to upgrade their cars or to pay off oppressively looming debts. I've bought used vehicles from both types of sellers, put as many as 60,000 miles on the cars, and then sold them two or three years later for the same price I paid.

On one occasion, I bought a low-mileage, 12-year-old Toyota van for $3,000. I drove it 4,000 miles from British Columbia, Canada, down the Mexican Baja peninsula, then on to Guadalajara, before driving back to Canada. After covering more than 8,000 miles in a single trip, I sold it for $3,500.

Here's one surprisingly simple strategy for buying used vehicles that can save you loads of time and money.

Imagine wandering onto a car lot. You're not generally given free rein to browse on your own or with a friend. A sharply dressed salesperson will soon be courting you through a variety of makes and models. They could have good intentions. But if you're anything like me, your pulse will race a bit faster as you're shadowed, and the pressure of being shadowed by a slick talker might throw you off. After all, you're on their turf.

A minnow like me needs an effective strategy against big, hungry, experienced fish—and this is mine: first, I identify exactly what I'm looking for. A few years ago, I wanted a Japanese car with a stick shift and original paint. I didn't want a new paint job because I'm not skilled enough to determine whether something had been covered up, such as rust or damage from an accident. I also wanted to ensure that the car had fewer than 80,000 miles on it, and I wanted to pay less than $3,000. It really didn't matter how old the car was as long as it had been properly maintained and hadn't been around the block too many times.

Like a secret agent wrapped up in the bravery of anonymity, I pulled out my hit list from the yellow pages to call every car lot within a 20-mile radius. Sticking to my guns, I told them exactly what I was looking for. I wouldn't entertain anything that didn't fit my criteria.

I did have to hold my ground with aggressive sales staff. But it was a lot easier to do over the telephone than it would have been in person. Most of the dealers told me that they had something I would be interested in, but they couldn't go as low as $3,000. Some tried tempting me into their lairs with alternatives; others referred to my price ceiling as delusional. But I wasn't bothered. My strategy was a knight's sword and the phone, my trusty shield. I also practiced chivalry—knowing that I might end up calling on them again.

Because my first round of phone calls didn't pan out, I called the dealers back when it got closer to the end of the month. I hoped the salespeople would be hungrier by then to meet their monthly quotas. As fortune would have it, at one dealership an elderly couple had traded in an older Toyota Tercel with 30,000 miles on it. The car hadn't been cleaned or inspected, but the dealership was willing to do a quick turn-around sale for $3,000.

This strategy doesn't have to be limited to a $3,000 purchase. The process makes sense for any make or model and it saves time. Over the past five years, I've become far less extreme. I no longer pinch pennies. But I still buy used cars. Typically, I now sell them for a little less than what I paid. But if I add up all the money that I've "lost" on cars over the past five years, it doesn't amount to much. The typical new car buyer will lose more money in five months than I've lost in five years.

If you save more money on cars, you can invest more money in wealth-building assets.

Leasing Cars Instead Of Buying Used Could Be A $1 Million Decision

My friend Nathan is a millionaire. But like most millionaires, he won't ever lease a car. "Leasing a car, instead of buying used," he says, "is a million-dollar decision."[14]

According to *The Millionaire Next Door* author Thomas Stanley, 80 percent of millionaires have never leased a car. Finance author Dave Ramsey isn't a fan of leasing either. He says, "Broke people think 'how much down and how much a month.' Rich people think 'how much.' If you can't pay cash for a car, then ride a bicycle. But don't lease a car."

But How Could Leasing Cars Cost $1 Million?

Nathan has never paid more than $6,000 for a car. Like me, he looks for cars with low mileage. The average American drives 12,000 miles a year. That means the typical 10-year-old car will have about 120,000 miles on it. Such cars may nickel-and-dime their owners as the cost of maintenance creeps up.

Nathan's most recent car typifies what he likes. It's a 2006 Honda Accord. He paid $5,500. When he bought it, the car had just 60,000 miles on it. That means it has as much wear and tear as the average five-year-old car. "A well- maintained car with 60,000 miles on it still has plenty of life left," says Nathan.

He typically drives his cars for three to five years. Then he sells them for a price that's not much lower than what he paid. "I should be able to get at least $3,500 for this Honda," he says, "if I sell it in three to five years."

Many people prefer to lease new cars. It allows them to get behind the wheel of a brand new car without saving a penny. They drive those cars for a few years. They make monthly pay-ments. But they don't get money back when they return those cars. In many cases, they even pay extra. Many dealers have mileage restrictions of 12,000 miles a year. Those who drive further pay the financial piper when they bring the car back.

According to Edmunds.com, the average midsized leased car costs $294 a month, or $3,528 a year.[15] But most households have two cars. That means leasing two cars costs the typical household about $7,056 per year.

Nathan, like most wealthy people, tracks what he spends. He and his wife's two cars cost them about $2,200 a year after calculating purchase price, maintenance costs, and resale value. The difference between buying low-cost, low-mileage used models versus leasing is about $4,856 a year for a two-car household.

The US stock market averaged a compound annual return of 9.2 percent from January 1990 through July 2016. If a couple invested $4,856 a year, and if they earned such a return, they would make a lot of money.

As seen in Table 1.1, over 15 years this investment would earn them $158,162. Over 35 years, they would have more than $1 million. That's why Nathan says that leasing cars is a $1-million decision.

Negative Nellies could find all kinds of reasons this wouldn't work. Perhaps your investments wouldn't gain 9.2 percent. Perhaps you couldn't find well-maintained, low-mileage used

Table 1.1   Benefits of Buying Used over Leasing (Based on 2 Cars per Household)

Time Duration	Used Cars Savings*	Leased Cars Savings*
15 years	$158,162	$0
20 years	$277,455	$0
25 years	$462,692	$0
30 years	$750,326	$0
35 years	$1,196,962	$0
40 years	$1,890,496	$0
Max purchase price per car	$6,000	$0
5-year maintenance costs per car	$3,000	$17,640 (lease payments at $294 per month over 5 years)
Total spent per car	$9,000	$17,640
Resale value per car (5 years later)	$3,500	$0 (sometimes it costs money to turn in a leased car if there's high wear and tear or if it exceeds mileage limitations)
Cost per car after resale	$5,500	$17,640
x 2 Cars	$11,000	$35,280
Savings per year	$4,856	$0

*Assuming $4,856 invested annually at 9.2 percent per year

cars. Perhaps your used vehicle maintenance costs would exceed an average of $3,000 every five years.

You might pay more than what Nathan pays for a good used car. But a lifetime of buying used cars over leasing cars will win—to the tune of (at least) a few hundred thousand dollars.

Careful Home Purchases

Most people realize that expensive automobile purchases can hinder wealth. But the global financial crisis of 2008–2009 taught us important lessons about homes as well.

One of the lessons that aspiring rich people have to learn is that the banks aren't their friends. They're out to make money for their shareholders. To do so, they often hire kind or convincing salespeople. Their jobs are to persuade you to buy lousy investment products (which I'll discuss in Chapter 3). They also sugarcoat bloated house loans, so you continue paying interest for years.

What caused the financial crisis of 2008–2009? The greed of the banks not looking after the best interests of their customers, coupled with the ignorance of those who bought homes they couldn't afford.

Caught up in the housing boom, buyers purchased homes they couldn't really pay for, and when the dangerously enticing, low interest rates finally rose, they couldn't make their mortgage payments. Unsurprisingly, many were forced to sell their homes, creating a surplus in the housing market. When there's a surplus of anything, people aren't willing to pay as much for those items—so they fall in price. Houses were no exception.

The banks had sold these mortgage loans to other institutions around the world. But when the original holders of the mortgages (the home purchasers) couldn't afford their mortgage payments, the financial institutions repossessed their houses—but at a significant loss, because housing prices were falling like a skydiver without a chute.

The banks had also bundled the loans up and sold them to other global institutions, which were then on the hook when the homeowners couldn't pay their mortgages, putting many of the world's most respected financial institutions in peril. With dwindling financial resources, the banks didn't loan as readily to other businesses, which in turn didn't have the funds to cover their day-to-day operations. The snowball effect resulted in a global slowdown and mass layoffs. Don't believe those who sugarcoat housing loans. The effects can be devastating.

It reminds me of a lesson my mom taught me when I took out my first mortgage on a piece of oceanfront land. She asked me: "If the interest rate doubled, could you still afford to make the payment?" According to the terms of the mortgage, I was being charged 7 percent in interest a year. She knew at the time that a 7 percent mortgage was historically cheap, especially compared with mortgage rates in the late 1970s and 1980s. As far as she was concerned, if I couldn't afford to pay double, or 14 percent interest, then rising interest rates could expose me. I would be one of those unfortunate guys caught swimming naked when the tide goes out.

Her advice is a good rule of thumb if you don't want to be stripped of your real estate. If you're considering purchasing a home, double the interest rate and figure out if you could still afford the payments. If you can, then you can afford the home.

Millionaire Handouts

There's a Chinese proverb suggesting that wealth doesn't last more than three generations. There's a generation that builds wealth, a generation that maintains it, and a generation that squanders it.

US studies suggest that—contrary to what we might think—most millionaires didn't inherit their wealth. More than 80 percent of those surveyed are first-generation rich.

I taught at a private school in Singapore where most of the expat students come from affluent families. I told my students (only half-jokingly) that they're on the financial endangered species list. It's natural for parents to want to help their children. But the Chinese have known for thousands of years what happens to money that's given to youngsters who had no hand in building that wealth. It gets squandered.

Adults who receive "helpful" financial gifts from their parents (stocks, cash, real estate) typically end up with lower levels of wealth than people in the same income bracket who don't receive financial assistance.[16]

It's a tough concept for many parents to grasp. They feel they can give their kids a strong financial head start by giving them money. Statistically speaking, easy money is wasted money. Thomas Stanley studied a broad cross section of educated professionals in their 40s and 50s. He categorized them by vocation. Then he split them up into two groups: those who had received financial assistance from their parents and those who hadn't. That assistance included cash gifts, help in paying off loans, help in buying a car, or help with a down payment on a home. He found that those who received help were more likely to have less wealth during their peak earning years than those who had not received financial help from their parents. Receiving financial handouts hinders a person's ability to create wealth.

For example, the average accountant who received financial help from his or her parents was 43 percent less wealthy than an average accountant who didn't receive handouts. In sharp contrast, the only two professional groups studied that became wealthier after receiving financial assistance were teachers and college professors.[17]

How Did I Become a Millionaire?

My dad was a mechanic. I was one of four kids being raised on his salary, so we didn't have a lot of money to throw around when I was growing up. From the age of 15, I bought my own clothes. At 16, I bought my own car with earnings from a part-time job at a supermarket. I had to work for what I wanted. But I didn't enjoy working. Like most kids, I would have preferred hanging out on a beach.

So for me, money was equated with work. I would see something I wanted that cost "just" $10. But then I would ask myself if I wanted to mop the supermarket floor and stack 50-pound sacks of potatoes to pay for it. If the answer was no, then I wouldn't buy it. Never receiving "free" money allowed me to adopt responsible spending habits.

Confessions of a Former Cheapskate

Today, my wife and I can afford to live well. In 2014, we retired from our teaching jobs. I was 44 years old. I still enjoy writing about investing, and one day I may choose to teach again. But we no longer have to work.

We travel prolifically, having visited more than 55 different countries. While working, we lived in a luxurious condominium with a swimming pool, squash courts, tennis courts, and a weight room. We also enjoyed massages every week, 52 weeks a year.

During the first year of our "retirement" we lived in Mexico, Thailand, Bali, Malaysia, and Vietnam. If our health holds out, we'll enjoy these fruits and travels for the next 40 years.

But an early aversion to debt put us in this position. I hate debt. It's going to sound extreme, but for me, owing money is like making a deal with the devil. Always thinking of the worst-case scenario, I would worry what would happen if I lost my job and couldn't meet my debt-obligation payments.

I'm not recommending that a young person who seeks early retirement should live the way I did in my early 20s. But thinking of debt as a life-threatening, contagious disease served me pretty well. Whether you find it inspirational or delusional, I think you'll get a kick out of my story.

I began teaching seventh grade a few months after graduating from university. Paying low rent and low food costs, I figured, were like roadmaps to student-loan obliteration. Sure, it sounds like a reasonable idea, but there are big-city panhandlers who might cringe at my form of minimalism.

Potatoes, pasta, and clams were the cheapest forms of sustenance I could find. Clams simply represented free protein. With a bucket in hand, I would wander to the beach with a retired fellow named Oscar, and we would load up on clams. While Oscar turned his catch into delicacies, my efforts were spartan: microwave some spuds or boil pasta, and toss in the clams with a bit of olive oil. Voila! Dinner for less than a dollar. It doesn't matter how well you can initially tolerate a bland meal. Keeping that diet up day after day is about as enticing as eating dog food. But my debt burden lessened as I lived on just 30 percent of my teacher's salary—allowing me to allocate 70 percent of my salary toward debt reduction.

Sharing accommodation with roommates also cut costs. I preferred, however, not paying rent at all, so I looked for people who needed someone to look after their homes because they were escaping to the Sunbelt for winter.

No matter how cold the rent-free homes got during the winter, I never turned on the heat. Wanting to keep costs down, I would walk around the house wearing layers of shirts and sweaters while the winter's snow piled up outside. If there was a fireplace, I used it. At night, I would make a roaring fire and then drag blankets in front of it to sleep. Waking up during winter mornings, I often saw my breath.

One December week, my father was in town on business, so I invited him to stay with me. Typically boisterous, he was uncharacteristically quiet when I told him: "No Dad, I'm not going to turn on the heat." I figured that snuggling up together at night next to a fireplace in a frosty living room would be a great father-son bonding moment. I guess he didn't think so. The next time he was in town, he stayed at a hotel.

Eventually, I craved the freedom of my own place, so I moved into a basement suite where the landlord charged $350 a month. But low rents can come with inconveniences. In this case, I was a long way from the school where I taught—35 miles door to door.

If I had been smart enough to drive a car to work, it wouldn't have been so bad. I owned a rusting, 20-year-old Volkswagen that I bought for $1,200 (which I sold two years later for $1,800), but I wasn't prepared to pay fuel prices for the 70-mile round-trip commute. So . . . I rode my bike.

Riding an old mountain bike 70 miles a day through rain and sleet on my way to work and back gave me a frontrunner's edge for the bonehead award. At the time, I had an investment portfolio that would have allowed me to buy a brand-new sports car with cash. I could have also rented an oceanside apartment. But the people I worked with probably thought I was broke.

One of my fellow teachers saw me at a gas station on my way home from work. We were both picking up fuel—but mine was of the edible kind. Rushing up to me as I straddled my bike and stuffed a PowerBar into my mouth she said: "We should really start a collection for you at the school, Andrew." If I thought she was kidding, I would have laughed.

After a while, even I decided my lifestyle was a little extreme. To make things easier, I moved closer to work after placing an advertisement in the local paper: Teacher looking for accommodation for no more than $450 a month. It was far below the going rate, but I reasoned an advertisement selling myself as employed and responsible—while leaving out a few other adjectives—might attract someone looking for a dependable tenant.

I got only a couple of calls. But one of the places was perfect, so I took it.

Because I had been investing money since I was 19, I already had a growing nest egg. But I wasn't willing to sell any of my investments to pay down my loans. Instead, I threw every extra income dollar I could toward reducing my student loans. One year after working full-time and living like a monk, I paid off my debts. That's when I redirected much of my income straight into my investments.

Six years after paying off my student loans, I bought a piece of oceanfront property and calculated how to aggressively pay down the mortgage. I even took a higher interest rate to increase my flexibility of mortgage payments.

Once I paid it off, I shoveled money, once again, into my investments.

Admittedly, few people despise debt as much as I do. But once you're debt free, there's no feeling like it.

Don't get me wrong. This part of my financial history isn't a "how to" manual for a young person to follow. It was a fun challenge at the time, but it wouldn't appeal to me today. And my wife, whom I married much later, admits it wouldn't have appealed to her—ever. That said, if you want to be wealthy, you dramatically increase your odds if you're frugal, especially when you're young.

Looking to the Future

Those who want to be rich often overlook responsible spending habits. It's one of the reasons many people nearing retirement age have to work when they would rather be traveling the world or spending time with their grandchildren. Naturally, not everyone has the same philosophy about work. But how many people on their deathbeds ever lament: "Gosh, I wish I had spent more time at the office," or "Geez, I really wish they had given me that promotion back in 2025."

Most people prefer their hobbies to their workplace, their children to their iPhones, and their quiet reflective moments to their office meetings. I'm certainly among them. That's why I learned to control my spending and invest my money.

If you're a young person starting out and you see someone with the latest expensive toys, think about how they might have acquired them. Too many of those items were probably bought on credit—with sleepless nights as a complementary accessory. Many of those people will never truly be rich. Instead, they will be stressed.

By learning how to spend like a rich person, you can eventually build wealth (and material possessions) without the added anxiety. You don't have to live like a pauper to do it either. Apply the investment rules that I'm willing to share, and you could feasibly invest half of what your neighbors do, take lower risks, and still end up with twice as much money as they do. Read on to find out how.

Notes

1. Odysseas Papadimitriou, "2015 Credit Card Debt Study: Trends & Insights," Cardhub.com, March 7, 2016, www.cardhub.com/edu/credit-card-debt-study/.
2. Quentin Fottrell, "Underwater American Homeowners Still Drowning in Mortgage Debt," *MarketWatch*, June 12, 2015, www.marketwatch.com/story/american-homeowners-still-drowning-in-mortgage-debt-2015–06–12.
3. "Property Prices Index Per Country 2016," Numbeo.com, www.numbeo.com/property-investment/rankings_by_country.jsp.
4. Thomas Stanley, *Stop Acting Rich* (Hoboken, NJ: John Wiley & Sons, 2009), 9.
5. Ibid., 45.
6. "State Median Income," U.S. Census Bureau, 2016, www.census.gov/hhes/www/income/data/statemedian/.

7. Philip L. Cooley, Carl M. Hubbard, and Daniel T. Walz, "Portfolio Success Rates: Where to Draw the Line," *Journal of Financial Planning*, www.onefpa.org/journal/Pages/Portfolio%20Success%20Rates%20Where%20to%20Draw%20the%20Line.aspx.

8. Andrew Hallam, "Retirement Fortunes That You Can't Control," AssetBuilder.com, June 6, 2016, https://assetbuilder.com/knowledge-center/articles/retirement-fortunes-that-you-cant-control.

9. Dave Feschuk, "NBA Players' Financial Security No Slam Dunk," *Toronto Star*, January 31, 2008, www.thestar.com/sports/article/299119.

10. Stanley, *Stop Acting Rich*, 204.

11. Ibid.

12. "Warren Buffett Vouches for GM with Caddy Purchase," Left-Lane, June 6, 2006, www.leftlanenews.com/warren-buffett-vouches-for-gm-with-caddy-purchase.html.

13. Stanley, *Stop Acting Rich*, 204.

14. Dave Ramsey, "Explain How a Car Lease Works," www.daveramsey.com/askdave/posts/10367.

15. Philip Reed, "Comparing Car Costs: Buy New, Buy Used Or Lease?" September 30, 2015, www.edmunds.com/car-buying/compare-the-costs-buying-vs-leasing-vs-buying-a-used-car.html.

16. Thomas Stanley and William Danko, *The Millionaire Next Door* (New York: Simon & Schuster, 1996), 9.

17. Ibid., 151.

RULE 2

Use the Greatest Investment Ally You Have

So much of what schools teach in a traditional mathematics class is . . . hmm, let me word this diplomatically, not likely to affect our day-to-day lives. Sure, learning the formulas for quadratic equations (and their abstract family members) might jazz the odd engineering student. But let's be honest. Few people get aroused by quadratic equations.

Perhaps I'm committing heresy in the eyes of the world's math teachers, but I think quadratic equations (a polynomial equation of the second degree, if that clears things up) are about as useful to most people as ingrown toenails and just as painful for some. Having said that, buried in the dull pages of most school math books is something that's actually useful: the magical premise of compound interest.

Warren Buffett applied it to become a billionaire. More important, you can apply it, too. I'll show you how.

Buffett has long jockeyed with Microsoft Chairman Bill Gates for the title of "World's Richest Man." He lives like a typical millionaire (he doesn't spend much on material things) and he mastered the secret of investing his money early. He bought his first stock when he was 11 years old, and the multi-billionaire jokes that he started too late.[1]

Starting early is the greatest gift you can give yourself. If you start early and if you invest efficiently (in a manner that I'll explain in this book) you can build a fortune over time, while spending just 60 minutes a year monitoring your investments.

Warren Buffett famously quips: "Preparation is everything. Noah did not start building the Ark when it was raining."[2]

Most of us are aware of the Biblical story about Noah's Ark. God told him to build an Ark and to collect a variety of animals, and eventually, when the rains came, they would sail off to a new beginning. Luckily for the animals, Noah started building that Ark right away. He didn't procrastinate.

But let's imagine Noah for a second. The guy probably had a similar nature to you and me, so even if God told him to keep the upcoming flood a secret, he might not have. After all, he was human, too. So I can imagine him wandering down to the local watering hole. After having a couple of forerunners to Budweiser beer, I can see him whispering to a friend: "Hey listen, God is saying that the rains are going to come and that I have to build an Ark and sail away once the land is flooded." Some of his buddies (maybe even all of them) might have figured that Noah had eaten some kind of naturally grown narcotic. A crazy story, they would think.

Yet, someone must have believed him. As far-fetched as Noah's flood story might have sounded to his buddies, it would have inspired at least one of his friends to build an Ark—or at least a decent-sized boat.

Despite the best of intentions, though, that person obviously never got around to it. Maybe he planned to build it when he acquired more money to pay for the materials. Maybe he wanted to be sure, waiting to see if the clouds grew dark and it started sprinkling. English naturalist Charles Darwin might call this guy's procrastination "natural selection." Needless to say, he wasn't selected.

For the best odds of amassing wealth in the stock and bond markets, it's best to start early.

Thankfully your friends—if they procrastinate—won't meet the same fate as Noah's friends. But your metaphorical ship will sail off into the distance while others scramble in the rain to assemble their own boats.

Starting early is more than just getting a head start. It's about using magic. You can sail away slowly, and your friends can come after you with racing boats. But thanks to the force described by Albert Einstein (some say) as more powerful than splitting the atom, they aren't likely to catch you.

In William Shakespeare's *Hamlet*, the protagonist says to his friend: "There are more things in heaven and earth, Horatio, than are dreamt of in your philosophy."

Hamlet was referring to ghosts. Einstein was referring to the magic of compound interest.

Compound Interest—The World's Most Powerful Financial Concept

Compound interest might sound like a complicated process. But it's simple.

If $100 attracts 10 percent interest in one year, then we know that it gained $10, turning $100 into $110.

You would start the second year with $110, and if it increases 10 percent, it would gain $11, turning $110 into $121.

You will go into the third year with $121 in your pocket, and if it increases 10 percent, it would gain $12.10, turning $121 into $133.10.

It isn't long before a snowball effect takes place. Have a look at what $100 invested at 10 percent annually can do.

$100 at 10 percent compounding interest a year turns into:

- $161.05 after 5 years

- $259.37 after 10 years

- $417.72 after 15 years

- $672.74 after 20 years

- $1,744.94 after 30 years

- $4,525.92 after 40 years

- $11,739.08 after 50 years

- $78,974.69 after 70 years

- $204,840.02 after 80 years

- $1,378,061.23 after 100 years

Some of the lengthier periods above might look dramatically unrealistic. But you don't have to be an immortal creep to benefit. Someone who starts to invest at 19 (like I did) and who lives until age 90 (which I hope to!) will have money compounding in the markets for 71 years. They will spend some of it along the way, but they'll always want to keep a portion of their money compounding in case they live to 100.

The Inspirational Realities of Starting Early

After paying off your high-interest loans (whether they are car loans or credit-card loans) you will be ready to put Buffett's Noah Principle to work. The earlier you start, the better—so if you're 18 years old, start now. If you're 50 years old, and you haven't begun, there's no better time than the present. You'll never be younger than you are right now.

The money that doesn't go toward expensive cars, the latest tech gadgets, and credit-card payments (assuming you have paid off your credit debts) can compound dramatically in the stock market if you're patient. And the longer your money is invested in the stock market, the lower the risk.

We know that stock markets can fluctuate dramatically. They can even move sideways for many years. But over the past 90 years, the US stock market has generated returns exceeding nine percent annually.[3] This includes the crashes of 1929, 1973–1974, 1987, and 2008–2009. In *Stocks for the Long Run*, University of Pennsylvania's Wharton School finance professor Jeremy Siegel suggests a dominant historical market, such as the United States, isn't the only source of impressive long-term returns. Despite the shrinking global importance of England, its stock market returns since 1926 have been very similar to that of the United States. Meanwhile, not even two devastating world wars for Germany have hurt its long-term stock market performance, which also rivals that of the United States.[4]

My suggestion isn't going to be to choose one country's stock market over another. Some stock markets will do better than others, but without mythical crystal balls we're not going to know ahead of time. Instead, to ensure the best chances of success, owning an interest in all of the world's stock markets is a good idea. And you can benefit most by investing right away. The younger you are when you start to invest, the better.

Grow Wealthier than Your Neighbor While Investing Less

The question below showcases how powerful the "Noah Principle" of starting early really is.

> **A.** Would you rather invest $32,400 and turn it into $1,050,180? Or,

> **B.** Would you rather invest $240,000 and turn it into $813,128?

Sure it's a dumb question. Anyone who can fog a mirror would choose A. But because most people haven't had a strong financial education, the vast majority would be lucky to face scenario B—never mind scenario A.

If you know anyone who's really young, they can benefit from your knowledge. They can feasibly turn $32,400 into more than a million dollars. But don't weaken them by giving them money. Make them earn it. Here's how it can be done.

The Bohemian Millionaire—The Best of Historical-Based Fiction

A five-year-old girl named Star is raised by her mother, Autumn, and brought up on a Bohemian island where the locals make their own clothes, where neither men nor women use razors to shave, and where no one tries to mask the aphrodisiac quality of good old-fashioned sweat.

Unfortunately, despite how appealing this might sound (especially at tightly congested town hall meetings), it isn't paradise. Islanders and locals often throw empty aluminum beverage cans into ditches. Autumn convinces Star that collecting those cans and recycling them can help the environment and eventually make her a millionaire. Autumn takes Star to the local recycling depot where Star collects an average of $1.45 a day from refunded cans and bottles. Although a Bohemian at heart, Autumn's no provincial bumpkin. She recognizes that if she persuades Star to earn $1.45 a day from can returns, she can invest the daily $1.45 to make Star a millionaire.

Putting it into the US stock market, Star earns an average of 9 percent a year (which is slightly less than what the stock market has averaged over the past 90 years). Autumn also understands what most parents do not: if she teaches Star to save, her daughter will become a financial powerhouse. But if she "gifts" Star money, rather than coaching her to earn it, then her daughter may become financially weak.

Fast-forward 20 years. Star is now 25 years old. She no longer collects cans from ditches. But her mother insists that Star sends her a $45 monthly check (roughly $1.45 per day). Autumn continues to invest Star's money while Star hawks her handmade Dream Catchers at the local farmer's market.

Living in New York City, Star's best friend Lucy works as an investment banker. (I know you're wondering how these two hooked up, but roll with it. It's my story.) Living the "good life," Lucy drives a BMW, dines at gourmet restaurants, and blows the rest of her significant income on clothing, theater shows, expensive shoes, and flashy jewelry.

At age 40, Lucy begins to save $800 a month. She gets on Star's case, via e-mail, about Star's limited $45-a-month contribution to her financial future.

Star doesn't want to brag but she needs to set Lucy straight.

"Lucy," she writes, "you're the one in financial trouble, not me. It's true that you're investing far more money than I am, but you'll need to invest more than $800 a month if you want as much as I'll have when I retire."

The e-mail puzzles Lucy, who assumes that Star must have ingested some very Bohemian mushrooms to write such cryptic nonsense.

Twenty-five years later, both women are 65 years old. They decide to rent a retirement home together in Lake Chapala, Mexico, where their money would go further.

"Well," inquires Star, "Did you invest more than $800 a month like I suggested?"

"This is coming from someone who invested just $45 a month?" asks Lucy with surprise.

"But Lucy, you ignored the Noah principle, so despite investing far more money, you ended up with a lot less than I did because you started investing so much later."

Both women achieved the same return in the stock market. Some years they gained money. Other years, they lost money. But overall, they each averaged a compound return of 9 percent per year.

Figure 2.1 shows that because Star started early, she was able to invest a total of $32,400 and turn it into more than $1 million. Lucy started later, invested nearly eight times more, but ended up with $237,052 less than Star.

I didn't start investing until I was 19, so Star would have had the jump on me. But I started far earlier than most, so I have had more time to let the Noah Principle work its magic. I put money in US and international stock markets that, from 1990 to 2016, have averaged more than 9 percent per year. The money that I put in the market in 1990 had grown to 10 times its original value by 2016.

When I tell young parents about the power of compounding money, they often want to set money aside for their children's future. "Setting aside" money for a child, however, is very different from encouraging a child to earn, save, and invest.

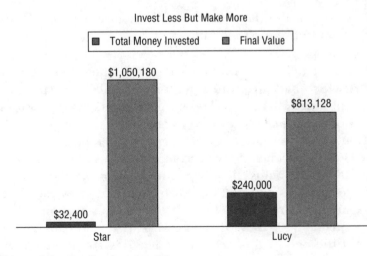

Figure 2.1   Turning Less into More

Giving money promotes weakness and dependence.

Teaching money lessons and cheerleading the struggle promotes strength, independence, and pride.

Gifting Money to Yourself

In 2005, I was having dinner with a couple of school teachers. We started to talk about saving money. They wanted to know how much they should save for their retirement. Unlike most public school teachers, who can look forward to pensions when they retire, these friends are in the same boat as me. As private school teachers, they're responsible for their own retirement money.

I threw out a minimum dollar figure that I thought they should save each month. It was double what they were currently saving.

The woman (who I'll call Julie) thought it was an attainable amount. Her husband (who I'll call Tom) thought it was crazy. So I asked them to do a couple of things:

1. Write down everything they spent money on for three months, including food costs, mortgage costs, gas for the car, and health insurance.

2. At the end of those three months, figure out what it cost them to live each month.

The next time we had dinner together, they told me their results, which had given them both a jolt. Julie was surprised at how much she was spending on eating out, buying clothes, and purchasing small items such as Starbucks coffee.

Tom was surprised at how much he was spending on beers at the clubhouse when he went golfing with his buddies.

After three months, they began to change. Pulling receipts from their wallets and writing down their expenses each evening made them realize how much they were squandering. As Tom explained: "I knew that I had to write those purchases down at the end of the day, which acted as an accountability measurement. So I started spending less."

Financially efficient households know what their costs are. By writing down expenses, two things occur. You get an idea of how much you spend in a month, providing an idea of how much you can invest. It also makes you accountable for your spending, which encourages most people to cut back.

The next step is to figure out exactly what you get paid in the average month.

When you subtract your average monthly expense costs from your income, you can get an idea of how much you can afford to invest. Don't wait until the end of the month to invest that money; instead, make the transfer payment to your investment of choice on the day you get paid. Otherwise, you might not have enough left at the end of the month (after a few too many nights out) to follow through with your new financial plan. My wife made that mistake before we were married. She invested whatever amount she had left in her account at the end of the month or the end of the year. When she switched things around and automatically had money transferred from her savings account on the date she was paid, she ended up investing twice as much.

My friends Julie and Tom had the same realization. After a year, they had doubled the amount that they were investing. Two years later when the same conversation came up, I found they had tripled the amount they were originally putting away. Both said the same thing: "We didn't know where that money was going each month. It doesn't feel like we live any differently than we did three years ago, but the deposits in our investment account don't lie. We've tripled our savings."

My wife and I document every penny we spend with an expense tracking app on our iPhone. It's easy. After coming out of a grocery store or restaurant, for example, we enter our costs right away. My wife rolls her eyes as I excitedly tell anyone within earshot, "This is the best thing ever!" Then she drags me outside before I embarrass her further.

By documenting what you spend, you'll fall into a healthy spending pattern. It will allow you to invest much more money over time.

Here's another useful tip. Over the years, your salary will most likely rise. If it increases by $1,000 in a given year, add at least half of it to your investment account, while putting the rest in a separate account for something special. That way, you'll get rewarded twice for the salary increase.

When You Definitely Shouldn't Invest

Before getting wrapped up in how much money you can save and invest, there's one thing to consider. Are you paying interest on credit cards? If you are, then investing money doesn't make sense. Most credit cards charge 18 to 24 percent in interest annually. Not paying them off in full at the end of the month means that your friendly card company (the one you'll never leave home without) is sucking your money from an intravenous drip attached to your femoral artery. You don't have to be a genius to realize that paying 18 percent interest on credit-card debt and investing money that you hope will provide returns of 8 to 10 percent makes as much sense as bathing fully clothed in a tub of Vaseline and then travelling home on the roof of a bus.

Paying off credit-card debt that's charging 18 percent in interest is like making a tax-free 18-percent gain on your money. And there's no way that your investments can guarantee a gain like that after tax. If any financial adviser, advertisement, or investment group of any kind promises a return of 18 percent annually, think of disgraced US financier Bernie Madoff and run. Nobody can guarantee those kinds of returns.

Well, nobody except the credit-card companies. They're making 18 to 24 percent annually *from* you (if you carry a balance), not *for* you.

How and Why Stocks Rise in Value

You might be wondering how I averaged about 9.5 percent a year on the stock market for 25 years. There were certainly years when my money dropped in value, but there were years when I earned a lot more than 9.5 percent as well.

Where does the money come from? How is it created?

Imagine Willy Wonka (from Roald Dahl's classic novel *Charlie and the Chocolate Factory*). Willy started out with a little chocolate shop. Having big dreams, he wanted to make ice cream that didn't melt, chewing gum that never lost its flavor, and chocolate that would make even the devil sell his soul.

But Willy didn't have limitless money to grow his business. He needed to buy a larger building, hire more of those creepy little workers, and purchase machinery that would make chocolate faster than he ever could before.

So Willy hired someone to approach the New York Stock Exchange. Before Willy knew it, he had investors in his business. They bought parts of his business, also known as "shares" or "stock." Willy was no longer the sole owner, but by selling part of his business to new shareholders, he was able to build a larger, more efficient factory with the shareholder proceeds. This increased the chocolate factory's profits because he was able to make more treats at a faster rate.

Willy's company was now "public," meaning that the shareowners (should they choose to) could sell their stakes in Willy's company to other willing buyers. When a publicly traded company has shares that trade on a stock market, the trading activity has a negligible effect on the business. So Willy, of course, was able to concentrate on what he did best: making chocolate. The shareholders didn't bother him because generally, minority shareholders don't have any influence in a company's day-to-day operations.

Willy's chocolate was amazing. Pleasing the shareholders, he began selling more and more chocolate. But they wanted more than a certificate from the New York Stock Exchange or their local brokerage firm to prove that they were partial owners of the chocolate factory. They wanted to share in the business profits that the factory generated. This made sense because shareholders in a company are technically owners.

So the board of directors (which was voted into their positions by the shareholders) decided to give the owners an annual percentage of the profits and everyone was happy. This is how it worked: Willy's factory sold about $100,000 worth of chocolate and goodies each year. After paying taxes on the earnings, employee wages, and maintenance costs, Willy Wonka's Chocolate Factory made an annual profit of $10,000, so the company's board of directors decided to pay its shareholders $5,000 of that annual $10,000 profit and split it among the shareholders. This is known as a dividend.

The remaining $5,000 profit would be reinvested back into the business—so Willy could pay for bigger and better machinery, advertise his chocolate far and wide, and make chocolate even faster, generating higher profits.

Those reinvested profits made Willy's business even more lucrative. As a result, the Chocolate Factory doubled its profits to $20,000 the following year, and it increased its dividend payout to shareholders.

This, of course, caused other potential investors to drool. They wanted to buy shares in the factory, too. Now there were more people wanting to buy shares than there were people who wanted to sell them. This created a demand for the shares, causing the share price on the New York Stock Exchange to rise. (If there are more buyers than sellers, the share price rises. If there are more sellers than buyers, the share price falls.)

Over time, the share price of Willy's business fluctuated: sometimes climbing, sometimes falling, depending on investor sentiment. If news about the company was good, it increased public demand for the shares, pushing up the price. On other days, investors grew pessimistic, causing the share price to fall.

Willy's factory continued to make more money over the years. And over the long term, when a company increases its profits, the stock price generally rises along with it.

Willy's shareholders were able to make money in two different ways. They could realize a profit from dividends (cash payments given to shareholders usually four times each year) or they could wait until their stock had increased substantially in value on the stock market and choose to sell some or all of their shares.

Here's how an investor could hypothetically make 10 percent a year from owning shares in Willy Wonka's business.

Montgomery Burns had his eye on Willy Wonka's Chocolate Factory shares, and he decided to buy $1,000 of the chocolate company's stock at $10 a share. After one year, if the share price rose to $10.50, this would amount to a 5 percent increase in the share price ($10.50 is 5 percent higher than the $10 that Burns paid).

And if Burns was given a $50 dividend, we could say that he had earned an additional 5 percent because a $50 dividend is five percent of his initial $1,000 investment.

So if his shares gain 5 percent in value from the share-price increase and he makes an extra 5 percent from the dividend payment, then after one year Burns potentially would have made a 10 percent profit on his shares. Of course, only the 5 percent dividend payout would go into his pocket as a "realized" profit. The 5 percent "profit" from the price appreciation (as the stock rose in value) would only be realized if Burns sold his Willy Wonka shares.

Montgomery Burns, however, didn't become the richest man in Springfield by buying and selling Willy Wonka shares when they fluctuated in price. Studies have shown that, on average, investors who buy shares and sell them again quickly don't tend to make profits as high as investors who hold onto their shares over the long term.

Burns held onto those shares for many years. Sometimes the share price rose and sometimes it fell. But the company kept increasing its profits, so the share price increased over time. The annual dividends kept a smile on Montgomery Burns' greedy little lips, as his profits from the rising stock price, coupled with dividends, earned him an average potential return of 10 percent a year.

However, Burns wasn't rubbing his bony hands together as gleefully as you might expect because at the same time he bought Willy Wonka shares, he also bought shares in Homer's donuts and Moe's Tavern. Neither business worked out, and Burns lost money.

Driving him really crazy, however, was missing out on shares in the joke-store company, Bart's Barf Gags. If Burns had bought shares in this business, he would be laughing— all the way to the bank. Share prices quadrupled in just four years.

In the following chapter, I'll show you that one of the best ways to invest in the stock market is to own every stock in the market, rather than trying to follow the strategy of Burns and guess which stocks will rise. Though it sounds impossible to buy virtually every stock in a given market, it's made easy by purchasing a single product that owns every stock within it.

Before getting to that, remember that you can invest half of what your neighbors invest over your lifetime and still end up with twice as much money—if you start early enough. For patient investors, the aggregate returns of the world's stock markets have dished out fabulous profits.

For example, the US stock market averaged 10.16 percent annually from 1920 to 2016. There were periods where it grew faster than that, while it dropped back at other times. But that 10.16 percent average return has provided some impressive long-term profits.

Of course, the stock market doesn't grow each and every year. Some years between 1920 and 2016, US stocks exceeded a growth rate of 10.16 percent. Other years, stocks fell. But patient investors get rewarded.

Here's an example. Assume you had invested $1,600 in the US stock market at the beginning of 1978. If you had added $100 per month, come hell or high water, you would have practiced something called dollar-cost averaging. Instead of speculating whether it was a "good time" or "bad time" to invest, you would have put your money on autopilot. Here's how that money would have grown in a tax-free account, if you had added $100 per month to the initial $1,600 investment between 1978 and August 2016 (the time of this writing).

Table 2.1 Dollar Cost Averaging with US Stocks Starting with $1,600 and Adding $100 Per Month

Year Ending	Total Cost of Cumulative Investments	Total Value after Growth
1978	$1,600	$1,699
1979	$2,800	$3,273
1980	$4000	$5,755
1981	$5,200	$6,630
1982	$6,400	$9,487
1983	$7,600	$12,783
1984	$8,800	$14,863
1985	$10,000	$20,905
1986	$11,200	$25,934
1987	$12,400	$28,221
1988	$13,600	$34,079
1989	$14,800	$46,126
1990	$16,000	$45,803
1991	$17,200	$61,009

Table 2.1 *(Cont'd)*

Year Ending	Total Cost of Cumulative Investments	Total Value after Growth
1992	$18,400	$66,816
1993	$19,600	$74,687
1994	$20,800	$76,779
1995	$22,000	$106,944
1996	$23,200	$132,767
1997	$24,400	$178,217
1998	$25,600	$230,619
1999	$26,800	$280,564
2000	$28,000	$256,271
2001	$29,200	$226,622
2002	$30,400	$177,503
2003	$31,600	$229,523
2004	$32,800	$255,479
2005	$34,000	$268,932
2006	$35,200	$312,317
2007	$36,400	$330,350
2008	$37,600	$208,940
2009	$38,800	$265,756
2010	$40,000	$301,098
2011	$41,200	$302,298
2012	$42,400	$344,459
2013	$43,600	$403,514
2014	$44,800	$458,028
2015	$46,000	$463,754
August 2016	$46,800	$498,904

Source: A Random Walk Down Wall Street (11th edition); Morningstar.com, using returns from the S&P 500.

Between 1978 and August 23, 2016, the investor would have added just $46,800. But the money would have grown to $498,904. To build such massive wealth, it's best to start early. Let me show you how.

Notes

1. Jay Steele, Warren Buffett, *Master of the Market* (New York: Avon Books, 1999), 17.
2. Andrew Kilpatrick, *Of Permanent Value, The Story of Warren Buffett* (Birmingham, AL: Andy Kilpatrick Publishing Empire, 2006), 226.

3. The Value Line Investment Survey—A Long-Term Perspective Chart 1920–2005 and Morningstar Performance Tracking of the S&P 500 from 2005 to 2016, www.morningstar.com.

4. Jeremy Siegel, *Stocks for the Long Run*, 3rd ed. (New York: McGraw-Hill, 2002), 18.

RULE 3
Small Fees Pack Big Punches

An out-of-town visitor was being shown the wonders of the New York financial district. When the party arrived at the Battery, one of his guides indicated some handsome ships riding at anchor. He said,

"Look, those are the bankers' and brokers' yachts."

"Where are the customers' yachts?" asked the naïve visitor.[1]

—Fred Schwed, *Where Are the Customer's Yachts?*

In 1971, when the great boxer Muhammad Ali was still undefeated, US basketball star Wilt Chamberlain suggested publicly that he stood a chance of beating Ali in the boxing ring. Promoters scrambled to organize a fight that Ali considered a joke. Whenever the ultra-confident Ali walked into a room with the towering Chamberlain within earshot, he would cup his hands and holler through them: "Timber-r-r-r!"

Chamberlain felt that one lucky punch could knock Ali out. He thought he had a chance. But the rest of the sporting world knew better. Chamberlain's odds of winning were ridiculously low, and his bravado could only lead to significant pain for the great basketball player.

As legend has it, Ali's "Timber-r-r-r!" taunts eventually rattled Chamberlain's nerves enough to put a stop to the pending fight.[2]

Most people don't like losing. For that reason there are certain things most of us won't do. If we're smart (sorry Wilt) we won't bet a professional boxer that we can beat him or her in the ring. We won't bet a prosecuting lawyer that we can defend ourselves in a court of law and win. We won't put our money down on the odds of beating a chess master at chess.

But would we dare challenge a professional financial adviser in a long-term investing contest? Common sense initially suggests that we shouldn't. However, this may be the only exception to the rule of challenging someone in their given profession—and beating them easily.

With Training, the Average Fifth Grader Can Take on Wall Street

Yes, it's easy for a fifth grader to take on Wall Street. The kid doesn't have to be smart. He just needs to learn that when following financial advice from most professional advisers, he won't be steered toward the best investments. The game is rigged against the average investor because most advisers make money for themselves—at their clients' expense.

The Selfish Reality of the Financial Service Industry

The vast majority of financial advisers are salespeople who will put their own financial interests ahead of yours. They sell investment products that pay them (or their employers) well, while you're a distant second on their priority list. Many of us know people who work as financial planners. They're fun to talk to at parties or on the golf course. But if they're buying actively managed mutual funds for their clients, they're doing their clients a disservice.

Instead of recommending actively managed mutual funds (which the vast number of advisers do), they should direct their clients toward index funds.

Index Funds—What Experts Love but Advisers Hate

Every nonfiction book has an index. Go ahead, flip to the back of this one. Scan all those referenced words representing this book's content. A book's index is a representation of everything that's inside it.

Now think of the stock market as a book. If you went to the back pages (the index) you could see a representation of everything that was inside that "book." For example, if you went to the back pages of the US stock market, you would see the names of companies such as Walmart, The Gap, Exxon Mobil, Procter & Gamble, and Colgate-Palmolive. The directory would go on and on until several thousand businesses were named.

In the world of investing, if you buy a US total stock market index fund, you're buying a single product that has thousands of stocks within it. It represents the entire US stock market.

With just three index funds, your money can be spread over nearly every available global money basket:

1. A home country stock market index (for Americans, this would be a US index; for Canadians, a Canadian stock index)

2. An international stock market index (holding the widest array of international stocks from around the world)

3. A government bond market index (made up of government bonds that guarantee an interest rate)

I'll explain the bond index in Chapter 5. In Chapter 6, I'll introduce you to four real people from across the globe. They created indexed investment portfolios. It was easy for them (as you'll see) and it will be easy for you.

That's it. With just three index funds, you'll beat the pants (and the shirts, socks, underwear, and shoes) off most financial professionals.

Financial Experts Backing the Irrefutable

Full-time professionals in other fields, let's say dentists, bring a lot to the layman. But in aggregate, people get nothing for their money from professional money managers. . . . The best way to own common stocks is through an index fund.[3]

—*Warren Buffett, Berkshire Hathaway Chairman*

If you were to ask Warren Buffett what you should invest in, he would suggest that you buy index funds. He has also instructed his estate's trustees to put his heirs' proceeds into index funds when he dies. He shared this information in Berkshire Hathaway's 2014 annual report. "My advice to the trustee could not be more simple: put 10 percent of the cash in short-term government bonds and 90 percent in a very low-cost S&P 500 index fund. (I suggest Vanguard's.)"[4]

As the world's greatest investor, you might think that Warren Buffett could find a great stock picker or mutual fund manager to invest his wife's money. But he's a smart man. The odds are against him finding anyone who can beat the market index after fees. That's why his wife's money will go into index funds.

I don't believe I would have amassed a million dollars on a teacher's salary while still in my 30s if I were unknowingly paying hidden fees to a typical financial adviser. Don't think I'm not a generous guy. I just don't want to be giving away hundreds of thousands of dollars during my investment life-time to a slick talker in a salesperson's cloak. And I don't think you should either.

What Would a Nobel Prize-Winning Economist Suggest?

The most efficient way to diversify a stock portfolio is with a low fee index fund.[5]

—Paul Samuelson, 1970 Nobel Prize in Economics

Arguably the most famous economist of our time, the late Paul Samuelson, was the first American to win a Nobel Prize in Economics. It's fair to say that he knew a heck of a lot more about money than the brokers who suffer from conflicts of interest at your neighborhood Merrill Lynch, Edward Jones, or Raymond James offices.

The typical financial planner won't want you to know this. But a dream team of Economic Nobel Laureates want you to know the truth. Investors aren't likely to find a professional money manager who can beat the stock market index.

They're just not going to do it. It's just not going to happen.[6]

—*Daniel Kahneman, 2002 Nobel Prize in Economics, when asked about investors' long-term chances of beating a broad-based index fund*

Kahneman won the Nobel Prize for his work on how natural human behaviors negatively affect investment decisions. Too many people, in his view, think they can find fund managers who can beat the market index, long term. But such thinking is wrong.

Any pension fund manager who doesn't have the vast majority—and I mean 70 percent or 80 percent of his or her portfolio—in passive investments [index funds] is guilty of malfeasance, nonfeasance, or some other kind of bad feasance! There's just no sense for most of them to have anything but a passive [indexed] investment policy.[7]

—*Merton Miller, 1990 Nobel Prize in Economics*

Pension fund managers are trusted to invest billions of dollars for governments and corporations. In the United States, more than half of them use indexed approaches. Those who don't are, according to Miller, setting an irresponsible policy.

I have a global index fund with all-in expenses at eight basis points.[8]

—*Robert Merton, 1997 Nobel Prize in Economics*

In 1994, Robert Merton, Professor Emeritus at Harvard Business School, probably thought he could beat the market. After all, he was a director of Long Term Capital Management, a US hedge fund (a type of mutual fund I will explain later) that reportedly earned 40 percent annual returns from 1994 to 1998. That was before the fund imploded. It lost most of its shareholders' money and shut down in 2000.[9]

Naturally, a Nobel Prize winner such as Merton is a brilliant man—and he's brilliant enough to learn from his mistakes. When asked to share his investment holdings in an interview with PBS News Hour in 2009, the first thing out of Merton's mouth was the global index fund that he owns. It charges eight basis points. That's just a fancy way of saying that the hidden annual fee for his index is 0.08 percent.

The average retail investor working with a financial adviser pays between 12 to 30 times more than that in fees. These fees can cost hundreds of thousands of dollars over an investment lifetime. I'll show you how to get your investment fees down very close to what Robert Merton pays. By doing so, you'll be able to learn from his mistakes.

More often (alas) the conclusions (supporting active management) can only be justified by assuming that the laws of arithmetic have been suspended for the convenience of those who choose to pursue careers as active managers.[10]

—*William F. Sharpe, 1990 Nobel Prize in Economics*

If you were lucky enough to have William Sharpe living across the street, he would tell you that he's a huge proponent of index funds and suggest that financial advisers and mutual fund managers who pursue other forms of stock market investing are deluding themselves.[11]

If a financial adviser tries to tell you not to invest in index funds, they're essentially suggesting that they're smarter than Warren Buffett and more brilliant than a Nobel Prize Laureate in Economics. What do you think?

What Causes Experts to Shake Their Heads

Advisers get paid well when you buy actively managed mutual funds (or unit trusts, as they're known outside of North America) so they love buying them for their clients' accounts. Advisers rarely get paid anything (if at all) when you buy stock market indexes. That's why they desperately try to steer their clients in another (more profitable) direction.

An actively managed mutual fund works like this:

1. Your adviser takes your money and sends it to a fund company.

2. That fund company combines your money with those of other investors into an active mutual fund.

3. The fund company has a fund manager who buys and sells stocks within that fund hoping that their buying and selling will result in profits for investors.

While a total US stock market index owns nearly all the stocks in the US market all of the time, an active mutual fund manager buys and sells selected stocks repeatedly.

For example, an active mutual fund manager might buy Coca-Cola Company shares today, sell Microsoft shares tomorrow, buy the stock back next week, and buy and sell General Electric Company shares two or three times within a 12-month period.

It sounds strategic. But academic evidence suggests that, statistically, buying an actively managed mutual fund is a loser's game when comparing it with buying index funds. Despite the strategic buying and selling of stocks by fund managers, the vast majority of actively managed mutual funds will lose to the indexes over the long term.

Economic Nobel Prize winner William F. Sharpe explained this in his Stanford published paper "The Arithmetic of Active Management."[12] Here's his explanation in a nutshell.

When the US stock market moves up by, say, 8 percent in a given year, it means the average dollar invested in the stock market increased by 8 percent that year. When the US stock market drops by, say, 8 percent in a given year, it means the average dollar invested in the stock market dropped in value by 8 percent that year.

But does it mean that if the stock market made (hypothetically speaking) 8 percent last year, every investor in US stocks made an 8 percent return on their investments that year? Of course not. Some made more, some made less. In a year where the markets made 8 percent, half of the money that was invested in the market that year would have made more than 8 percent and half of the money invested in the markets would have made less than 8 percent. When averaging all the "successes" and "losses" (in terms of individual stocks moving up or down that year), the average return would have been 8 percent.

Most of the money that's in the stock market comes from mutual funds (and index funds), pension funds, hedge funds and endowment money.

So if the markets made 8 percent this year, what do you think the average mutual fund, pension fund, hedge fund and college endowment fund would have made on their stock market assets during that year?

The answer, of course, is going to be very close to 8 percent. Before fees.

We know that a broad-based index fund would have made roughly 8 percent during this hypothetical year because it would own every stock in the market—giving it the "average" return of the market. There's no mathematical possibility that a total stock market index can ever beat the return of the stock market. If the stock market makes 25 percent in a given year, a total stock market index fund would make about 24.8 percent after factoring in the small cost (about 0.2 percent) of running the index. If the stock market made 13 percent the following year, a total stock market index would make about 12.8 percent.

A financial adviser selling mutual funds seems, at first glance, to have a high prospect of getting his or her hand on your wallet right now. The adviser might suggest that earning the same return that the stock market makes (and not more) would represent an "average" return—and that he or she could beat the average return through purchasing superior actively managed mutual funds.

If actively managed mutual funds didn't cost money to run, and if advisers worked for free, investors' odds of finding funds that would beat the broad-based index would be close to 50–50. In a 15-year-long US study published in the *Journal of Portfolio Management*, actively managed stock market mutual funds were compared with the Standard & Poor's 500 stock market index. The study concluded that 96 percent of actively managed mutual funds underperformed the US market index after fees, taxes, and survivorship bias.[13]

What's a Survivorship Bias?

When a mutual fund performs terribly, it doesn't typically attract new investors and many of its current customers flee the fund for healthier pastures. Often, the poorly performing fund is merged with another fund or it is shut down.

In November 2009, I underwent bone cancer surgery— where large pieces of three of my ribs were removed, as well as chunks of my vertebrae. But you want to know something? My five-year survivorship odds were better than that of the average mutual fund. Examining two decades of actively managed mutual fund data, investment researchers Robert Arnott, Andrew Berkin, and Jia Ye tracked 195 actively managed funds before reporting that the funds had a 17 percent mortality. According to the article they published with the *Journal of Portfolio Management* in 2000 called "How Well Have Taxable Investors Been Served in the 1980s and 1990s?," 33 of the 195 funds they tracked disappeared between 1979 and 1999.[14] No one can predict which funds are going to survive and which won't. The odds of picking an actively managed fund that you think will survive are no better than predicting which bone cancer survivor will last the longest.

When the Best Funds Turn Malignant

You might think that the very best funds (those with long established track records) are large enough and strong enough to have a predictable longevity. They can't suddenly turn sour and disappear, can they?

That's what investors in the 44 Wall Street Fund thought. It was the top-ranked fund of the 1970s—outperforming every diversified fund in the industry and beating the S&P 500 index for 11 years in a row. Its success was temporary, however, and it went from being the best-performing fund in one decade to being the worst-performing fund in the next, losing 73 percent of its value in the 1980s. Consequently, its brand name was mud, so it was merged into the Cumberland Growth Fund in 1993, which then was merged into the Matterhorn Growth Fund in 1996. Today, it's as if it never existed.[15]

Then there was the Lindner Large-Cap Fund, another stellar performer that attracted a huge following of investors as it beat the S&P 500 index for each of the 11 years from 1974 to 1984. But you won't find it today. Over the next 18 years (from 1984 to 2002) it made its investors just 4.1 percent annually, compared with the 12.6 percent annual gain for investors in the S&P 500 index. Finally, the dismal track record of the Lindner Large-Cap Fund was erased when it was merged into the Hennessy Total Return Fund.[16]

You can read countless books on index-performance track records versus actively managed funds. Most say index funds have the advantage over 80 percent of actively managed funds over a period of 10 years or more. But they don't typically account for survivorship bias (or taxes, which I'll discuss later in this chapter) when making the comparisons. Doing so gives index funds an even larger advantage.

When accounting for fees, survivorship bias, and taxes, most actively managed mutual funds dramatically underperform index funds.

Mark Kritzman is president and chief executive of Windham Capital Management of Boston. He also teaches a graduate course in financial engineering at M.I.T.'s Sloan School of Management. In 2009, he calculated that the typical actively managed mutual fund, in a taxable account, would have to beat an index fund by an average of 4.3 percent per year, before fees and taxes, just to break even with an index fund. *The New York Times* reported his study in 2009.[17]

Holes in the Hulls of Actively Managed Mutual Funds

There are five factors dragging down the returns of actively managed US mutual funds: expense ratios, 12B1 fees, trading costs, sales commissions, and taxes. Many people ask me why they don't see these fee liabilities mentioned on their mutual fund statements. With the possible exception of expense ratios and sales commissions—in very small print—the rest are hidden from view. Buying these products over an investment lifetime can be like entering a swimming race while towing a hunk of carpet.

1. Expense Ratios

Expense ratios are costs associated with running a mutual fund. You might not realize this, but if you buy an actively managed mutual fund, hidden fees pay the salaries of the analysts and/or traders to choose which stocks to buy and sell. These folks are some of the highest paid professionals in the world; as such, they are expensive to employ. There's also the cost of maintaining their computers, paying office leases, ordering the paper they shuffle, using electricity, and compensating the advisers/salespeople for recommending their funds.

Then there are the owners of the fund company. They receive profits based on the costs skimmed from mutual fund expense ratios. I'm not referring to the average Joe who buys fund units in the mutual fund. I'm referring to the fund company's owners.

A US fund that holds a collective $30 billion would cost its investors (the average Joe) about $450 million every year (or 1.5 percent of its total assets) in expense-ratio fees. That money is sifted out of the mutual fund's value. But it isn't itemized for investors to see.[18] And the cash comes out whether the mutual fund makes money or not.

2. 12B1 Fees

Not every actively managed fund company charges 12B1 fees, but roughly 60 percent in the United States do. They can cost up to 0.25 percent, or a further $75 million a year for a $30 billion fund. These pay for marketing expenses including magazine, newspaper, television, and online advertising that's meant to lure new investors. That money has to come from somewhere. So current investors pay for new investors to join the party.[19] It's like a masked phantom pulling money from the wallets of mutual fund investors every night. Financial advisory statements don't itemize these expenses either.

3. Trading Costs

A third fee includes the fund's trading costs. They fluctuate year to year, based on how much buying and selling the fund managers do. Remember, actively managed mutual funds have traders at the helm who buy and sell stocks within the fund to try and gain an edge. But on average, according to the global research company Lipper, the average actively managed stock market mutual fund accrues trading costs of 0.2 percent annually, or $60 million a year on a $30 billion fund.[20] The costs of trading, 12B1 fees, and expense ratios aren't the only invisible albatrosses around the necks of mutual fund investors.

4. Sales Commissions

If the three hidden fees above are bringing you back in time to the nightmarish bottom of an elementary school dog pile, I have worse news for you. Many fund companies charge load fees: either a percentage up front to buy the fund (which goes directly to the salesperson) or a fee to sell the fund (which also goes directly to the salesperson). These fees can be as high as 6 percent. Many financial advisers love selling "loaded funds," which add a pretty nice kick to their own personal accounts. But they aren't such a great deal for investors. A fund charging a sales fee of 5.75 percent, for example, has to gain 6.1 percent the following year just to break even on the deposited money. That might sound like strange math at first, but if you lose a given percentage to fees, you have to gain back a higher percentage to get your head back above water. For example, losing 50 percent in one year (turning $100 into $50) ensures that you will need to double your money the following year to get back to the original $100. Advisers choosing loaded funds for their clients put a whole new spin on "Piggy Bank," don't you think?

5. Taxes

More than 60 percent of the money in US mutual funds is in taxable accounts.[21] This means when an actively managed mutual fund makes money in a given year, the investor has to pay taxes on that gain if the fund is held in a taxable account. There's a reason for that. Actively managed stock market mutual funds have fund managers who buy and sell stocks within their funds. If the stocks they sell generate an overall profit for the fund, then the investors in that fund (if they hold the fund in a taxable account) get handed a tax bill at the end of the year for the realized capital gain. The more trading a fund manager does, the less tax efficient the fund is.

In the case of a total stock market index fund, there's virtually no trading. The gains that are made on the stocks held don't generate a taxable hit for the funds' investors unless the investor sells the fund at a higher price than he or she paid. Rather than paying a high rate of capital gains tax every year, the index investor is able to defer his or her gains, paying them when he or she eventually sells the fund. Doing so allows for significantly higher compounding profits.

Mutual fund managers know that few people are going to compare their "after-tax" results with other mutual funds. For example, a fund making 11 percent a year might end up beating a fund making 12 percent a year—after taxes.[22] What makes one fund less tax efficient than another? It's the frequency of their buying and selling. The average actively managed mutual fund trades every stock it has during an average year. This is called a "100 percent turnover."[23] The trading practices of most mutual fund managers trigger short-term capital gains to the owners of those funds (when the funds make money). In the United States, the short-term capital gain tax is a hefty penalty. But few actively managed fund managers seem to care.

In comparison, index-fund investors pay far fewer taxes in taxable accounts because index funds follow a "buy and hold" strategy. The more trading that occurs within a mutual fund, the higher the taxes incurred by the investor.

In the Bogle Financial Markets Research Center's 15-year study on after-tax mutual fund performances (from 1994 to 2009), it found actively managed stock market mutual funds were dramatically less tax efficient than a stock market index. For example, if you had invested in a fund (for your taxable account) that equaled the performance of the stock market index from 1994 to 2009, you would have paradoxically made less money than if you had invested in an index fund. But why would you have made less money if your fund had matched the performance of the stock index?

Before taxes, if your fund matched the performance of the US index, you would have averaged 6.7 percent per year. After taxes though, for the actively managed fund to make as much money as a US index fund, it would have needed to beat the index by a total of 16.2 percent over the 15-year period. This is assuming that the mutual fund manager bought and sold stocks with a regularity that equaled the average actively managed fund "turnover."[24]

Let's look at an actively managed fund with a track record of strong performance and low portfolio turnover (remember that performance is rarely sustainable). Fidelity's Contrafund (FCNTX) fits the bill. When I accessed Morningstar, mid-2016, the fund ratings company posted the Fidelity Contrafund's turnover at just 35 percent. That's good. It's far below the industry average. It means that the fund would have traded just 35 percent of its holdings the previous year.

By April 30, 2016, Fidelity's Contrafund had earned an average pre-tax annual compound return of 11.57 percent over the previous three years. This beat the pre-tax return of Vanguard's S&P 500 index. It averaged 11.09 percent per year during the same time period. But the index fund's taxable turnover was just 3 percent. This gave it an after-tax advantage.

Morningstar estimated that the Fidelity Contrafund's three-year, post-tax performance was 9.82 percent per year. Vanguard's S&P 500 index did better. It averaged an estimated post-tax compound annual return of 10.38 percent per year.[25]

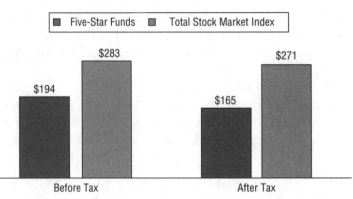

Figure 3.1   Five-Star Funds vs. Total Stock Market Index (1994–2004)
Source: John C. Bogle, *The Little Book of Common Sense Investing*

A post-tax comparison of a mutual fund's performance against the performance of a stock market index isn't something that you will likely see on a typical mutual fund statement. But the post-tax gain is the only number that should count. This also applies to Canadians and those of other nationalities who invest in taxable accounts.

Adding high expense ratios, 12B1 fees, trading costs, sales commissions, and taxes to your investment is a bit like a boxer standing blindfolded in a ring and asking his opponent to hit him five times on the jaw before the opening bell. It's tough to put up a fair fight when you're already bleeding.

Figure 3.1 illustrates that if you learned this in school, it's likely that you would never consider investing in actively managed funds as an adult.

The Futility of Picking Top Mutual Funds

You've just told your financial adviser that you'd like to invest in index funds—and now she's desperate. She won't make money (or not much) if you invest in indexes. It's far more lucrative for advisers to sell actively managed mutual funds instead. She needs you to buy the products for which she will be compensated handsomely, so here's the card she plays:

"Look, I'm a professional. And our company has access to researchers who will help me choose actively managed funds

that will beat the indexes. Just look at these top-rated funds. I can show you dozens of them that have beaten the stock market index over the past 10 years. Of course I would only buy you top-rated funds."

Are there dozens of funds that have beaten the stock market indexes over the past 5, 10, or 15 years? Sure there are. But those funds, despite their track records, aren't likely to repeat their winning streaks. Mutual fund investing is a rare example of how, paradoxically, historical excellence means nothing.

Reality Check

Morningstar is an investment-research firm in the United States that awards funds based on a five-star system: five stars for a fund with a remarkable track record, all the way down to one star for a fund with a poor track record. Five-star funds tend to be those that have beaten the indexes over the previous five or ten years.

The problem is that fund rankings change all the time, and so do fund performances. Just because a fund has a five-star rating today doesn't mean that it will outperform the index over the next year, five years, or 10 years. It's easy to look back in time and see great performing funds, but trying to pick them based on their historical performance is an expensive game.

Academics refer to something they call "reversion to the mean." In practical terms, actively managed funds that outperform the indexes typically revert to the mean or worse. In other words, buying the top historically performing funds can end up being the kiss of death.

If an adviser had decided to purchase Morningstar's five-star rated funds for you in 1994, and if he sold them as the funds slipped in the rankings (replacing them with the newly selected five-star funds), how do you think the investor would have performed from 1994 to 2004 compared with a broad-based US stock market index fund?

Thanks to *Hulbert's Financial Digest*, an investment newsletter that rates the performance predictions of other newsletters, we have the answer. It's emphasized in Figure 3.1.

One hundred dollars invested and continually adjusted to only hold the highest rated Morningstar funds from 1994 to 2004 would have turned into roughly $194. It would have averaged 6.9 percent per year in a tax-deferred portfolio.

One hundred dollars invested in a broad-based US stock market index from 1994 to 2004 would have turned into roughly $283. It would have averaged 11 percent per year in a tax-deferred portfolio.[26]

Many investors invest more than what their tax-deferred accounts will allow each year. To do so, they must invest in a taxable account. In such accounts, the after-tax performance difference between an actively managed fund and an index grows even wider. You might as well be running with a monkey on your back.

One hundred dollars invested and continually adjusted to hold only the highest rated Morningstar funds from 1994 to 2004 would have turned into roughly $165 in a taxable account. After taxes, it would have averaged 5.15 percent per year.

One hundred dollars invested in a broad-based US stock market index from 1994 to 2004 would have turned into roughly $271 in a taxable account. After taxes, it would have averaged 10.5 percent per year.

Interestingly, more than 98 percent of invested mutual fund money gets pushed into Morningstar's top-rated funds.[27]

But choosing which actively managed mutual fund will perform well in the future is, in Burton Malkiel's words, ". . . like an obstacle course through hell's kitchen."[28] Malkiel, a professor of economics at Princeton University and the best-selling author of *A Random Walk Guide to Investing*, adds:

> *There is no way to choose the best [actively managed mutual fund] managers in advance. I have calculated the results of employing strategies of buying the funds with the best recent-year performance, best recent two-year performance, best five-year and ten-year performance, and not one of these strategies produced above average returns. I calculated the returns from buying the best funds selected by* Forbes *magazine . . . and found that these funds subsequently produced below average returns.*[29]

Studies routinely show that you can't pick winning mutual funds based on how they performed last month, last year, or over the past decade. Funds that win during one time period usually get thumped the next.

The SPIVA Persistence Scorecard gets published twice a year. It looks at actively managed funds that are among the top 25 percent of performers. Then it determines what percentage of those funds remains among the top 25 percent of performers. There were 682 US stock market funds among the top 25 percent of performers as of March 2013. By March 2015, just 5.28 percent of them remained among the top quartile. Look for these reports every six months. They always present a similar eye-opening tale.[30]

Many financial writers wish for one thing at Christmas. They want their readers to suffer from classic, daytime soap opera amnesia. Steve Forbes should know. The publishing executive for *Forbes* magazine said, "You make more money selling advice than following it. It's one of the things we count on in the magazine business—along with the short memory of our readers."[31]

Take the article written by *Business Insider*'s Nick Levis on July 20, 2011.[32] He boldly pumped "7 Top Mutual Funds with Long Term Solid Track Records." None were stock market indexes. That would be boring. Instead, he promoted cotton candy over broccoli.

He chose seven actively managed mutual funds with strong historical track records. I asked Russel Kinnel, Morningstar's director of mutual fund research, what to look for when picking mutual funds that we hoped would do well in the future. He said, "Low fees are the best predictor. . . so go with a low-fee fund every time."[33] The funds with the lowest fees, of course, are indexes. That's why Warren Buffett instructed his estate's trustees to put his heirs' proceeds into index funds when he dies.

Those following Nick Levis's advice, however, are likely crying over their wallets. Since the article was published, the S&P 500 has scorched all seven of his recommendations. According to Morningstar, investors splitting $10,000 evenly into each of the former hot tickets would have seen their money grow to $12,219 by November 13, 2015. By comparison, a $10,000 investment in Vanguard's S&P 500 index fund would have been worth 36 percent more. It would have grown to $16,625.[34]

Academics call this "reversion to the mean." Winning funds rarely continue to win. And when they disappoint, investors pay the price. By the end of 2015, the S&P 500 had a better 5-year track record than each of Mr. Levis's former hot funds. The index also reported a better 10-year track record.

I don't mean to pick on Mr. Levis. Finance writers need to push a bit of excitement. That's their bread and butter. A *Fortune* magazine writer once said, "By day, we write about, 'Six Funds to Buy NOW!'... By night, we invest in sensible index funds. Unfortunately, pro-index fund stories don't sell magazines."[35]

When Best Mutual Fund Lists Can Strip You Naked

Here's an example from May 2010. *US News and World Report* published, "The 100 Best Mutual Funds for the Long Term." Each year, most finance magazines publish something similar. They should carry x-rated warnings.

The writer's opening line stated, "When it comes to choosing a mutual fund, there's nothing better than a solid track record." This would shock most mutual fund academics.

It's like saying, "When it comes to running on glass, nothing beats bare feet." "The 100 Best Mutual Funds for the Long Term" listed 50 US stock market mutual funds (the remaining 50 were bond funds, balanced funds, and international funds). *US News* broke them into five different categories: Value, Growth, Small-Cap, Mid-Cap, and Large-Cap.

What Exactly Are These Categories Of Funds?

You don't need to know what Value Funds, Growth Funds, Small-Cap, Mid-Cap, and Large-Cap Funds are, but here's a primer. A Value Fund is made up of cheap stocks. A Growth Fund is made up of stocks with

(Cont'd)

high expected business earnings. Small-Cap, Mid-Cap, and Large-Cap funds are those defined by the stocks within them. For example, a Large-Cap Fund is made up of large stocks (like Coca-Cola, Walmart, and Apple). A Small-Cap fund is made up of smaller company stocks. Medium-Cap funds represent medium-sized stocks.

Investors could theoretically buy an actively managed Small-Cap Fund or a Small-Cap Index Fund. But I don't think you should bother. Instead, the portfolios of funds that I recommend (and those that I own myself) keep things simple. They're made up of broad-based index funds that own a little bit of everything.

The author wrote:

We chose funds with positive 10-year trailing returns and, for stock funds, names that beat the S&P 500 over that time frame. . . . Our score is based on the ratings of some of the mutual fund industry's best-known analysts . . . [36]

He should have written:

We have ignored financial academic studies. Instead, we chose yesterday's winning funds and fortunetellers' picks. Those purchasing these funds will likely underperform their respective benchmark indexes by an average of 2.31 percent per year. Over a 30-year period, a retirement nest egg's potential could be reduced by a third.

Where am I getting this 2.31 percent? I tore at the forecaster's toga. I used portfoliovisualizer.com to see how these recommended funds performed since the article's May 2010 publication.

Some of the funds changed names (as a result of poor performance, company mergers, or acquisitions). But with the exception of the Madison Mosaic Disciplined Equity Fund, I tracked down every one. Keep in mind, these were index-beating funds when *US News* had listed them.

Ticker	Name
YACKX	AMG Yacktman Fund
ACGIX	Invesco Growth & Income Fund Class A
EQTIX	Shelton Core Value Fund Class S
AMANX	Amana Mutual Funds Trust - Income Fund
VAFGX	Valley Forge Fund, Inc.
FVALX	Forester Value Fund
FDSAX	Focused Dividend Strategy Portfolio Class A
AGOCX	Prudential Jennison Equity Income Fund Class C
AUXFX	Auxier Focus Fd Investor Shares
HOVLX	Homestead Funds, Inc. - Value Fund

Figure 3.2 *US News and World Report*: Recommended US Value Funds
Source: US News and World Report; portfoliovisualizer.com

But after the article was published, index funds crushed them in all five categories. The recommended value funds, listed on Figure 3.2, averaged a compound annual return of 8.77 percent between May 2010 and May 2016. Vanguard's Value Index (VIVAX) averaged a compound annual return of 11.13 percent during the same time period.

The writer's US Growth fund recommendations, listed in Figure 3.3, averaged a compound annual return of 10.73 percent per year. Vanguard's Growth Index (VIGRX) stomped them. It averaged a compound annual return of 12.35 percent.

Ticker	Name
JENSX	Jensen Quality Growth Fund Cl J
FKGRX	Franklin Growth Fund Class A
LHGFX	American Beacon Holland Large Cap Growth Fd Inv Cl
VHCOX	Vanguard Capital Opportunity Fund
PTWAX	Prudential Jennison 20/20 Focus Fund Class A
FCNTX	Fidelity Contra Fund
PROVX	Provident Trust Strategy Fund
MINVX	Madison Investors Fund Cl Y
BUFEX	Buffalo Large Cap Fund, Inc.
AMCPX	AMCAP Fund, Class A Shares A

Figure 3.3 *US News and World Report*: Recommended US Growth Funds
Source: US News and World Report; portfoliovisualizer.com

Ticker	Name
RYOTX	Royce Micro-Cap Fund Investment Class
FSLCX	Fidelity Commonwealth Trust Fidelity Small Cap Stock Fund
OTCFX	T. Rowe Price Small-Cap Stock Fund
RGFAX	Royce Heritage Fund Service Class
FOSCX	Tributary Small Company Fd Instl
LZSCX	Lazard US Small-Mid Cap Equity Portfolio Institutional Shares
LRSCX	Lord Abbett Research Fund, Inc. - Small-Cap Series - A Shares
PENNX	Royce Pennsylvania Mutual Fd, Investment Class
BVAOX	Broadview Opportunity Fund
NBGNX	Neuberger Berman Genesis Fd

Figure 3.4   *US News and World Report*: Recommended US Small-Cap Funds
Source: US News and World Report; portfoliovisualizer.com

The recommended US Small Cap stock market funds, listed in Figure 3.4, really got thumped. They averaged a compound annual return of 8.39 percent per year. Vanguard's Small Cap Index (NAESX) averaged a compound annual return of 10.79 percent per year.

The recommended Mid-Cap stock funds also dragged the market. Listed in Figure 3.5, they averaged a compound annual return of 9.71 percent. Vanguard's US Mid-Cap Index (VIMSX) averaged a compound annual return of 11.69 percent.

Ticker	Name
WPFRX	Westport Fd Cl R
FLPSX	Fidelity Low-Priced Stock Fund
CHTTX	Anton/Fairpointe Mid Cap Fund Class N
FMIMX	FMI Common Stock Fund
WPSRX	The Westport Select Cap Fund Class R
CAAPX	Ariel Appreciation Fund Investor Cl
GTAGX	Invesco Mid Cap Core Equity Fund Class A
DMCVX	Dreyfus Opportunistic Midcap Value Fund Class A
SPMIX	S&P MidCap Index Fund Class S
PESPX	Dreyfus Midcap Index Fund

Figure 3.5   *US News and World Report*: Recommended US Mid-Cap Funds
Source: US News and World Report; portfoliovisualizer.com

Ticker	Name
FAIRX	Fairholme Fd
PRBLX	Parnassus Core Equity Fund-Investor Shares
OAKMX	Oakmark Fund Cl I
PBFDX	Payson Total Return
ACEHX	Invesco Exchange Fund Shs
MPGFX	Mairs & Power Growth Fund
EXTAX	Manning & Napier Fd, Inc. Tax Managed Srs Cl A
CLVFX	Croft Value Fd Cl R
HEQFX	Henssler Equity Fund

Figure 3.6   *US News and World Report*: Recommended US Large-Cap Funds
Source: US News and World Report; portfoliovisualizer.com

They also recommended the 10 US Large-Cap funds in Figure 3.6. One is missing in action, so I averaged the returns of the nine that remain. As a group, they performed poorly. They averaged a compound annual return of 8.77 percent between May 2010 and May 2016. Vanguard's Large-Cap Index (VLISX) averaged a compound annual return of 11.73 percent. Vanguard's S&P 500 Index (VFINX) averaged 11.86 percent.

As seen in Figure 3.7, the five categories of recommended US stock market funds underperformed their benchmark indexes by 2.31 percent annually over the six years ending May 2016. That's far worse than the typical actively managed fund performed during the same time period. So much for forecasts.

Most of these funds won't appear in a future story of "Mutual Funds to Buy!" Many financial advisers will also pass them over.

Instead, many writers and advisers will search out the funds that beat the indexes during the most recent year or decade. The cycle will repeat. Investors, who follow such suggestions, will be those who pay the price.

Jason Zweig, however, probably said it best. *The Wall Street Journal* writer published an excellent book, *Your Money and Your Brain*. In it, he wrote, "The ancient Scythians discouraged frivolous prophecies by burning to death any soothsayer whose

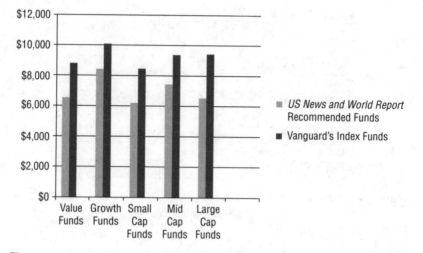

Figure 3.7 *US News and World Report*'s Recommended US Stock Funds Versus Benchmark Index Funds: Six-Year Profits Made on a $10,000 Investment, May 2010–May 2016

Source: US News and World Reports; portfoliovisualizer.com

predictions failed to come true."[37] He added that investors might be better off if modern forms of divination were held to biblical standards.

His theme echoes what Warren Buffett once said. People will pay a lot more money to be entertained than they will to be educated.

Still, most financial advisers won't give up. Their livelihood depends on you believing that they can find mutual funds that will beat the market indexes.

Before we were married, my wife Pele was being "helped" by the US-based financial services company Raymond James. They sold her actively managed mutual funds. On top of the standard, hidden mutual fund fees, she was charged an additional 1.75 percent of her account value every year. An ongoing annual fee such as this—called a wrap fee, adviser fee, or account fee—is like a package of arsenic-laced cookies sold at your local health food store. Why did her adviser charge this extra fee? Let's just say the adviser was servicing my wife the way the infamous Jesse James used to service train passengers—by taking the money and running.

According to a 2007 article published in the US weekly industry newspaper *Investment News*, Raymond James representatives are rewarded more for generating higher fees:

> *In the style of a 401(k) plan, the new deferred-compen-sation program this year gives a bonus of 1 percent to affiliated [Raymond James] reps who produce $450,000 in fees and commissions, a 2 percent bonus for $750,000 producers, and 3 percent for reps and advisers who produce $1 million.*[38]

The article adds that Raymond James pays advisers a percentage point bonus for every additional $500,000 that's produced for the firm. It tops out at a 10 percent bonus for advisers who produce $3.5 million in fees and commissions. With pilfering incentives like these, salespeople and advisers make out like sultans.

Looking at my wife's investment portfolio in 2004, after tracking her account's performance, I calculated that her $200,000 account would have been $20,000 better off if she had been with an index fund over the previous five years, instead of with her adviser's actively managed mutual funds. In my calculation, I included the 1.75 percent annual "fleecing" fee her adviser charged, on top of the mutual funds' regular expenses.

When Pele asked her adviser about her account's relatively poor performance, he suggested some new mutual funds. When Pele asked about index funds, he dismissed the idea. Perhaps he had his eye on a big prize: a Porsche or an Audi convertible. He couldn't afford either if he bought his client index funds. So he switched her into a group of different actively managed funds that had beaten the indexes over the previous five years—all had Morningstar five-star ratings.

And how did those new funds do from 2004 to 2007? Badly. Despite the strong track records of those funds, they performed poorly, relative to the market indexes, after he selected them for Pele's account. So Pele fired the guy, and I married Pele.

Over an investment lifetime, it's a virtual certainty that a portfolio of index funds will beat a portfolio of actively managed mutual funds, after all expenses. But over a one-, three-, or even a five-year period, there's always a chance that a person's actively managed funds will outperform the indexes.

At a seminar I gave in 2010, a man I'll call Charlie, after seeing the returns of an index-based portfolio, said: "My investment adviser has beaten those returns over the past five years."

That's possible. But the statistical realities are clear. Over his investment lifetime, the odds are that Charlie's account will fall far behind an indexed portfolio.

In July 1993, *The New York Times* decided to run a 20-year contest pitting high-profile financial advisers (and their mutual fund selections) against the returns of the S&P 500 stock market index.

Every three months, the newspaper would report the results, as if the money were invested in tax-free accounts. The advisers were allowed to switch their funds, at no cost, whenever they wished.

What started out as a great publicity coup for these high-profile moneymen quickly turned into what must have felt like a quarterly tarring and feathering. After just seven years, the S&P 500 index was like a Ferrari to the advisers' Hyundai Sonatas, as revealed in Figure 3.8.

An initial $50,000 with the index fund in 1993 (compared with the following respective advisers' mutual fund selections) would have turned into the preceding sums by 2000.[39]

Mysteriously, after just seven years, *The New York Times* discontinued the contest. Perhaps the competitive advisers in the study grew tired of the humiliation.

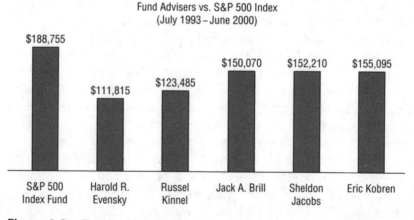

Fund Advisers vs. S&P 500 Index
(July 1993 – June 2000)

Figure 3.8 *The New York Times* Investment Contest

What's Under the Hood of an Index Fund?

Perhaps the best way to understand the differences between an actively managed mutual fund and an index fund is to put them side by side.

Table 3.1 has a point-by-point comparison.

Table 3.1   Differences between Actively Managed Funds and Index Funds

Actively Managed Mutual Funds	Total Stock Market Index Fund
1. A fund manager buys and sells (trades) dozens or hundreds of stocks. The average fund has very few of the same stocks at the end of the year that it held at the beginning of the year.	1. A fund manager buys a large group of stocks—often more than a thousand. More than 96 percent of the stocks are the same from one year to the next. No "trading" occurs. Poor businesses that get dropped from the stock exchange get dropped from the index. New businesses get added.
2. The fund manager and his or her team conduct extensive research. Their high salaries compensate them for this service, adding to the cost of the fund. This added cost is paid by investors.	2. No research is done on individual stocks. A total market index fund can literally be run by a computer with no research costs. Its goal is to virtually own everything on the stock market so there are no "trading" decisions to make.
3. Stock trading (the buying and selling of stocks) within the fund generates commission expenses, which are taken out of the value of the mutual fund. The investors pay for these.	3. Because there's no "trading" involved, commissions for buying and/or selling are extremely low. The savings are passed down to investors.
4. Trading triggers tax consequences that are passed down to the investor when the fund is held in a taxable account. The taxman sends you a bill.	4. The lack of trading means that, even in a taxable account, capital gains can grow with minimal annual taxation. You keep the taxman at bay.
5. The fund manager focuses on certain stock sizes and sectors. For example, a small-cap fund would own small companies only; a large-cap fund would own large companies only; a value fund would own cheap companies only; a growth fund would own growth companies only.	5. A total stock market index would own stock in every category listed on the left—all wrapped up into one fund—because it owns "the entire stock market."
6. Companies offering mutual funds have owners who profit from the funds' fees. More fees raked from investors mean higher profits for the fund company's owners.	6. A fund company such as Vanguard is a "nonprofit" company. Vanguard is the world's largest provider of index funds, serving Americans, Australians, and the British. Low-cost indexes are also available to Asians, Canadians, and Europeans.

(continued)

Table 3.1 *(Cont'd)*

Actively Managed Mutual Funds	Total Stock Market Index Fund
7. Because mutual fund companies have "owners" who seek profits for their fund company, there are aggressive sales campaigns and incentives paid to salespeople (advisers) to recommend their funds for clients. Investors pay for these.	7. Salespeople rarely tout indexes because they are less profitable for financial service companies to sell.
8. Actively managed fund companies pay annual "trailer fees" to advisers, rewarding them for selling their funds to investors—who end up paying for these.	8. Index funds rarely pay trailer fees to advisers.
9. Most US fund companies charge sales or redemption fees—which go directly to the broker/adviser who sold you the fund. The investor pays for these.	9. Most index funds do not charge sales or redemption fees.
10. Actively managed mutual fund companies are extremely well liked by advisers and brokers.	10. Index funds are not well liked by most advisers and brokers.

Captain America Calls for Government Action

David Swensen is one of America's most famous investors. He runs Yale University's endowment fund. Like the marvel comic hero Captain America, he fights for justice. In this case, he rallies against high mutual fund fees. In his book, *Unconventional Success*, he wrote, "The fund industry's systemic exploitation of individual investors requires government action."[40]

As high as US actively managed stock mutual fund costs can run, the average non-US fund is even more expensive. In a study presented in 2008 by Oxford University Press, Ajay Khorana, Henri Servaes, and Peter Tufano compared international fund costs, including estimated sales fees. According to the study, the country with the most expensive stock market mutual funds is Canada.[41]

High global investment costs make it even more important for global citizens outside of the United States to buy indexes for their investment accounts rather than pay the heavy fees associated with actively managed mutual funds.

In June 2015, Morningstar published its Global Fund Investor Experience Study. Country cost rankings hadn't changed much since the 2008 study, "Mutual Fund Fees Around the World."

Investors who buy actively managed funds in Canada and India end up the biggest losers. Not including the damages of sales commissions (which were included in the Oxford University Press study in Table 3.2), Canadian and Indian investors are still paying more than 2 percent per year in mutual fund fees.[42]

Sadly, actively managed mutual fund investors from Belgium, China, Denmark, Finland, France, Germany, Hong Kong, Italy, Korea, Norway, Singapore, South Africa, Spain, Sweden, Taiwan, Thailand, and the United Kingdom aren't far behind. Not including sales commissions, the Morningstar study pegs their actively managed mutual fund costs at 1.75 to

Table 3.2 The World's Actively Managed Stock Market Mutual Fund Fees

Country	Total Estimated Expenses, Including Sales Costs	Ranking of Least Expensive to Most Expensive Actively Managed Funds
Netherlands	0.82%	#1
Australia	1.41%	#2
Sweden	1.51%	#3
United States	1.53%	#4
Belgium	1.76%	#5
Denmark	1.85%	#6
France	1.88%	#7
Finland	1.91%	#8
Germany	1.97%	#9
Switzerland	2.03%	#10
Austria	2.26%	#11
United Kingdom	2.28%	#12
Ireland (Dublin)	2.40%	#13
Norway	2.43%	#14
Italy	2.44%	#15
Luxembourg	2.63%	#16
Spain	2.70%	#17
Canada	3.00%	#18

Source: "Mutual Fund Fees Around the World," Oxford University Press, 2008

2.0 percent per year.[43] After accounting for sales commissions, most of them pay much more.

Why Donald Trump Should Have Bought Index Funds

In 1982, the first year *Forbes* published its list of the wealthiest Americans, the magazine calculated Donald Trump's net worth at $200 million. He inherited most of the money from his father. By 2014, *Forbes* said his wealth had jumped to $4.1 billion. That's a compounding annual return of 9.9 percent. But Trump cries foul.

He complains that *Forbes* downplays his wealth. According to *Business Insider,* he recently said his net worth is $8.7 billion. In 1999, *Forbes* said, "We love Donald. He returns our calls. He usually pays for lunch. He even estimates his own net worth. But no matter how hard we try, we just can't prove it."

Let's assume that *Forbes* is wrong—and that Trump has the money he says he does. According to Timothy L. O'Brien's book *TrumpNation: The Art of Being The Donald,* Mr. Trump said he was worth $500 million in 1982, not the $200 million reported by *Forbes.* If we ignore *Forbes'* data and base Trump's wealth on his own figure ($8.7 billion) we find that his net worth has increased by an average compounding rate of 9.05 percent per year.

If Trump had invested that initial $500 million in Vanguard's S&P 500 index fund, he would have compounded his money by 11.3 percent annually over 33 years. His $500 million would have grown to $17.11 billion. That's $8.41 billion more than Trump says he has.

Between 1982 and 2014, he could have sat on his butt, spent a few million dollars every year, and ended up a lot wealthier than he is right now.

Who's Arguing against Indexes?

There are three types of people who argue that a portfolio of actively managed funds has a better chance of keeping pace with a diversified portfolio of indexes after taxes and fees over the long term.

Introduced first, dancing across the stage of improbability is your friendly neighborhood financial adviser. Pulling all kinds of tricks out of his bag, he needs to convince you that the world is flat, that the sun revolves around the Earth, and that he is better at predicting the future than a gypsy at a carnival. Mentioning index funds to him is like somebody sneezing on his birthday cake. He wants to eat that cake, and he wants a chunk of your cake, too.

He exits, stage left, and a bigger hotshot strolls in front of the captive audience. Wearing a professionally pressed suit, she works for a financial advisory public relations department. Part of her job is to compose confusing market-summary commentaries that often accompany mutual fund statements. They read something like this:

Stocks fell this month because retail sales were off 2.5 percent, creating a surplus of gold buyers over denim, which will likely raise Chinese futures on the backs of the growing federal deficit, which caused two Wall Street Bankers to streak through Central Park because of the narrowing bond yield curve.

Saying stock markets rose this year because more polar bears were able to find suitable mates before November has as much merit as the confusing economic drivel that these representatives write and distribute.

If you ask her, she will tell you that actively managed mutual funds are the way to go. But she won't mention the killer mortgage payments on her $17 million Hawaiian beachside summer home. You need to help her pay it.

Sadly, the third type of person who might tell you actively managed mutual funds have a better statistical long-term chance at profit (over indexes) are the prideful, or gullible, folks who won't want to admit their advisers put their own financial interests above their clients.

Let's consider Peter Lynch, the man who was arguably one of history's greatest mutual fund managers. Before retiring at age 46, he managed the Fidelity Magellan fund, which captured public interest as it averaged 29 percent a year from 1977 to 1990.[44] Since then, however, Lynch's former fund has disappointed investors. If $10,000 were invested in the fund in January 1990, it would have grown to $83,640 by May 16, 2016.[45] The same $10,000 invested in Vanguard's S&P 500 Index Fund would have grown to $99,760. Hammering the industry's faults, Peter Lynch says:

> *So it's getting worse, the deterioration by professionals is getting worse. The public would be better off in an index fund.*[46]

As the industry's idol from the 1980s, you might suggest that Lynch is a relic of a bygone era. Perhaps. But let's turn our attention forward and look at Bill Miller. He was the fund manager of Legg Mason Value Trust. In 2006, *Fortune* magazine writer Andy Serwer called Miller "the greatest money manager of our time," after Miller's fund had beaten the S&P 500 index for the fifteenth straight year.[47] Yet, when *Money* magazine's Jason Zweig interviewed Miller in July 2007, Miller recommended index funds:

> *[A] significant portion of one's assets in equities should be comprised of index funds. . . . Unless you are lucky, or extremely skillful in the selection of managers, you're going to have a much better experience going with the index fund.*[48]

Miller's quote was timely. Since 2007, his fund has performed horribly. Between January 2007 and May 17, 2016 (the time of this writing), it gained a total of 2.6 percent. During the same time period, Vanguard's S&P 500 index gained 78.2 percent.[49]

Poor performing funds often change their names. Such was the case with Bill Miller's Legg Mason Value Trust. Miller was once considered "the greatest money manager of our time." But today, the fund's name brings nothing but pain. In 2011, Miller stepped down.[50] The fund is now called ClearBridge Value Trust.[51]

Some mutual fund managers, of course (these are people who actually run the funds), are required by their employers to buy shares in the funds they run. But in taxable accounts—if fund managers don't have to commit their own money, they generally won't. Ted Aronson actively manages more than $7 billion for retirement portfolios, endowments, and corporate pension fund accounts. He's one of the best in the business. But what does he do with his own taxable money? As he told Jason Zweig, who was writing for *CNN Money* in 1999, all of his taxable money is invested with Vanguard's index funds:

> *Once you throw in taxes, it just skewers the argument for active [mutual fund] management ... indexing wins hands-down. After tax, active management just can't win.*[52]

Or, in the words of a real heavy hitter, Arthur Levitt, former chairman of the US Securities and Exchange Commission:

> *The deadliest sin of all is the high cost of owning some mutual funds. What might seem to be low fees, expressed in tenths of 1 percent, can easily cost an investor tens of thousands of dollars over a lifetime.*[53]

You don't have to be disappointed with your investment results. With disciplined savings and a willingness to invest regularly in low-cost, tax-efficient index funds, you can feasibly invest half of what your neighbors invest—over your lifetime—while still ending up with more money.

You may not have learned these lessons in school. But you can learn them now.

1. Index fund investing will provide the highest statistical chance of success, compared with actively managed mutual fund investing.

2. Nobody yet has devised a system of choosing which actively managed mutual funds will consistently beat stock market indexes. Ignore people who suggest otherwise.

3. Don't be impressed by the historical returns of any actively managed mutual fund. Choosing to invest in a fund based on its past performance is one of the silliest things an investor can do.

4. Index funds extend their superiority over actively managed funds when the invested money is in a taxable
account.

5. Remember the conflict of interest that most advisers
face. They don't want you to buy index funds because
they (the brokers) make far more money in commissions
and trailer fees when they convince you to buy actively
managed funds.

Notes

1. Fred Schwed, *Where Are the Customers' Yachts?, Or, A Good
   Hard Look at Wall Street* (New York: John Wiley & Sons,
   1995), 1.
2. W. Gregory Guedel, "Ali versus Wilt Chamberlain—The Fight
   That Almost Was," EastSideBoxing, May 29, 2006, www
   .boxing247.com/weblog/archives/109022.
3. Linda Grant, "Striking Out at Wall Street," *US News & World
   Report*, June 20, 1994, 58.
4. Warren Buffett, Berkshire Hathaway 2014 Annual Report,
   accessed May 18, 2016, www.berkshirehathaway.com/
   2014ar/2014ar.pdf.
5. Mel Lindauer, Michael LeBoeuf, and Taylor Larimore, *The
   Bogleheads Guide to Investing* (Hoboken, NJ: John Wiley &
   Sons, 2007), 83.
6. "Investors Can't Beat the Market, Scholar Says," *Orange
   County Register*, January 2, 2002, www.ifa.com/articles/
   investors_cant_beat_market_scholar_ says_hope_yen/.
7. Peter Tanous, "An Interview with Merton Miller," Index
   Fund Advisors, February 1, 1997, www.ifa.com/Articles/An_
   Interview_with_Merton_Miller.aspx.
8. "Where Nobel Economists Put Their Money," accessed October
   30, 2010, www.youtube.com/watch?v = -HrTD5J2qP0.
9. Ibid.
10. "Arithmetic of Active Management," *Financial Analysts'
    Journal* 47, no. 1 (January/February 1991): 7.
11. Ibid.
12. Ibid.

13. David F. Swensen, *Unconventional Success, a Fundamental Approach to Personal Investment* (New York: Free Press, 2005), 217.

14. Robert D. Arnott, Andrew L. Berkin, and Jia Ye, "How Well Have Taxable Investors Been Served in the 1980s and 1990s?" *The Journal of Portfolio Management* 26, no. 4 (Summer 2000): 86.

15. Larry Swedroe, *The Quest For Alpha* (Hoboken, NJ: John Wiley & Sons, 2011), 13.

16. Larry Swedroe, *The Quest For Alpha*, 13–14.

17. Mark Hulbert, "Index Funds Win Again," February 21, 2009, *The New York Times*, www.nytimes.com/2009/02/22/your-money/stocks-and-bonds/22stra.html?_r = 0.

18. David F. Swensen, *Unconventional Success, a Fundamental Approach to Personal Investment*, 266.

19. Ibid.

20. John C. Bogle, *Common Sense on Mutual Funds* (Hoboken, NJ: John Wiley & Sons, 2010), 376.

21. Ibid., 384.

22. John C. Bogle, *The Little Book of Common Sense Investing*, 61.

23. John C. Bogle, *Common Sense on Mutual Funds*, 376.

24. Ibid.

25. Morningstar.com, accessed May 16, 2016.

26. John C. Bogle, *The Little Book of Common Sense Investing*, 90.

27. John C. Bogle, *Don't Count On It!* (Hoboken, NJ: John Wiley & Sons, 2011), 382.

28. Burton Malkiel, *The Random Walk Guide to Investing* (New York: Norton, 2003), 130.

29. Ibid.

30. "Does Past Performance Matter," S&P Dow Jones Indices, January 2016, us.spindices.com/documents/spiva/persistence-scorecard-january-2016.pdf.

31. Larry Swedroe, "You Make More Money Selling Advice Than Following It," *CBS MarketWatch*, May 21, 2010, www.cbsnews.com/news/you-make-more-money-selling-advice-than-following-it/.

32. Nick Levis, "7 Top Mutual Funds with Long Term Track Records," *Business Insider*, July 20, 2011, 2016, www.businessinsider.com/mutual-funds-with-solid-long-term-track-records-2011-7.

33. "Interview with Russel Kinnel," interview by author, September 10, 2015.

34. Morningstar.com, accessed November 13, 2015.

35. "Confessions of a Former Mutual Funds Reporter," *Fortune* magazine archives, April 26, 1999, archive.fortune.com/magazines/fortune/fortune_archive/1999/04/26/258745/index.htm.

36. "The 100 Best Mutual Funds for the Long Term," *US News & World Report*, May 19, 2010, http://money.usnews.com/money/personal-finance/mutual-funds/articles/2010/05/19/the-100-best-mutual-funds-for-the-long-term.

37. Jason Zweig, *Your Money and Your Brain: How the New Science of Neuroeconomics Can Help Make You Rich* (New York: Simon & Schuster, 2007).

38. Bruce Kelly, "Raymond James Unit Gives Bonuses to Big Producers," *Investment News—The Leading Source for Financial Advisors*, June 18, 2007.

39. Carole Gould, "Mutual Funds Report; A Seven-Year Lesson in Investing: Expect the Unexpected, and More," *The New York Times*, July 9, 2000, www.nytimes.com/2000/07/09/business/mutual-funds-report-seven-year-lesson-investing-expect-unexpected-more.html?.

40. David F. Swensen, *Unconventional Success, A Fundamental Approach to Personal Investment* (New York: Free Press, 2005), 1.

41. Ajay Khorana, Henri Servaes, and Peter Tufano, "Mutual Fund Fees Around the World," *The Review of Financial Studies* 22, no. 3 (2008), Oxford University Press, faculty.london.edu/hservaes/rfs2009.pdf.

42. "Global Fund Investor Experience Study," Morningstar, June 2015, corporate.morningstar.com/us/documents/2015%20Global%20Fund%20Investor%20Experience.pdf.

43. Ibid.

44. "The Greatest Investors: Peter Lynch," Investopedia, accessed April 15, 2011, www.investopedia.com/university/greatest/peterlynch.asp.

45. Morningstar.com, accessed May 16, 2016.

46. John C. Bogle, *The Little Book of Common Sense Investing*, 47–48.

47. Andy Serwer, "The Greatest Money Manager of Our Time," *Fortune*, November 15, 2006, money.cnn.com/2006/11/14/magazines/fortune/Bill_miller.fortune/index.htm.

48. Jason Zweig, "What's Luck Got to Do with It?" *Money*, July 18, 2007, money.cnn.com/2007/07/17/pf/miller_interview_full.moneymag/.

49. Morningstar.com, accessed May 16, 2016.

50. Joe Light and Tom Lauricella, "A Star Exits after Value Falls," *The Wall Street Journal*, November 11, 2011, www.wsj.com/articles/SB10001424052970203611404577043910758867408.

51. Morningstar.com, accessed May 16, 2016, www.morningstar.com/funds/XNAS/LMVTX/quote.html.

52. Paul B. Farrell, "'Laziest Portfolio' 2004 Winner Ted Aronson Scores Repeat Win with 15 Percent Returns," CBS Marketwatch.com, January 11, 2005, www.tsptalk.com/mb/longer-term-strategies/1047-laziest-portfolio-2004-winner-print.html?imz_s = llndr74at79s89u1mjuje7p321.

53. Mel Lindauer, Michael LeBoeuf, and Taylor Larimore, *The Bogleheads Guide to Investing*, 118.

RULE 4

Conquer the Enemy in the Mirror

My brother Ian is a huge fan of the 1999 movie *Fight Club*, particularly the scene where the lead character Tyler, played by Edward Norton, is shown throwing haymaker punches at his own swollen face. Norton's character is metaphorically battling his materialistic urges. Most investors fight similar battles in a war against themselves.

Much of that internal grappling comes from misunderstanding the stock market. I can't promise to collar your inner doppelganger. But when you understand how the stock market works—and how human emotions can sabotage the best-laid plans—you'll become a better investor.

When a 10 Percent Gain Isn't a 10 Percent Gain

Imagine a mutual fund that has averaged 10 percent a year over the past 20 years after all fees and expenses. Some years it might have lost money; other years it might have profited beyond expectation. It's a roller coaster ride, right? But imagine, on average, that it gained 10 percent annually even after the bumps, rises, twists, and turns. If you found a thousand investors who had invested in that fund from 1996 to 2016, you would expect that each would have netted a 10 percent annual return.

On average, however, they wouldn't have made anything close to that. When the fund had a couple of bad years, most investors react by putting less money in the fund or they stop contributing to it entirely. Many investment advisers would say:

"This fund hasn't been doing well lately. Because we're looking after your best interests, we're going to move your money to another fund that is doing better at the moment." And when the fund had a great year, most individual investors and financial advisers scramble to put more money in the fund, like feral cats around a fat salmon.

This behavior is self-destructive. They sell or cease to buy after the fund becomes cheap, and they buy like lunatics when the fund becomes expensive. If there weren't so many people doing it, we would call it a "disorder" and name it after some dead Teutonic psychologist. This kind of investment behavior ensures that investors pay higher-than-average prices for their funds over time. Whether it's an index fund or an actively managed mutual fund, most investors perform worse than the funds they own—because they like to buy high, and they hate buying low. That's a pity.

Morningstar says most investors do this. In a 2014 study, they looked at average mutual fund returns over the 10-year period ending December 31, 2013. The typical fund averaged 7.3 percent per year after fees. The typical fund investor averaged 4.8 percent per year.[1]

Their fear of low prices prevented them from buying when the funds were low, while their elation at high prices encouraged purchases when fund prices were high. Such bizarre behavior has devastating consequences.

Over a 30-year period, the financial difference would be huge:

$500 invested per month at 7.3 percent a year for 30 years = $641,971

$500 invested per month at 4.8 percent a year for 30 years = $403,699

Cost of irrationality = $238,272

What If You Didn't Care What the Stock Market Was Doing?

As investors, you really don't have to watch the stock market to see if it's going up or down. In fact, if you bought a market index fund for 25 years, with an equal dollar amount going into that fund each month (called "dollar-cost averaging") and if that fund averaged 10 percent annually, you would have averaged 10 percent or more. Why more?

If the stock market crashes, dollar cost averaging could actually juice returns. Here's an example.

Assume that somebody started to invest $100 into Vanguard's US Total Stock Market Index in January 2008. We know what came next: the crash of 2008–2009. You can see it on Figure 4.1. Stocks fell hard in 2008. Part way through 2009, stocks began to recover. But by January 2011, the market was still below its January 2008 level. You can see the chart below.

Investors who started to invest in January 2008 might curse their bad luck. But if they stuck to the plan and dollar-cost averaged, they would have done okay.

If they added $100 a month between January 2008 and January 2011, they would have added a total of $3,600. But their investment would have grown to a value of $4,886.[2]

If the investors had continued to add $100 a month until August 2016 (the time of this writing), they would have added a total of $9,200 since January 2008. Their investment would have grown to $19,228.

By adding equal dollar sums to their index each month, the investors would have bought a greater number of units when the markets were low and fewer units when the market rose. This allowed them to pay a below-average price over time.

Figure 4.1   Vanguard's US Stock Market Index: January 2008–January 2011
Source: © The Vanguard Group, Inc., used with permission

Much will depend on the stock market's volatility. If stocks bounce around a lot, investors who dollar-cost average get rewarded for their discipline—they can actually beat the return of their index. If stock market returns are more stable, someone who dollar-cost averages will still do well—but they won't beat the market's return.

Should You Invest a Lump Sum or Dollar Cost Average?

You've inherited a windfall. Should you invest it all at once? Or should you add the money to the markets, month by month, dollar-cost averaging? Nobody knows for sure. But earlier lump sum investments usually win. In other words it's usually best to invest as soon as you have the money.

A Vanguard case study found that investing a lump sum, as soon as you have it, usually beats dollar-cost averaging. Vanguard compared a series of historical scenarios. They assumed that someone had invested a $1 million lump sum. They wanted to find out if, 10 years later, that investment would have grown higher than if the deposits were spaced out over 6, 12, 18, 24, 30, or 36 months.

Vanguard compared rolling 10-year periods for the US market between 1926 and 2011. They analyzed the same scenario for the UK market (1976–2011) and for the Australian market (1984–2011). Lump sum investing won 67 percent of the time. It's usually best to invest as soon as you have the money.

Few investors, however, stick to a disciplined plan. Most underperform their funds.

Most Investors Exhibit Nutty Behavior

Combine the crazy behavior of the average investor with the fees associated with actively managed mutual funds. The average investor ends up with a comparatively puny portfolio compared with the disciplined investor who puts in the same amount of money every month into index funds. Table 4.1 categorizes investors who will be working—and adding to their investments—for at least the next five years.

Table 4.1 The Average Investor Compared with the Evolved Investor

The Average Investor	The Evolved Investor
Buys actively managed mutual funds.	Buys index funds.
Feels good about his or her fund when the price increases so buys more of it.	Buys equal dollar amounts of the indexes and knows, happily, that this buys fewer units as the stock market rises.
Feels bad about his or her fund when the price decreases, so the person limits purchases or sells the fund.	Loves to see the stock index fall in value. If he or she has the money, the person increases purchases.

I'm not going to suggest that all indexed investors are evolved enough to ignore the market's fearful roller coaster while shunning the self-sabotaging caused by fear and greed. But if you can learn to invest regularly in indexes and remain calm when the markets fly upward or downward, you'll grow far wealthier. In Table 4.2, you can see examples based on actual US returns between 1980 and 2005.

The figure on the left side ($84,909.01) is probably a little generous. The 10 percent annual return for the average actively managed fund has been historically overstated because it doesn't include sales fees, adviser wrap fees, or the added liability of taxes in a taxable account.

Table 4.2 Historical Differences Between the Average Investor and the Evolved Investor

The Average Investor	The Evolved Investor
$100 a month invested from 1980 to 2005 in the average US mutual fund (roughly $3.33 a day). 10% annual average.	$100 a month invested from 1980 to 2005 in the US stock market index (roughly $3.33 a day). 12.3% annual average.
Minus 2.7% annually for the average investor's self-sabotaging behavior.	No deficit for silly behavior.
25-year average annual return for investors: 7.3%	25-year average annual return for investors: 12.3%
Portfolio value after 25 years = $84,909.01	Portfolio value after 25 years = $198,181.90

Note: Although the US stock market has averaged about 10 percent annually over the past 100 years, there are periods where it performs better and there are periods where it performs worse. From 1980 to 2005, the US stock market averaged slightly more than 12.3 percent a year.[3]

Disciplined index investors who don't self-sabotage their accounts can end up with a portfolio that's easily twice as large as that of the average investor over a 25-year period.

Are Index Fund Investors Smarter?

Many financial advisers fall prey to the same weakness. Many like to recommend "hot" funds. They also sometimes think that they can time the market. There's a US actively managed mutual fund company called American Funds. Investors can't buy these funds directly. Such funds must be purchased through a financial adviser or broker. You might think that these professionals can advise investors to stay invested and not jump from fund to fund. But that isn't the case.

Using data from Morningstar, I compared all of the firm's funds with 10-year track records. I wanted to see how the funds had performed compared to how the funds' investors had performed.

I examined four fund categories between October 31, 2004, and October 31, 2014. They included US Large Cap, Emerging Markets, Broad International, and Small Cap funds. When averaging investors' returns in each of the four categories, I found that the American Fund investors underperformed their funds by an average of 1.75 percent per year. If the funds' investors were rational, they would have earned the same returns as those posted by their funds.

For example, if a fund averaged 10 percent per year over a designated period, then the funds' investors, over that same time period, should have done the same. But poor behavior (chasing winners, buying high and selling low) cost the American Funds' investors 1.75 percent per year between October 31, 2004, and October 31, 2014. Once again, investors can't buy these funds without an adviser. So much for the advisers' smart guidance!

I made the same category comparisons with the fund company Fidelity. Investors *can* buy Fidelity's funds without a financial adviser. But in many cases, financial advisers stuff Fidelity's actively managed funds into client accounts. Comparing the same four categories over the same time period, Fidelity's investors underperformed their funds by an average of 2.53 percent per year. As with the American Funds' investors, they shot themselves in the feet.

Most index fund investors fly solo, without a financial adviser. When I compared the returns of Vanguard's index fund investors over the same time period in the same four categories, they underperformed their funds by just 0.71 percent per year. Index fund investors didn't behave perfectly. But they were far less foolish.

I detailed the findings in my December 2014 AssetBuilder article, "Are Index Fund Investors Simply Smarter?"[4]

Three and a half months later, *The Wall Street Journal's* Jonathan Clements published a similar story, "Are Index Fund Investors Smarter?" He asked Morningstar to conduct a broader study. It revealed the same results. Index fund investors appeared to have more discipline. He also offered an explanation:

> *I suspect it is less about greater intelligence and more about greater conviction. When you buy an index fund, your only worry is the market's performance. But when you buy an active fund, you have to worry about both the market's direction and your fund's performance relative to the market.*[5]

Investors and advisers shouldn't speculate. They should commit to staying invested. Such discipline, coupled with low-cost index funds, can allow people with middle-class incomes to amass wealth more effectively than their high-salaried neighbors—especially if the middle-class earners think twice about spending more than they can afford.

Even if your neighbors invest twice as much as you each month, if they are average, they will buy actively managed mutual funds. They will also either chase hot-performing funds or fail to keep a regular commitment to their investments when the markets fall. They'll feel good about buying into the markets when they're expensive. They won't be as keen to buy when stocks are on sale.

Don't be like your neighbors. Avoid that kind of self-destructive behavior and you'll increase your odds of building wealth as an investor.

It's Not Timing the Market That Matters; It's Time in the Market

There are smart people (and people who aren't so smart) who mistakenly think they can jump in and out of the stock market at opportune moments. It seems simple. Get in before the market rises and get out before the market drops. This is referred to as "market timing." But most financial advisers have a better chance beating Roger Federer in a tennis match than effectively timing the market for your account.

Vanguard's Bogle, who was named by *Fortune* magazine as one of the four investment giants of the twentieth century, has this to say about market timing:

> *After nearly 50 years in this business, I do not know of anybody who has done it successfully and consistently. I don't even know anybody who knows anybody who has done it successfully and consistently.*[6]

When the markets go raving mad, dramatically jumping in and out can be tempting. But stock markets are highly irrational and characterized by short-term swings. The stock market will often fly higher than most people expect during a euphoric phase, while plunging further than anticipated during times of economic duress. There's a simple, annual, mechanical strategy that you can follow to protect your money from excessive crashes, which I'll outline in Chapter 5. Your investment will still fall in value when the stock market falls, but not as much as your neighbor's—and that can help you sleep when stocks go crazy.

The strategy that I'll show you doesn't involve trying to guess the stock market's direction. Forecasting where it's going to go over a short period is like trying to guess which frantic, nightly moth is going to get singed by the light bulb first.

Doing nothing but holding onto your total stock market index fund might sound boring during a financial boom. It might also sound terrifying during a financial meltdown. But the vast majority of people (including professionals) who jump in and out of the stock market end up paying the piper. They often end up buying high and selling low.

What Can You Miss by Guessing Wrong?

Studies show that most market moves are like the flu you got last year or like the mysterious $10 bill you found in the pocket of your jeans. In each case, you don't see it coming. Even when looking back at the stock market's biggest historical returns, Jeremy Siegel, a professor of business at University of Pennsylvania's Wharton School, suggests that there's no rhyme or reason when it comes to market activity. He looked back at the biggest stock market moves since 1885 (focusing on trading sessions where the markets moved by 5 percent or more in a single day). He tried to connect each of them to a world event.[7]

In most instances, he couldn't find logical explanations for such large stock market movements—and he had the luxury of looking back in time and trying to match the market's behavior with historical world news. If a smart man like Siegel can't make connections between world events and the stock market movements with the benefit of hindsight, then how is someone supposed to predict future movements based on economic events—or the prediction of economic events to come?

If you're ever convinced to act on somebody's short-term stock market prediction, you could end up kicking yourself. Big stock market gains are usually concentrated during just a handful of trading days each year.

During the 20-year period between 1994 and 2013 (5,037 trading days), US stocks averaged a compound annual return of 9.22 percent. But investors who missed the best five trading days would have averaged just 7 percent per year. If they missed the best 20 days, their average return would have been just 3.02 percent per year. If they missed the best 40 trading days, the investor would have lost money. In Table 4.3, you can see the kind of effect it would have on your money.

Table 4.3   Costs of Speculation, 1994–2013

	Average Annual Return	$10,000 Would Have Grown To
Stock Market's Return	9.22%	$58,352
Best 5 Days Missed	7%	$38,710
Best 20 Days Missed	3.02%	$18,131
Best 40 Days Missed	−1.02%	$8,149

Source: IFA Advisors[8]

Markets can move so unpredictably and so quickly. If you take money out of the stock market for a day, a week, a month, or a year, you could miss the best trading days of the decade. You'll never see them coming. They just happen. More important, as I said before, neither you nor your broker are going to be able to predict them.

Legendary investor and self-made billionaire Kenneth Fisher, has this to say about market timing:

> *Never forget how fast a market moves. Your annual return can come from just a few big moves. Do you know which days those will be? I sure don't and I've been managing money for a third of a century.*[9]

The easiest way to build a responsible, diversified investment account is with stock and bond index funds. I'll discuss bond indexes in Chapter 5, but for now, just recognize them as instruments that generally create stability in a portfolio. Many people view them as boring because they don't produce the same kind of long-term returns that stocks do. But they don't fall like stocks do either. They're the steadier, slower, and more dependable part of an investment portfolio. A responsible portfolio has a certain percentage allocated to the stock market and a certain percentage allocated to the bond market, with an increasing emphasis on bonds as the investor ages.

But when stocks start racing upward and everyone's getting giddy on the profits they're making, most people ignore their bonds (if they own any at all) and they buy more stocks. Many others chase whichever fund has recently done well.

How can you ensure that you're never a victim? It's far easier than you might think. If you understand exactly what stocks are—and what you can expect from them—you'll fortify your odds of success.

On Stocks . . . What You Really Should Have Learned in School

The stock market is a collection of businesses. It isn't just a squiggly bunch of lines on a chart or quotes in the newspaper. When you own shares in a stock market index fund, you own something that's as real as the land you're standing on. You become an indirect owner of all kinds of industries and businesses via the companies you own within your index: land, buildings, brand names, machinery, transportation systems, and products, to name a few. Just understanding this key concept can give you a huge advantage as an investor.

Business earnings and stock price growth are two separate things. But long term, they tend to reflect the same result. For example, if a business grew its profits by 1,000 percent over a 30-year period, we could expect the stock price of that business to appreciate similarly over the same period.

It's the same for a stock market index. If the average company within an index grew by 1,000 percent over 30 years (that's 8.32 percent annually) we could expect the stock market index to perform similarly. Long term, stock markets predictably reflect the fortunes of the businesses within them. But over shorter periods, the stock market can be as irrational as a crazy dog on a leash. And it's the crazy dog's movements that can—if we let them—lure us closer to poverty than to wealth.

True Stock Market Experts Understand Dogs on Leashes

I used to have a dog named Sue. She behaved as if we were feeding her rocket fuel instead of dog food. If you turned your back on her in the backyard, she'd enact a scene from the US television show *Prison Break*, bounding over the 5-foot-high fence in our yard and straining diplomatic relations between our family and those whose gardens she would destroy.

When I took her for extended runs on wide, open fields, she burned off some octane. I would run in a single direction while she darted upward, backward, right, then left. But collared by a very long rope, she couldn't escape.

If I ran from the lake to the barn with Sue on a leash, and if it took me 10 minutes to get there, then any observer would realize it would take the dog 10 minutes to get there as well. True, the dog could bolt ahead or lag behind while sticking its nose in a gift left behind by another canine. But ultimately, it can't cover the distance much slower or much faster than I do—because of the leash.

Now imagine a bunch of emotional gamblers who watch and bet money on leashed dogs. When a dog bursts ahead of its owner, the gamblers put money on the sprinting dog, betting that it will sprint far off into the distance. But the dog's on a leash, so it can't get too far ahead of its owner. When the leashed dog gets ahead, it's destined to either slow down or stop—so that the owner can catch up.

But the gamblers don't think about that. If they see the dog bounding along without noticing the leash, they place presumptuous bets that the dog will maintain its frenetic pace. Their greed wraps itself around their brains and squeezes. Without that cranial compression, they would see that the leashed dog couldn't outpace its owner.

It sounds so obvious, doesn't it? Now get this: the stock market is exactly like a dog on a leash. If the stock market races at twice the pace of business earnings for a few years, then it has to either wait for business earnings to catch up, or it will get choke-chained back in a hurry. But a rapidly rising stock market can cause people to forget that reality. I'll use an individual stock to prove the point.

Coca-Cola Bounds from Its Owner

From 1988 to 1998, the Coca-Cola Company increased its profits as a business by 294 percent. During this short period (and yes, 10 years is a stock market blip) Coca-Cola's stock price increased by 966 percent. Because it was rising rapidly, investors (including mutual fund managers) fell over themselves to buy Coca-Cola shares. That pushed the share price even higher. Greed might be the greatest hallucinogenic known to man.

The dog (Coca-Cola's stock price) was racing ahead of its master (Coca-Cola's business earnings). A rational share price increase must fall in line with profits. If Coca-Cola's business earnings increased by 294 percent from 1988 to 1998, we would assume that its stock price would grow by a percentage that was at least somewhat similar, maybe a little higher or maybe a little lower. But Coca-Cola's stock price growth of 966 percent was irrational, compared with its business earnings increase of 294 percent.[10]

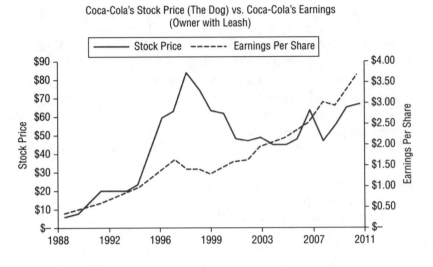

Figure 4.2   Coca-Cola's Stock Price vs. Coca-Cola's Earnings
Source: Value Line Investment Survey

Can you see what happened to the blazing Coca-Cola share price when it got far ahead of Coca-Cola's business profits?

The dog eventually dropped back to meet its owner. After blazing ahead at 29 percent a year for a decade (from 1988 to 1998), Coca-Cola's stock price eventually "heeled." It had to. You can see in Figure 4.2 that the stock price was lower in 2011 than it was in 1998.

Coca-Cola's earnings growth and stock price were realigned, much like a leashed dog with its owner.

You can look at the earnings growth of any stock you choose. Over a long period, the stock's price might jump around, but it will never disconnect itself from the business earnings. To see a few examples for yourself, you can log on to *The Value Line Investment Survey*. The US research company offers free, online historical data of the 30 Dow Jones Industrial stocks.

The Madness of People

Coca-Cola wasn't the only business with a share price that was out of step with its business earnings. Stock market investors worldwide euphorically flocked to stocks in the late 1990s, as they were motivated by rising prices. The stock buying grew more frenzied during the latter part of the decade as stock prices reached lofty new heights. The United States (for example) went through a period of strong economic growth during the 1990s. But the prices of stocks were rising twice as fast as the level of business earnings. It couldn't last forever, however. The decade that followed saw the racing, leashed dogs eventually fall in line with their owners who were moving at a much slower rate.

Global stock markets also took a breather between the year 2000 and 2010. They rose just 21 percent for the decade, after climbing 250 percent between 1989 and 1999, as measured by the MSCI index of developed country stock markets.[11]

Stocks Go Crazy Every Generation

Long term, whether we're talking about Coca-Cola or a stock market index, there's one reality: the growth of stock market prices will closely match the growth of the businesses they represent. It's supply and demand that pushes stock prices over the short term. If there are more buyers than sellers, the stock price (or the stock market index in general) will rise. If there are more sellers than buyers, stocks will drop. And when prices rise, people feel more confident about that investment. They buy more, pushing the price even higher. People become drunk on their own greed, not recognizing that bubbles form when price levels dramatically exceed business profit growth.

"History Doesn't Repeat Itself, But It Does Rhyme"—Mark Twain[12]

As far back as we have records, at least once every generation, the stock market goes bonkers. Table 4.4 presents three periods from the past 90 years showing the US market as represented by the Dow Jones Industrial stocks. You can see, in each case, share price levels that grossly exceeded earnings levels, and the terrible returns that followed as the "dogs" were caught by their "owners."

Table 4.4   Prices of Stocks Can't Outpace Business Earnings for Long

Years When Stock Prices Exceeded Business Earnings	Growth in Business Earnings (the Pace of the Dog's Owner)	Growth in Stock Prices (the Pace of the Dog)	Stock Price Decline/ Gain (the Dog's Overall Progress) During the Following Decade
1920–1929	118%	271.2%	-40.9%
1955–1965	150%	198.5%	29.3%
1990–2000	152%	290%	20.17%

Note: Figures do not include dividends.

Source: The Value Line Investment Survey[13]

Note from 1920 to 1929, the Dow stocks' average business growth amounted to 118 percent over the 10-year period. But the prices of the Dow stocks increased by 271.2 percent over that decade, so if someone invested in all 30 Dow stocks in 1920 and held them until 1929, he would have gained more than 271 percent not including dividends and close to 300 percent including dividends. Because stock prices can't exceed business growth for long, the decade that followed (1930–1940) saw the stock market fall by an overall total of 40.9 percent. Again, the leashed dog can't escape its owner.

The two other time periods during the past 90 years where investors lost sight of the connections between business earnings and stock price appreciation occurred from 1955 to 1965 and from 1990 to 2000. You can see the results in Table 4.4.

Anyone investing in a broad US stock market index would have gained more than 300 percent (including dividends) in the 10 short years between 1990 and 2000. Did business earnings increase by 300 percent? Not even close. That's the main reason the markets stalled from 2000 to 2010.

How Does this Relate to You?

Every generation, it happens again. Stock prices go haywire. When they do, many people abandon responsible investment strategies. The more rapidly the markets rise, the more reckless most investors become. They pile more and more money into stocks, ignoring their bonds. And when the markets eventually fall or stagnate, they curse their bad luck. But luck has little to do with it.

Internet Madness and the Damage It Caused

The greatest Titanic period of delusion sailed during the technology stock mania of the late 1990s. The stocks that were riskiest were those companies with the greatest disconnection between their business earnings and their stock prices.

Many Internet-based businesses weren't even making profits but their stock prices were soaring, pushed upward by the media and the scintillating stories of Silicon Valley's super-rich. Most of their investors probably didn't know that there's a direct long-term connection between stock prices and business earnings. They probably didn't know that it's not realistic for businesses to grow their earnings by 150 percent a year—year after year, no matter what the business is. And if businesses can't grow earnings by 150 percent on an annual basis, then their stocks can't either.

Some of the more famous promoters at the time were such high-profile financial analysts as Morgan Stanley's Mary Meeker, Merrill Lynch's Henry Blodgett, and Solomon Smith Barney's Jack Grubman. But they might have a tough time showing their faces today. For all I know, the top Internet stock analysts of the 1990s are now hiding in an African jungle, hoping that angry investors won't find them. Their voices tossed buckets of gas on the flames of madness when technology-based companies without profits were priced in the stratosphere. Meeker, Blodgett, and Grubman were encouraging the average person to buy, buy, buy.

One difference between this period and the bubbles of previous generations was the speed at which the bubble grew, thanks to the Internet as a rapid communication channel. One transgenerational similarity, however, was the investors' attitude that "this time it would be different." In each period where stock prices disconnect from earnings levels, you find people who think that history is going to rewrite itself, that stock prices no longer need to reflect earnings, and that

Table 4.5   How Investors Were Punished

Formerly Hot Stocks	$10,000 Invested at the Market High in 2000	Value of the Same $10,000 at the Low of 2001–2002
Amazon.com	$10,000	$700
Cisco Systems	$10,000	$990
Corning Inc.	$10,000	$100
JDS Uniphase	$10,000	$50
Lucent Technologies	$10,000	$70
Nortel Networks	$10,000	$30
Priceline.com	$10,000	$60
Yahoo!	$10,000	$360

Source: Morningstar and Burton Malkiel, *A Random Walk Down Wall Street,* 2003[14]

leashed dogs everywhere can develop mutations, grow wings, and lead flocks of Canadian geese on their way to Florida. In the long term, stock prices reflect business earnings. When they don't, it spells trouble.

Even shares of the world's largest technology companies sold at nosebleed prices as they defied business profit levels. And, as shown in Table 4.5, when cold, hard business earnings eventually yanked the price leashes back to Earth, people who had ignored the age-old premise (that business growth and stock growth is directly proportional) eventually lost their shirts. Investing $10,000 in a few of the new millennium's most popular stocks during 2000 would have resulted in some devastating losses for investors.

The stories of wealth enticed individual investors and fund management firms alike before the eventual collapse of the dot-com bubble.

Mutual fund companies rushed to create technology-based funds that they could sell. The job of fund companies, of course, isn't to make money for you or me. Their primary job is to make money for their companies' owners or share-holders.

There's a saying that "Wall Street will sell what Wall Street can sell." In this case, newly introduced technology-stock mutual funds were first-class tickets on airplanes with near-empty fuel tanks. Passengers giggled with delight as they soared into the clouds . . . until the fuel ran out.

Sadly, there were plenty of regular middle-class folk who climbed aboard this soon-to-be-plunging craft. When the plane hurtled into the ground, many investors in technology funds and Internet stocks lost nearly everything they had invested.

Few players in the Internet stock fiasco escaped unscathed. You might imagine loads of people getting out on top, or near the top, but the hysterical era of easily quadrupling your money within a matter of months swept through amateur and professional investors alike. Nobody really knew where that "top" was going to be, so loads of people kept climbing into tech stocks.

I'd be lying if I claimed to avoid the tech sector's sirens. In 1999, I succumbed to buying shares in one of the technology stock darlings of the day, Nortel Networks.

It was silly of me to buy it, but watching my friends making bucket loads of easy money on Internet stocks while I sat on the sidelines was more than I could take. Swept up in the madness, it didn't matter that I didn't really know what the company did.

Eventually getting around to reading Nortel's annual report, I recognized that the company had been losing more and more money since 1996. But I didn't care. Sure, it made me nervous, but the stock price was rising and I didn't want to be left behind.

What was worse was that every year since 1996, the business was losing more and more money while its stock price was going in the opposite direction: up! I paid $83 a share. When that stock price rose to $118, I had made a 42 percent profit. Late getting onto the Nortel train, I couldn't believe the money I had made in such a short time. Recognizing a quick profit, I figured it would be wise to sell, which is exactly what I did at $118 a share. If only the story ended there. No sooner did I sell than the price rose to $124 a share.

Then I read an analyst's report suggesting that the share price was going to rise to $150 before the year was up. What was I doing, selling at $118?

Shortly after the stock price dipped to $120, and like a knucklehead, I bought back the shares I had previously sold. I was watching the dog while ignoring the owner's rigor mortis.

And that's when gravity hurtled the stock price down to $100 a share...then $80 a share...then $50 a share. Suddenly, people noticed the smell.

I sold at $48, losing almost half of what I put into my investment. I got burned for buying a stock I never should have bought in the first place because—despite the meteoric rise in its stock price—the business itself hadn't made a dime in years.

But I was lucky. Today, those same shares are worthless.

Many of my friends never sold. It's a shameful reminder of what can happen when we mix greed and ignorance.

Taking Advantage of Fear and Greed

Buying a total stock market index fund needn't be boring. If you can be greedy when others are fearful and fearful when others are greedy, you can add a touch of nitrate to your investment portfolio. You don't need to follow investment news or follow the markets. You just need to utilize the safest component of your investment portfolio—your bonds.

The disastrous events of September 11, 2001, invoked tremendous fear in the American people when terrorists hijacked two airliners and flew them into New York's World Trade Center. After the twin towers collapsed, the stock markets were temporarily closed. Sadly, nearly 3,000 people were killed in the terrorist attack.

But long term, how would the attack affect American business profits? As catastrophic as the event had been, it wasn't likely to have a permanent effect on the number of Coca-Cola cans or McDonald's hamburgers sold worldwide or Safeway's food sales. Americans are resilient, and so are their businesses.

And yet, when the stock markets re-opened after the terrorist attack, US stock prices dropped.

Short Term, Most Investors Prove Their Irrationality

Many investors don't think about the stock market as a representation of something real—like true business earnings. Fear and greed rule the short-term irrationality of stock markets.

But thinking about the market as a group of businesses, and not a squiggly line on a chart or a quote in the paper, can fertilize your wealth. When there's a disconnection between business profits and stock prices, you can easily take advantage of the circumstances. What happened in the stock markets after 9/11 was the antithesis of the boom times of the late 1990s. Stock prices fell like football-sized chunks of hail. But business earnings were hardly affected.

When the New York Stock Exchange reopened after the 9/11 attacks, it might as well have held up a giant neon sign: "Stocks on sale today!" The US stock market opened 20 percent lower than its opening level the previous month. Scraping together every penny I could muster, I dumped money into the stock market like a crazed shopper at a "going out of business" sale. Speculators hate doing that because they're continually worried the markets will fall further. Real investors never think like that. They care more about what the markets will be doing in 20 years, not next week.

Worrying about the immediate future is letting the stock market lead you by the gonads.

Most People Have a Backward View of the Markets

The Oracle of Omaha, Warren Buffett, laid out a quiz in his 1997 letter to Berkshire Hathaway shareholders. If you can pass this quiz, you'll be on your way to doing well in the stock market. But most investors and most financial advisers would fail this little quiz, and that's one of the reasons most people are poor investors.

He asked his readers whether they would prefer to pay higher or lower prices for items like hamburgers or cars in the future. Of course, it makes more sense to wish for lower prices. He then asks another question. If you expect to buy stock market products over at least the next five years, should you wish for higher or lower stock prices? Buffett says that most investors get this one wrong. They prefer to pay higher prices. Instead, he says people should think about stock prices the same way they would think about the prices of hamburgers or cars:

Only those who will be sellers of equities [stock market investments] in the near future should be happy at seeing stocks rise. Prospective purchasers should much prefer sinking prices.[15]

Young People Should Salivate When Stocks Sputter

William Bernstein, the former neurologist turned financial adviser, says investors in their 20s or early 30s should *"pray for a long, awful [bear] market."* He wrote *If You Can*, a short e-book about investing for Millennials.

Most young people want their investments to rise right away. They want immediate confirmation that they're doing the right thing. But instead, they should hope for stocks to sag or limp.

Think of stocks as cans of nonperishable food. Workers buy these cans and stuff them in the cellar. Once retired, they eat that food. If the price of those items rises rapidly after they retire, the retirees can celebrate. After all, they've already bought their cans.

That isn't the same for young investors. They're in the collecting phase. They get less for their money when prices rise quickly.

We can't control stock market levels. But we can control how we feel about market prices. Young investors should smile—and keep investing—when stocks don't rise.

Imagine a young investor named Lisa. She starts her career at age 22. She invests every year. Over the next 30 years, should Lisa prefer to see stocks rise by a compound annual return of 15 percent annually for 15 years, followed by an equal time period when stocks average a compound annual return of 2 percent? Or should she prefer stocks to compound annually at 2 percent per year for the first 15 years, followed by 11 percent per year for the next 15 years?

Instinctively, most people would choose option 1. They would want to see their investments make money right away. After 30 years, that would give Lisa $922,817.99. But Warren

Buffett and William Bernstein are right. Young investors benefit when markets are weak. The second option is better. With it, as seen in Table 4.6, Lisa's money would grow to $1,235,866.87.

Table 4.6 $10,000 Invested Annually

	Scenario 1: Stocks Gain 15% Per Year for 15 Years, Followed by 2% Per Year for 15 Years		Scenario 2: Stocks Gain 2% Per Year for 15 Years, Followed by 11% Per Year for 15 Years	
Year	Account Balance	Compound Annual Growth Rate	Account Balance	Compound Annual Growth Rate
	$10,000.00		$10,000.00	
1.	$21,500.00	15%	$20,200.00	2%
2.	$34,725.00	15%	$30,604.00	2%
3.	$49,933.75	15%	$41,216.08	2%
4.	$67,423.81	15%	$52,040.40	2%
5.	$87,537.38	15%	$63,081.21	2%
6.	$110,667.99	15%	$74,342.83	2%
7.	$137,268.19	15%	$85,829.69	2%
8.	$167,858.42	15%	$97,546.28	2%
9.	$203,037.18	15%	$109,497.21	2%
10.	$243,492.76	15%	$121,687.15	2%
11.	$290,016.67	15%	$134,120.90	2%
12.	$343,519.17	15%	$146,803.32	2%
13.	$405,047.05	15%	$159,739.38	2%
14.	$475,804.11	15%	$172,934.17	2%
15.	$557,174.72	15%	$186,392.85	2%
16.	$578,318.22	2%	$216,896.07	11%
17.	$599,884.58	2%	$250,754.63	11%
18.	$621,882.28	2%	$288,337.64	11%
19.	$644,319.92	2%	$330,054.78	11%
20.	$667,206.32	2%	$376,360.81	11%
21.	$690,550.45	2%	$427,760.50	11%
22.	$714,361.45	2%	$484,814.15	11%
23.	$738,648.68	2%	$548,143.71	11%
24.	$763,421.66	2%	$618,439.52	11%
25.	$788,690.09	2%	$696,467.87	11%
26.	$814,463.89	2%	$783,079.33	11%
27.	$840,753.17	2%	$879,218.06	11%
28.	$867,568.23	2%	$985,932.05	11%
29.	$894,919.60	2%	$1,104,384.57	11%
30.	$922,817.99	2%	$1,235,866.87	11%

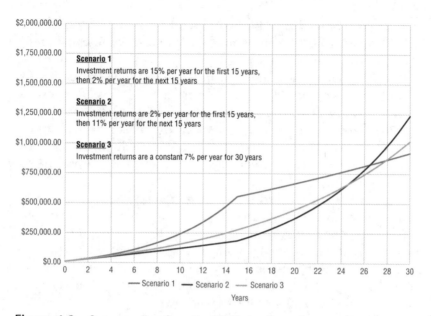

Figure 4.3   Compounding Growth of Differing Scenarios

How about a constant annual compound return of 7 percent over 30 years? It would be easier on the nerves. Instinctively, it also looks better than facing weak stock returns for the first 15 years. But the market laughs at instinct. As seen in Figure 4.3, this third scenario would see that money grow to $1,020,730.41.

Facing the first 15 years of horrible returns, followed by 11 percent per year, would provide $215,136.46 more.

Nobody can control stock prices. But people can control their behavior and perspective. Young people, especially, shouldn't be afraid to invest when the markets sputter.

Instead, they should invest every month—and smile when markets lag.

Opportunities after Chaos

When the stock market reopened after 9/11, it was trading at a discount. As a result, I added more money. But where did I get it?

I sold some of my bonds. It didn't take any kind of special judgment on my part. I just stuck to a mechanical strategy, which I'll explain further in Chapter 5.

Unfortunately, the money I invested in the US stock market index in September 2001 went on to gain 15 percent over just a few months. By January 2016 (even after the financial crisis of 2008–2009), the value of my stock purchases in the autumn of 2001 was up more than 158 percent, including dividends. But that upset me. Yes, you read that right. I was upset to see my stock market investments rise.

After 9/11, I wanted the markets to stay down. I was hoping to keep buying into the stock markets for many years at a discounted rate. It's a bit like betting that a sleeping dog on a long leash is eventually going to have to get up and run to catch its sprinting owner. The longer the leash and the longer that dog sleeps, the more money I can put on the dog, which will eventually tear after its owner up the hill, pulling my wheelbarrow load of money behind it. Sadly for me, the stock market didn't sleep in its discounted state for long.

Of course, not everybody is going to be happy about a sinking or stagnating stock market. My apologies to retirees. If you're retired, there's no way you're going to want to see plummeting stock prices. You're no longer able to buy cheap stocks when you're not making a salary. And, you'll be regularly selling small pieces of your investments every year to cover living expenses.

Younger people who will be adding to their portfolios for at least five years or more need to celebrate when markets fall. I didn't think I would get another opportunity to benefit from irrational fear after September 2001. A plunging stock market is a special treat for a wage earner—one that doesn't come along every day. But another opportunity fell on my lap again between 2002 and 2003 (as shown in Figure 4.4), with the stock market eventually selling at a 40 percent discount from its 2001 high, after the United States announced it was going to war with Iraq.

Was the average US business going to make 40 percent less money? Were businesses like PepsiCo, Walmart, Exxon Mobil, and Microsoft going to see a 40 percent drop in profits? Even at the time, it would have been really tough to find anyone

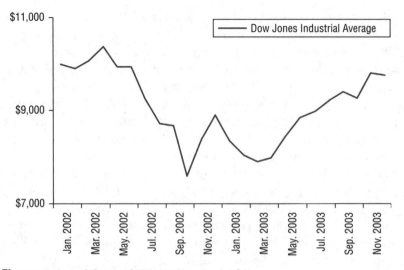

Figure 4.4   US Stocks Offered a Wonderful Sale
Source: Yahoo! Finance historical price tables for Dow Jones Industrials

who believed that. Yet, US businesses were trading at a 40 percent discount on the stock market. I was salivating, and hoping
that the markets would stay down this time—for years if possible. I wanted to load up.

I didn't know how low the markets would fall, so I wasn't
lucky enough to buy stock indexes at the very bottom of the
market's plunge. But it didn't matter to me. Once the "20 percent off" flags were waving in my face, I was a chocoholic
stowaway in Willy Wonka's factory. The stock market continued to fall as I continued to buy. If I could have taken an
extra job to give me more money to take advantage of cheap
stock prices, I probably would have done it. For some reason,
most investors were doing what they typically do: they over-
react when prices fall, sending stocks to mouthwatering levels.
They sell when they should be buying. They become afraid of
a discounted sale, hoping (and yes, this is a true representation of insanity) that they can soon pay higher prices for their
stock market products. They miss the point of what stocks are.
Stocks represent ownership in real businesses.

Again, I hoped that the stock markets would keep falling
in 2003, or that they would stay low for a few years so I could
gorge at the buffet.

It was not to be. I was disappointed as the US stock market index began a long recovery from 2002–2003 until the end of 2007, rising more than 100 percent from its low point in just four years. Retirees would have been celebrating, but I was crying in my oatmeal. The big supermarket sale was over.

As the stock market roared ahead in 2007, I didn't put a penny in my stock indexes. I bought bond indexes instead. Following a general rule of thumb, I wanted my bond allocation to equal my age. For example, I was 37 years old and I wanted 35 to 40 percent of my portfolio to be comprised of bonds. But the rapidly rising stock market in 2007 was sending my stock indexes far higher than the allocation I set for them. As a result, my bonds represented far less than 35 percent of my total account, so I spent 2007 buying bonds—even selling some of my stock indexes to do it.

I resumed my aggressive stock-buying plan in 2008 when the stock market traded at a 20 percent discount to its 2007 peak. Figure 4.5 shows what kind of hammering the stock market took in 2008. And I happily increased my purchases with my monthly savings as the markets plummeted by 50 percent from 2007 to a low point in March 2009. It was like wandering into an Apple computer dealership and seeing the

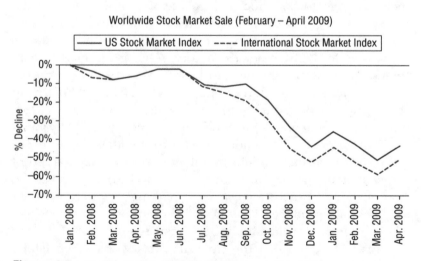

Figure 4.5 Worldwide Stock Market Sale
Source: Vanguard historical prices for total US and international indexes

discount bins filled to the brim with the latest iPhones. Stocks were selling at 50 percent off—and nobody was lining up to buy them! At one point, the stock indexes had fallen so far that I sold a large amount of my bond index so I could buy more of my stock index, mindful of keeping a balanced allocation of stocks and bonds. When the stock markets fell, my bond allocation ended up being significantly higher than 35 percent of my total portfolio. Selling off some of my bond index to buy more of my stock index also helped bring my portfolio back to the desired allocation.

With stock prices falling so heavily, I finally understood Buffett's comments in 1974, when he was interviewed by *Forbes* magazine. Faced at the time with a stock market drop of a similar magnitude, he said he felt like an oversexed guy in a harem.[16]

Again, did the economic crash in 2008–2009 eat into the profits of US businesses? Certainly some of them lost money, but not all. If stock prices fall by 50 percent, it can be justified only if business earnings have fallen (or expect to fall) by 50 percent. As always with the stock market, investors' fear and greed can produce irrational price levels. In 2008–2009, I prayed stocks would remain cheap.

Obviously, praying for something so nonspiritual was the wrong thing to do. Perhaps divine intervention punished me for it when the markets rose. Between March 2009 and January 2016, the US stock market index rose 223 percent and the international stock market index, which I was also buying, rose 104 percent. I'm not the sort of guy who normally gets depressed, but the indexes I was buying were getting pricier by the month. I would have preferred it if the markets had stayed low.

People don't normally get such wonderful opportunities to take advantage of crazy, short-term discounts. But with sensational financial television programs based on financial Armageddon, with a rough economic period, and with the Internet spreading news of emotional market sentiment far and wide, we had a recipe for some remarkable stock market volatility over the past decade.

Unfortunately, the enemy in the mirror thrashes most investors. They like buying stock market investments when prices are rising, and they shrink away in horror when they see bargains. How do we know? We just need to observe what most investors do when stock markets are falling or rising. John Bogle, in his classic text, *Common Sense on Mutual Funds*, reveals the startling data while asking the rhetorical question: "Will investors never learn?"

In the late 1990s, when stock markets were defying gravity, investors piled more money into the stock market than they ever had before, adding $650 billion to stock mutual funds during this period. Then when stock prices became cheap in 2008 and 2009, with the biggest market decline since 1929–1933, what do you think most American mutual fund investors were doing? When they should have been enthusiastically buying, they were selling off more than $228 billion of stock market mutual funds.[17]

What we do know about the future is that we will once again experience unpredictable stock market shockers. The markets will either fall, seemingly off a cliff, or they'll catch hold of a rocket to soar into the stratosphere. Armed with the knowledge of how stock markets reflect business earnings you won't be seduced to take silly risks, and you won't be as fearful when markets fall. By building a responsible portfolio of stock and bond indexes, you'll create more stability in your account while providing opportunities to take advantage of stock market silliness.

The next chapter will show you how to do this.

Notes

1. "Mind The Gap 2014," February 27, 2014, Morningstar.com, http://www.morningstar.com/advisor/t/88015528/mind-the-gap-2014.htm.
2. Portfoliovisualizer.com, accessed July 7, 2016.
3. John C. Bogle, *The Little Book of Common Sense Investing* (Hoboken, NJ: John Wiley & Sons, 2007), 51.
4. Andrew Hallam, "Are Index Fund Investors Simply Smarter?" AssetBuilder.com, December 8, 2014, assetbuilder.com/knowledge-center/articles/are-index-fund-investors-simply-smarter.

5. Jonathan Clements, "Are Index Fund Investors Smarter?" *The Wall Street Journal* blog, March 26, 2015, blogs.wsj.com/totalreturn/2015/03/26/are-index-fund-investors-smarter/.

6. John C. Bogle, *Common Sense on Mutual Funds* (Hoboken, NJ: John Wiley & Sons, 2010), 28.

7. Jeremy Siegel, *Stocks for the Long Run* (New York: McGraw-Hill, 2002), 217–218.

8. "Missing the Best and Worst Days," IFA Advisors, accessed July 7, 2016, www.ifa.com/12steps/step 4/missing_the_best_and_worst_days/.

9. Ken Fisher, *The Only Three Questions That Count* (Hoboken, NJ: John Wiley & Sons, 2007), 279.

10. "Coca-Cola Report," The Value Line Investment Survey, November 9, 2001, 1551.

11. "Long Term Performance of Major Developed Equity Markets," Management and Factset Research Systems, accessed April 15, 2011, www.fulcrumasset.com/files/Long%20Term%20Equity%20Performance.pdf.

12. Quote DB, accessed April 15, 2011, www.quotedb.com/quotes/3038.

13. "A Long-Term Perspective Chart," The Value Line Investment Survey, 1920–2005.

14. Burton Malkiel, *A Random Walk Down Wall Street* (New York: WW Norton & Company, 2003), 86.

15. Lawrence Cunningham, *The Essays of Warren Buffett* (Singapore: John Wiley & Sons, 2009), 86–87.

16. Forbes, from the archives, "Warren Buffett—1974," accessed January 5, 2011, www.forbes.com/2008/04/30/warren-buffett-profile-invest-oped-cx_hs_0430buffett.html.

17. John C. Bogle, *Common Sense on Mutual Funds* (Hoboken, New Jersey: John Wiley & Sons, 2010), 32.

Build Mountains of Money with a Responsible Portfolio

"Eat your Brussels sprouts," I used to hear when I was a kid, "and you'll grow into a big, strong boy."

So I ate a bowl of Brussels sprouts for breakfast, a plate of Brussels sprouts for lunch, and a casserole dish of Brussels sprouts for dinner—seven days a week.

If that were true, I'd probably resemble a green, leafy ball with legs by now. Brussels sprouts might be good for you, but you need to eat more than a bunch of tiny cabbages if you want to be healthy.

In the same vein, a total stock market index fund might be good for you as well, but it doesn't represent a balanced portfolio.

If that were all you bought, your portfolio would gyrate wildly with the stock market. If the market dropped 20 percent, so would your overall portfolio. If the market dropped 50 percent, so would your total investments.

This isn't good for any investor, especially those approaching retirement and needing more stability. If a 60-year-old plans to use her portfolio as a nest egg, she's not going to be comfortable seeing all of her hard-earned money plunge into what might look like a bottomless crater during a sharp market decline.

Only an irresponsible portfolio would fall 50 percent if the stock market value were cut in half. That's because bonds become parachutes when stock markets fall.

What Are Bonds?

Bond is a secret British agent with a license to kill. He sleeps with multiple women, never dies, and every 15 years or so, gets a body transplant to look like a completely different guy.

Financial bonds are just as riveting.

Bonds Get Less Shaken and Stirred

In the long term, bonds don't make as much money as stocks. But they're less volatile, so they can save your account from falling to the bottom of a stock market canyon if the market gods want a hearty laugh.

A bond is a loan that you make to a government or a corporation. Your money is safe as long as that entity (the government or the corporation receiving the loan) is able to pay the money back, plus annual interest.

The safest ones you can buy are first-world government bonds from high-income industrial countries. Slightly riskier bonds can be bought from strong blue-chip businesses such as Coca-Cola, Walmart, and Johnson & Johnson. Bonds from smaller, less established companies usually offer the highest rates of interest. But there's a higher chance that they might forfeit on their loans. The higher the interest paid by a corporate bond, the higher the risk associated with it.

If you're looking for a safe place for your money, it's best to keep it in short-term or intermediate-term government bonds or high-quality corporate bonds.

Why short term or intermediate term? If you buy a bond paying 4 percent annually over the next 10 years, there's always a chance that inflation could make a meal out of it. If that happens, you're essentially losing money. Sure, the bond is paying you 4 percent annually, but if you're buying breakfast cereal that increases in price every year by 6 percent, then your 4 percent bond interest is losing to a box of cornflakes.

For this reason, buying bonds with shorter maturities (such as one- to five-year bonds) is wiser than buying longer-term bonds (such as 20- to 30-year bonds). If inflation rears its head, you won't be saddled with a commitment to a certain interest rate. When a short-term or intermediate-term bond expires, and you get your money back, you can buy another short-term or intermediate-term bond at the higher interest rate.

If this sounds complicated, don't worry. You can buy a short-term or intermediate-term government bond index, and you never have to worry about an expiration date. It will keep pace with inflation over time, and you can sell it whenever you want. It's easy.

If You Want to Know How Bonds Work, Here's the Skinny

You don't need to know the intricacies of how bonds work. You can just buy a government bond index (which I'll show you how to do in the next chapter) and that bond index can represent the temperate part of your investment account. But if you want to know how bonds work, here it is in a half-page nutshell.

If you buy a five-year government bond, you know immediately what the interest rate is and that the rate is guaranteed by the government. If you loan a government say, $10,000, they promise to give you that $10,000 back. Along the way, you are guaranteed to earn $500 each year in interest payments, assuming that the interest rate was 5 percent annually.

If you choose to sell that bond before the five years are up, you can do that, but bond prices fluctuate every day. Instead of getting back your $10,000, you might get back $10,500 or $9,500, if you sell before the maturity date.

When inflation/interest rates rise, bond prices fall. If inflation were running at 3 percent annually when you bought a bond that yields 5 percent in interest, and if inflation suddenly jumped to 5 percent, then no new investors would want to buy a bond like yours (paying 5 percent interest with inflation at 5 percent). If they did, they wouldn't make any money after the increase in the cost of living. But if the price of that bond dropped, the new investor would be lured by the idea of paying $9,500 for the same bond that you paid

$10,000. When that bond expired, the new investor would get $10,000 back.

If interest rates dropped, a friend of yours might be dying to buy your $10,000 bond that pays 5 percent in interest annually. But he wouldn't be alone. Institutional bond traders would rush to buy that bond quickly, resulting in a price increase for it—perhaps from $10,000 to $10,300. Bond-price adjustments are similar to stock-price adjustments. If there's more demand, the price will rise.

Your friend, however, would earn 5 percent annually on $10,000 (not on the $10,300 he paid for the bond). When the bond expired, he would receive $10,000 back. You'd brag. He'd get upset. And if your friend were anything like my dad, you might find cat food in your shoes.

You can see why there's a bond "trading market" as people try to take advantage of these price movements. It only follows that there are actively managed mutual funds focused on buying and selling bonds as well.

Bond Index Funds Are the Winner

In case you're tempted to buy an actively managed bond fund, remember this: bond index funds beat them silly. Costs matter even more in the world of bond funds.

Figure 5.1 reveals that from 2003 to 2008, the average actively managed government bond fund with a sales load (that crafty commission paid to advisers) made 3.7 percent annually and the average actively managed bond fund without a sales load made 4.9 percent annually. As with actively managed stock market mutual funds, those without sales-load fees outperform, on average, those with sales-load fees.

During the same period, a US government bond index averaged 7.1 percent annually.

The SPIVA Persistence Scorecard measures what percentage of actively managed bond funds beat their bond index counterparts. When measuring three categories of government bond funds (long term, intermediate term, and short term) they found that just 17.67 percent of them beat their index fund counterparts during the 10-year period that ended December 31, 2015.[1]

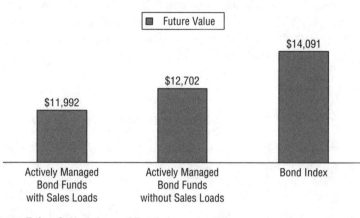

Actively Managed Bond Funds vs.
Indexed Bond Funds (2003–2008)

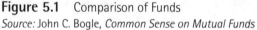

Figure 5.1 Comparison of Funds
Source: John C. Bogle, *Common Sense on Mutual Funds*

Whether you're buying stock indexes or bond indexes, active management puts a drag on your returns because of the extra fees.

If your account has a bond index, a domestic stock index, and an international stock index, you'll have a good chance of success.

What Percentage of Your Portfolio Should You Have in Bonds?

The debate over what percentage you should own in stocks and what percentage you should own in bonds is livelier than an Italian family reunion.

A rule of thumb is that you should have a bond allocation that's roughly equivalent to your age. Some experts suggest that it should be your age minus 10, or if you want a riskier portfolio, your age minus 20; for example, a 50-year-old would have between 30 and 50 percent of his or her investment portfolio in bonds.

Common sense should be used here. A 50-year-old government employee expecting a guaranteed pension when he retires can afford to invest less than 50 percent of his portfolio in bonds. He can take on greater risk (for the promise of higher returns). Stock returns don't always beat bond returns over the short term, but over long periods, stocks run circles around bonds. That said, bonds could be your secret weapon when stocks hit the skids.

Trounce the Professionals with a Balanced Portfolio

If you're adding $200 a month to a portfolio, you could add $60 a month to a bond index ($60 is 30 percent of $200) and $140 a month ($140 is 70 percent of $200) to your stock indexes.

In any given year, as you know, the stock market can go crazy, rising or dropping by 30 percent or more. Dispassionate, intelligent investors can rebalance their portfolios if they're too far from the stock/bond allocation they set for themselves.

For example, if a 30-year-old man has 30 percent in bonds and 70 percent in stocks, he will want to maintain that allocation.

If the stock market falls heavily in a given month, the investor will find that his portfolio (which started out with 70 percent in stocks) now has a lower percentage in stocks than his goal allocation of 70 percent. So what should that investor do when adding fresh money to the account? He should add to his stock indexes.

If the stock market rose considerably during another month, the investor might find that stocks now make up more than 70 percent of his total portfolio. What should he do with fresh money? He should add to his bond index.

Profiting from Panic—Stock Market Crash, 2008–2009

When stock markets fall, most people panic, sending stocks to lower levels. Calm investors, however, can lay seeds for future profits. My personal portfolio was far larger just one year after

My Portfolio–January 2008

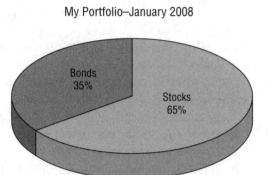

Figure 5.2   Portfolio at Age 37

the financial crisis compared with its level before the crisis scuttled the markets. It helped that I kept a constant allocation of stocks and bonds. As I mentioned in the previous chapter, I started 2008 (before the stock market crash) with a bond allocation at roughly 35 percent of my total portfolio, as shown in Figure 5.2.

Then the stock markets started to fall, giving me a disproportionate percentage in bonds. I invest monthly, so when the markets fell—to keep me close to my desired stock/bond allocation—I bought nothing but stocks and stock indexes. But no matter how much money I was adding to my stock indexes, the markets continued to drop until March 2009.

Figure 5.3 shows how my portfolio looked during the first few months of 2009.

My Portfolio–January 2009

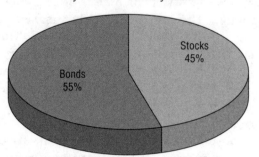

Figure 5.3   Portfolio at Age 38

Despite my monthly stock market purchases, I couldn't get my stock allocation back to 65 percent of my total. As a result, I had to sell some of my bonds in early 2009 to bring my portfolio back to my desired allocation.

Naturally, I was hoping the markets would stay low. But they didn't. As the stock markets began to recover that year, I switched tactics again and bought nothing but bonds for more than a year. I was low on bonds because I had sold bonds to buy stocks, and my stocks were rising in value.

This kind of rebalancing is common practice among university endowment funds and pension funds.

Usually investors don't need to address their stock/bond allocation more than once a year. But when the stock markets go completely nuts—dropping by 20 percent or more—it's a good idea to take advantage of it if you can.

Having a Foreign Affair

Americans should have a nice chunk of money in a US index; Canadians should have a good-sized chunk in a Canadian index; and so it should follow for Australians, Brits, Singaporeans, or any other nationality with an established stock market. An investor's portfolio should always have the home country index represented. After all, it makes sense to keep much of your money in the currency with which you pay your bills.

After adding a government bond index to your portfolio, you really could stop right there.

But many investors (me included) like having an international component. The US stock market makes up about 50 percent of the world's stock market exposure. There are also stock markets in Canada, Australia, England, France, Japan, and China, just to mention a few. Investors can increase their diversification by building a portfolio with global exposure. A total international stock market index would fit the bill.

There are many trains of thought relating to how much of your stock exposure should be international. To keep it simple, you could split your stock market money between your home country index and an international index.

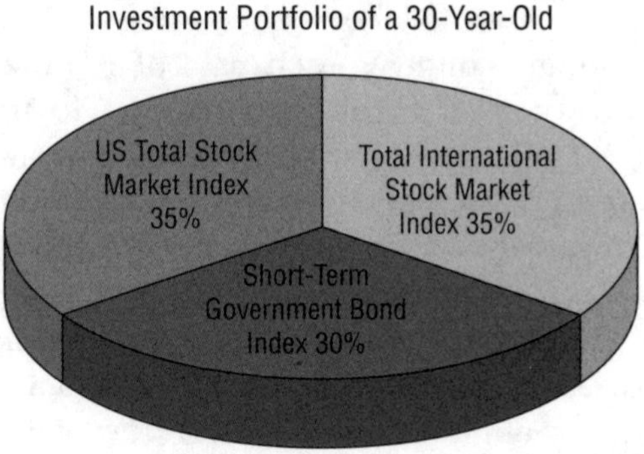

Investment Portfolio of a 30-Year-Old

Figure 5.4 Investment Portfolio Percentages

In that case, a 30-year-old American investor (without an upcoming pension) could have a portfolio that looks like the one on Figure 5.4.

If you're making monthly investment purchases, you need to look at your home country stock index and your international stock index and determine which one has done better over the previous month. When you figure it out (hold on for this!) you need to add newly invested money to the index that hasn't done as well. That should keep your account close to your desired allocation.

What do most people do? You guessed it. Metaphorically speaking, they sign long-term contracts to empty their wallets into the toilet—buying more of the high-performing index and less of the underperforming index. Over an investment lifetime, behavior such as this can cost hundreds of thousands of dollars.

Over my lifetime, the total US stock market index and the total international stock market index have performed similarly. There has been about 1 percent compounding difference between the two since 1970.[2] But there are times when one will lag the other. Take advantage of that.

Please note that I'm not talking about chasing individual stocks or individual foreign markets into the gutter. For example, just because the share price of company "Random X" has fallen doesn't mean that investors should throw good money after bad, thinking that it's a great deal just because it has dropped in value. Who knows what's going to happen to "Random X?" It could vaporize like a San Francisco fog.

Likewise, you take a large risk buying an index focusing on a single foreign country, such as Chile, Brazil, or China. Who really knows what's going to happen to those markets over the next 30 years? They might do really well, but it's better to diversify and go with the total international stock market index (if you want foreign exposure). Within it, you'll have exposure to older world economies such as England, France, and Germany, as well as the younger, fast-growing economies of China, India, Brazil, and Thailand. Just remember to rebalance. If the international stock market goes on a tear, don't chase it with fresh money. If your domestic stock index and the international stock index both shoot skyward, add fresh money to your bond index.

If that sounds too complicated, Scott Burns has popularized an even simpler strategy.

Introducing the Couch Potato Portfolio

A former columnist with *The Dallas Morning News*, Burns now works with AssetBuilder, a US-based investment company that manages money with indexed strategies. Recognizing that actively managed mutual fund purchases didn't make sense (thanks to high fees, high-tax consequences, and poor performance), he popularized a simple investment strategy called the Couch Potato Portfolio.

It's comprised of an equal commitment to a US total stock market index and a total bond market index. In other words, if you were investing $200 a month, you would put $100 a month into the stock market index and $100 a month into the bond market index. You don't even have to open your investment statements more than once a year.

After one year is up, look at your investment account and figure out whether you now have more money in stocks or bonds. If there's more money in the bond index, sell some of it to get equal weighting in your portfolio, buying the stock index with the proceeds. If there's more money in the stock index, sell some of your stock market index and buy the bond index with the proceeds.

Without allowing yourself to fall victim to the market's crazy "ups and downs," you would be buying low and selling high once a year.

With a 50 percent bond component, this would be a pretty conservative account. If the stock markets fell by 50 percent in a given year, your account would fall far less than that and you would have a chance to even out your account 12 months later by buying the underpriced stock index with proceeds from the bond index.

Such a strategy, despite its very conservative nature, would have averaged 10.96 percent annually from 1986 to 2001.[3]

This would have turned $1,000 into $4,758.79 over that 15-year period.

But a drunken monkey tossing darts at the stock market page could have made decent money from 1986 to 2001, because most of the world's stock markets rose like a hot air balloon. How did the indexed couch potato strategy perform when stock markets went through their gut-wrenching dives and rises (and dives again) during the next 10 years—a decade that many stock market investors have coined "the lost decade?" For starters, the indexed couch potato strategy let investors sleep more soundly during market drops, thanks to the large bond component.

During 2002, the US stock market was hammered. The average US stock market mutual fund declined 22.8 percent in value. In other words, an investment of $10,000 would have fallen to $7,723. But during that devastating year, the markets were able to knock the couch potato strategy down only 6.9 percent. A $10,000 investment would have dropped to $9,310.[4]

Between the beginning of 2003 and the beginning of 2008, the US and international stock market indexes rose dramatically, gaining 91 percent and 186 percent, respectively.[5] If you had money in the markets during these five years, you probably would have increased your portfolio size a lot, no matter who was managing it. But let's have a look at one of the ugliest years in modern financial history: 2008.

With the global economic crisis, world stock markets took a beating. Of course, long-term investors should have gleefully rubbed their hands. They could take advantage of lower prices. But let's see how the average US mutual fund and the couch potato portfolio would have fared during that falling market.

If you thought the average professional could have weathered the storm, you'd be disappointed. Table 5.1 shows that the average actively managed stock market mutual fund (comprised of stocks, without bonds) dropped 29.1 percent in 2008, compared to a drop of 20.4 percent for the indexed couch potato portfolio. And how about the average actively managed balanced fund? Balanced funds don't have the same kind of exposure to the stock market that regular stock market mutual funds have. Balanced funds are usually comprised of 60 percent stocks and 40 percent bonds. When stocks fell dramatically in 2008, the bond component of the average actively managed balanced fund should have cushioned the fall. But that wasn't the case. The average actively managed balanced fund dropped a whopping 28 percent during 2008.[6] Why did the average balanced fund manager lose so much money even though 40 percent to 50 percent of their funds' assets were in bonds? The only explanation is that they were afraid, and they sold stocks when the markets fell. As mentioned in my previous chapter, nobody can predict the short-term movements of the stock markets. Following a disciplined couch potato strategy is likely to be far more profitable than allowing a fund manager to mess with your money.

Another nice thing about using the couch potato portfolio strategy is that (despite the market crash of 2008–2009) you would have still made money from 2006 to 2011. During this five-year period—when many actively managed balanced mutual funds lost money—a $10,000 investment in the couch potato portfolio would have grown to more than $12,521.56. That's an overall gain of 25.2 percent.[7]

As an investor, I loved the stock market decline of 2008–2009. But as a consultant, it was disheartening. Many people brought their portfolios to me during the economic crisis, revealing investments that had collapsed 40 percent or more in value.

Table 5.1 The Couch Potato Portfolio vs. the Average US Mutual Fund in 2008

Average US mutual fund	−29.1% drop	$10,000 dropped to $7,090
Indexed Couch Potato Portfolio concept	−20.4% drop	$10,000 dropped to $7,960

When I looked at their investment holdings, I found something pretty shocking: their investment advisers obviously had little respect for bonds. Most of the people who showed me their statements were older than me, so they should have had bond components that equaled or exceeded mine. But none did. In some cases, they had no bonds at all! Their accounts fell far further than mine when the markets declined and they couldn't take advantage of cheap stock market prices because they didn't have any bonds to sell.

Investors in their 50s and 60s, especially, require bonds in their portfolios. It would be tough to find an investment book that didn't include this fundamental principle. But many of the accounts I saw were fully exposed to the market's gyrations without a protective bond component.

I taught with one fellow whom I refer to as a "cowboy investor." He's in his mid-50s and won't have a pension because he spent his career teaching in private schools overseas. He says bonds are for wimps, so he doesn't own any. Instead, he buys whatever rises in value (after it rises) and he sells whatever falls (after it falls). This gives him the distinction of a cowboy who'll never have enough money to leave the ranch.

Combinations of Stocks and Bonds Can Have Powerful Returns

Even when stock markets are rising, a portfolio with a bond component isn't the "party pooper" most cowboy investors think it is. Financial author Daniel Solin notes that from 1973 to 2004, an investor with an allocation of 60 percent in a US stock market index and 40 percent in a total bond market index would have earned an average return of 10.49 percent annually.

An investor taking much more risk and having 100 percent of their portfolio in a stock index would have returns averaging 11.19 percent annually during this period.[8]

The cowboy investor would have taken more risk, and for what? An extra 0.7 percent annual return? He would have needed a strong stomach. His worst year during this 31-year time period would have seen his account plunge by 20.15 percent. In contrast, an account with 40 percent bonds and

60 percent stocks wouldn't have fallen further than 9.15 percent during its worst 12 months.[9]

Using portfoliovisualizer.com, we can see how different Couch Potato portfolios would have performed between 1986 and 2016. The Classic Couch Potato portfolio, 50 percent stocks, 50 percent bonds, would have averaged a compound annual return of 8.04 percent. That would have turned $10,000 into $105,374.

Investors who wished to take a bit more risk may have chosen 60 percent stocks, 40 percent bonds. Such a portfolio would have been slightly more volatile. But it would have earned a higher average return, gaining an average of 8.82 percent during the same time period. That would have turned a $10,000 investment into $116,171.

Those choosing a portfolio with 70 percent stocks, 30 percent bonds would have seen even better long-term results. They would have averaged a compound annual return of 9.16 percent. That would have turned a $10,000 investment into $126,941.

Higher allocations of stocks in the portfolio increase returns over long time periods, as you can see in Table 5.2. But such portfolios fall further when markets fall. And there will always be periods (sometimes years at a time) when bonds beat stocks.

When Scott Burns first created the Couch Potato portfolio in 1991, he recommended Vanguard's S&P 500 Index (VFINX) and Vanguard's Total Bond Market Index (VBMFX). Since then, two other index funds have been introduced that he feels are better. Investors can get broader stock diversification with Vanguard's Total Stock Market Index (VTSMX). For the bond component, he says investors will have higher odds of beating inflation with Vanguard's Inflation-Protected Securities Fund (VIPSX).

Table 5.2   Couch Potato Portfolios, 1986–2016.

	Compound Annual Return	Best Year	Worst Year	$10,000 Would Have Grown to . . .
Portfolio 1 50% Stocks/50% Bonds	8.04%	+27.82%	-15.98%	$105,374
Portfolio 2 60% Stocks/40% Bonds	8.82%	+29.75%	-20.19%	$116,171
Portfolio 3 70% Stocks/30% Bonds	9.16%	+31.67%	-24.39%	$126,941

Source: portfoliovisualizer.com

When Bonds Whip Cowboys

The premise of rebalancing stock and bond indexes doesn't just work in the United States. It works no matter where you live. *MoneySense* magazine's founding editor, Ian McGugan, won a Canadian National Magazine Award for an article adapting the couch potato strategy for Canadians. His method was simple. An investor splits money evenly between a US stock market index, a Canadian stock market index, and a bond market index.

At the end of the calendar year, the investor simply rebalances the portfolio back to the original allocation. If the US stock market index did better than the Canadian index, then the investor would sell some of the US index to even things out with the Canadian index.

If the bond index beat both stock indexes, then some of the bond index would be sold to buy some of the Canadian and US stock market indexes. Of course, if you're making monthly contributions to the account, you could rebalance monthly by simply buying the laggard—to keep your allocation evenly split three ways.

You can see in Table 5.3 how $100 invested in 1975 would have grown if it were rebalanced annually with equal allocations to the Canadian stock index, the US stock index, and the Canadian bond index. Note that from 1975 to the end of 2015, a combination of bond indexes and stock market indexes wasn't just "for wimps." The rebalancing combination of indexes with bonds actually beat the returns of the Canadian stock market index (largely thanks to a strong performing US stock market).

Table 5.3 Invested in the Canadian Couch Potato Portfolio vs. Canadian Stock Index (1975–2015)

Year	Canadian Couch Potato Portfolio	Canadian Stock Index
1975	$100	$100
1976	$118	$100
1981	$195	$257
1986	$475	$469
1991	$730	$615
1996	$1,430	$1,134

(continued)

Table 5.3   *(Cont'd)*

Year	Canadian Couch Potato Portfolio	Canadian Stock Index
2001	$2,268	$1,525
2006	$3,163	$2,725
2010	$3,493	$3,157
2015	$5,371	$4,125
Compound Annual Average Return	+10.34%	+9.74%

Source: Moneysense.ca (1976–2010 data) Portfoliovisualizer (2010–2015 data, using iShares ETFs, XSP, XBB, XIC)[10]

Creating a disciplined plan to rebalance a portfolio removes the guesswork from investing, and it forces investors to ignore their hearts. As I mentioned before, we don't tend to be rational. Most people like buying shares that have risen in value and they like selling shares that have fallen in value.

Smart investors don't do that. They add money to their investments every month. They rebalance once a year.

If they have a moderate or conservative tolerance for risk, they also add bonds.

Notes

1. SPIVA U.S. Scorecard, accessed July 11, 2016, us.spindices .com/documents/spiva/spiva-us-yearend-2015.pdf.
2. David Swensen, *Pioneering Portfolio Management* (New York: Free Press, 2009), 170.
3. Paul Farrell, *The Lazy Person's Guide to Investing* (New York: Warner Business Books, 2004), 12.
4. Scott Burns, "Couch Potato Didn't Do the Market Mash," February 2, 2003, *Dallas News* online, www.dallasnews.com.
5. Morningstar data for VTSMX (Vanguard total stock market index) and VGTSX (Vanguard total international stock market index), 2003–2008.
6. Scott Burns, "Sloth Triumphs Again," UExpress.com, February 15, 2009, www.uexpress.com/scottburns/index.html?uc_full_ date = 20090215.

7. "Monthly Self Managed Couch Potato Returns," AssetBuilder, assetbuilder.com.
8. Daniel Solin, *The Smartest Investment Book You'll Ever Read* (New York: Penguin, 2006), 63–64.
9. Ibid., 63.
10. "Couch Potato Performance," MoneySense online, www .moneysense.ca/2006/04/05/classic-couch-potato-portfolio-historical-performance-tables/; Moneysense.ca (1976–2010 data); Portfoliovisualizer 2010–2015 data, using iShares ETFs, XSP, XBB, XIC.

RULE 6

Sample a "Round-the-World" Ticket to Indexing

Index funds have boarded ships and airplanes to find happy homes outside of the United States. In this section, I'll give you examples of how to build a portfolio of index funds whether you live in the United States, Canada, Great Britain, Australia, or Singapore. Feel free to check out the section relating to your geographic area, or read with interest how our international brothers and sisters can create indexed accounts. Even if you live in a country not mentioned here, as long as you have the ability to open a brokerage account in your home country, you can build a portfolio of indexes.

This chapter shows how to invest on your own. Going solo is the cheapest (and potentially most profitable) way to invest in index funds. It's simple. But if hell has to freeze before you go solo, you'll prefer the next chapter. It describes how to get help through a financial advisory firm.

Still with me? Great! Before getting into the profiles of some real people and how they're investing, let's answer a few important questions.

What's the Difference between an Index Fund and an ETF?

Index funds and ETFs (exchange traded funds) are like identical twins in the same royal family. If they wore t-shirts they would say "Same Same" on one side, "But Different" on the other. They each contain stocks that track a given market. For example, the Vanguard 500 Index fund (VFINX) is an index fund that holds 500 large American stocks. It's available to Americans who open an account with Vanguard. There are no commissions to buy or sell it.

Each trading day, stocks fluctuate. Anyone buying an index fund can place an order to purchase such a fund. They pay the closing price at the end of the trading day.

ETFs are different. They trade on a stock exchange, much like individual stocks. Theoretically (although this would be foolish) a trader could buy and sell them throughout the day. An ETF, like Vanguard's S&P 500 ETF (VOO) would earn almost the same return as Vanguard's 500 Index Fund (VFINX) because it holds the exact same shares in the same proportions. How could returns differ? Vanguard's 500 Index Fund (VFINX) has an expense ratio of 0.16 percent per year. Costs drop to 0.05 percent per year when the investor has more than $10,000 invested in the fund.

Vanguard's S&P 500 ETF (VOO) has an expense ratio cost of 0.05 percent, regardless of the amount invested. In theory, investors with less than $10,000 to invest would have a slight cost edge if they bought the S&P 500 in its ETF form.

But ETFs Have Drawbacks

In most cases, investors must pay commissions to buy and sell ETFs.* If they regularly purchase ETFs with small monthly sums, they may pay more in costs (thanks to commissions) than they would with a regular index fund.

Also, most stocks pay cash dividends. When an ETF receives those dividends, the dividends may or may not be reinvested automatically for free. It may depend on the brokerage used. With traditional index funds, however, dividends can be reinvested automatically at no extra cost.

---

* Investors with Vanguard USA can buy Vanguard's ETFs commission free.

The American Dream Lives With Index Funds

The United States still leads the global pack when it comes to index fund offerings. Investors with relatively small sums can buy index funds through Vanguard. Such costs rival those of the cheapest ETFs. Non-Americans have different options. In many cases, they can also buy index funds. But they cost more than their US-based cousins, or they carry higher minimum investment requirements. Low-cost ETFs, however, are globally available. Investors can purchase them off any of the world's stock market exchanges. Here are the steps to buying one.

How Do You Buy an ETF?

An ETF that tracks the entire global market is an excellent choice. Most of the model portfolios that I've listed later in the book include such a product. It would include stocks from each of the world's geographic regions. Its weightings are usually broken down into something called global market capitalization. For example, the US stock market makes up nearly half of the total worth of all global stocks. That's why a global stock market ETF would have nearly half of its exposure in US stocks. Other countries' stocks would also be represented based on their global market capitalization.

Investors could buy a Global ETF from any variety of different stock exchanges. Whether an investor buys an ETF off the US stock market, UK stock market, Australian, Canadian, or virtually any other market, the process is similar.

Step 1: Open a Brokerage Account

The first step is to open a brokerage account and send cash into that account.

Step 2: Identify the ETF symbol

If you want to buy an ETF, you need to identify the ticker symbol representing such a product on that given stock exchange. Table 6.1 lists some ETF ticker symbols for global stock market ETFs.

Table 6.1   Sample Global ETF Ticker Symbols

Stock Exchange	ETF Name	ETF Symbol	Annual Expense Ratio
US	Vanguard Total World Stock ETF	VT	0.14%
Canadian	Vanguard FTSE Global All Cap ex Canada Index ETF	VXC	0.25%
UK	Vanguard FTSE All World UCITS ETF	VWRL	0.25%

For example, Americans would buy the ETF that trades on the US stock exchange. Its symbol is VT. Canadians would buy the ETF that trades on the Canadian stock exchange. Its symbol is VXC.

Step 3: Identify the Price Per Share

Find the unit price (also known as the share price) for your ETF. Your online brokerage platform should show a price. If it doesn't, look it up. Americans could use Morningstar USA, Canadians could use Morningstar Canada, and Australians could use Morningstar Australia. When purchasing an ETF, enter the ETF's symbol where it asks for ticker, unit, or symbol.

Unit prices for different ETFs will vary. But that doesn't mean one ETF is cheaper than the other. If two ETFs track the exact same market (Vanguard isn't the only ETF provider), then the underlying values of the ETFs would be the same, even if one trades at $10 per unit and the other trades at $15 per unit.

Think of two 20-inch pizzas. Each of them costs $20. You're happy to buy $20 worth of pizza. One of the pizzas is cut into 10 different slices. The other is cut into 15 slices. Only a knucklehead would say, "I'm buying the pizza that's cut into 15 different slices because I get more pizza for my $20."

It's the same for ETFs that track the same market. The true cost variations can only be seen when looking at each respective ETF's expense ratio.

Vanguard FTSE Global All Cap ex Canada Index ETF VXC

Last Price	Day Change		NAV	Open Price	Day Range	52-Week Range	12-Mo.	Total Assets	MER
$28.24	↑0.43 | 1.55%		28.23 CAD	28.18	28.12-28.28	26.00-31.04	Yield 1.92%	406.51 mil CAD	0.27%

Figure 6.1   Vanguard Canada's Global Stock Market ETF Price
Source: Morningstar.ca

If I go to Morningstar Canada, I can see that Vanguard's FTSE Global All Cap ex Canada Index ETF (try saying that with a mouthful of cheese and pepperoni) traded at $28.24 on June 29, 2016. It's shown in Figure 6.1. The ticker symbol is VXC.

Ignore everything else that you see on the page. Just focus on the last price. In this case, it was $28.24 per share.

Step 4: How Many Shares Can You Buy?

Determine how much you'll be investing. Keep commissions in mind. If you want to buy an ETF with $100 but the commission price is $9.99 per trade, you would be giving up almost 10 percent in commissions. Anyone who does that twice should be tossed in a padded room.

Try to keep commissions below 1 percent. If it costs $9.99 per trade, don't invest less than $1,000 at a time. Let's assume that a Canadian investor has $4,000 to invest in Vanguard's global stock ETF. If the price is $28.24, the investor can afford 141 shares. The investor may want to round down to ensure that they have enough money to cover the commission for the trade. They should also determine a margin of safety in case the ETF's price jumps before the trade is executed. To be safe, they could choose to buy 130 shares.

Using the Canadian brokerage QTrade Investor, here's how it would look. Other international (and US) brokerages have similar looking trading platforms. When you understand how to make a purchase off one brokerage or exchange, you can do it anywhere. It's just like riding a different bike.

You can see what the trading platform looks like in Figure 6.2.

Because this ETF trades on the Canadian market, I entered **Canada** for the market.

Market	Canada	‡
Symbol	VXC	🔍
Action	Buy	‡
Quantity	130|	
Order Type	Market	‡
Good Through	Jun 30, Thursday	‡

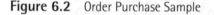

Figure 6.2   Order Purchase Sample

I then entered the ticker symbol for the ETF, **VXC**.

I placed an action to **Buy**.

For the quantity of shares, I entered **130**.

For Order Type, I selected **Market**. This means I am willing to accept the market price. I might also select Limit. Please see the sidebar explanation for the difference.

Then I selected submit or confirm.

Not everybody has to buy ETFs. Americans, for example, can invest just as cheaply with traditional index funds. Here's an example.

Should You Choose A Market Order Or A Limit Order?

When investors buy an ETF, they are asked to determine an order type. The two options will be a limit order and a market order. With a limit order, investors can enter the maximum price that they would pay that day. If, for example, the price opens for the morning at $45 per share, and the investor places a limit order to pay $44 per share, then they'll automatically pay $44 if the price dips to $44 during trading hours.

Investors shouldn't initiate a trade if the market isn't open. But if the ETF price closed at $45 the previous day, and the investor places a limit order before the next day's opening bell, to pay no more than $44 per share, and if the ETF opens its price for the day at $43, then the order might be filled at $43.

Many investors prefer limit orders. But they have to do it right. They shouldn't set low limit prices. That's like gambling. If their order doesn't get filled, the investor could end up chasing an ever-increasing price, day after day. In the August 2010 edition of *The Journal of Finance*, Juhani T. Linnain-maa published "Do Limit Orders Alter Inferences about Investor Performance and Behavior?" The researcher found that investors who use market orders usually do better than those who place limit orders.[1]

PWL Capital's Dan Bortolotti says there's a smarter way to do it. He places numerous limit orders on behalf of his clients every day. He confirms that investors shouldn't place any kind of order when the market isn't open. Dan always uses limit orders when trading ETFs on behalf of his clients. He says investors should get an up-to-date quote and then place a limit order a penny or two above the ask price (when buying) or below the bid price (when selling). Orders like this should get filled immediately at the best available price.

Sometimes, ETFs get mispriced. This means investors who place market orders could be in for a surprise if an ETF's price goes a little haywire during trading hours. They could end up paying an unusual, inflated price.

Historically, I've preferred market orders. I've liked knowing that my order will get filled and that I won't ever have to chase a higher price the next day. But Dan Bortolotti makes some excellent points. They're concepts I could learn from. They're especially important if you invest large amounts or if your ETF is thinly traded.

Indexing in the United States—An American Father of Triplets

When Kris Olson's wife, Erica, had triplets in 2006, she single-handedly gave birth to a quarter of a soccer team. Suddenly, there were three more mouths to feed, a minivan to buy, and three college educations to save for.

I'm not suggesting that anyone would hold a charitable benefit with accompanying violin music for a well-paid specialist in pediatrics and internal medicine. But if you're American and suddenly more aware of your own financial obligations, Kris's story of opening an indexed investing account could provide some direction.

The 46-year-old doctor realized that investing money was similar, in many ways, to the global health work he does in the poverty-stricken, tsunami-affected regions of Sumatra, Indonesia, where he occasionally flies to train midwives. This latest passion comes on the tail of his volunteer work along the Thai-Burmese border, as well as in Darfur, Cambodia, Kenya, and Ethiopia.

Realizing that donations to developing countries are best done in person, he and his wife Erica (a registered nurse) often brought their own medical supplies to the countries they visited. Simply sending supplies was an invitation for third-world middlemen to plunder the goods before they arrived.

In 2004, he recognized that something similar was happening to his investments at home, which had been laboring in actively managed mutual funds for years.

"My financial adviser was a really nice guy, but I realize that he skimmed money off me like guys at a third-world country border. I was flushing money down the toilet in tiny sums that were adding up," he said.

On a trip to Indonesia, Kris made a stopover in Singapore, where he purchased cardiopulmonary resuscitation (CPR) training material to take to midwives in Aceh. I met him for lunch at a Japanese restaurant. Over sushi, he asked me what indexes he should buy for his investment account.[2]

The largest index provider in the United States is Vanguard. If you go to their website, the array of indexes can be confusing. But I suggested that Kris—who was 35-years-old at the time—should keep things simple: buy the broadest stock index he could for his US exposure, the broadest international index he could for his "world" exposure, and a total bond market index fund that approximated his age. I call it the Global Couch Potato Portfolio. Here's the allocation I recommended:

- 35 percent Vanguard US Bond Index (Symbol VBMFX)

- 35 percent Vanguard Total US Stock Market Index (Symbol VTSMX)

- 30 percent Vanguard Total International Stock Market Index (Symbol VGTSX)

I gave my advice on this basis: Vanguard doesn't charge commissions to buy or sell; he would be diversified across the entire US stock market and the international stock markets; and he would have a bond allocation that would allow him to rebalance his account once a year.

"Kris," I said, "Don't listen to Wall Street, don't read financial newspapers, and don't watch stock-market-based news. If you rebalance a portfolio like this just once a year, you'll beat 90 percent of investment professionals over time."

When Kris got back home to the United States, he put his old mutual fund investment statements on the dining room table. He then logged on to the Vanguard site and telephoned the company from the website's contact information.

A Vanguard employee walked Kris through the account opening process as they navigated the website together. She simply asked for his existing mutual fund account numbers— for both his IRA account (a tax-sheltered individual retirement account) and for his non-IRA mutual funds.

Over the telephone, the Vanguard representative then transferred his assets from his previous fund company to Vanguard where he diversified his money into the three index funds. Then, after taking his regular bank account information, she set up automatic deposits into Kris's index funds according to the allocation he wanted.

At the end of each calendar year, Kris took a look at his investments. "It didn't take much," he said. "I just rebalanced the portfolio back to the original allocation at the end of each year [as seen in Figure 6.3], selling off a bit of the 'winners' to bolster the 'losers.' It was the only time I ever looked at my investment statements—just when it was time to consider rebalancing." I was able to confirm Kris's investment returns (in US dollars) using the fund-tracking function at portfoliovisualizer.com.

January 2007

Kris noticed that the portfolio he established one year earlier had gained 15.4 percent during the course of the year. Most of the gains came from his international and US stock market indexes.

Kris's Portfolio

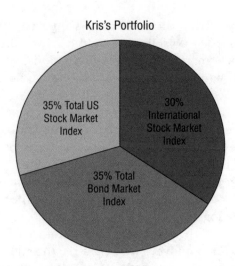

Figure 6.3   Kris Olson's Account Allocation

He called Vanguard on the phone, logged on to his account online, and the Vanguard representative guided him through the process of selling off some of his stock indexes to buy his bond index. This brought his portfolio back to its original allocation.

January 2008

Worldwide, stock markets continued to rise from 2007 to 2008. At this point, Kris's profits had really increased, gaining 25.86 percent from the initial 2006 value and 9 percent for the 2007 calendar year. Fighting the urge to buy more of what was propelling his portfolio (his stock indexes), Kris sold off portions of his international and US stock indexes to buy more of his bond index with the proceeds. It didn't require any judgment on his part. He just adjusted his account back to its original allocation.

January 2009

When Kris looked at his statements at the beginning of 2009, he noticed his total portfolio had dropped in value as the biggest stock market decline since 1929–1933 was starting to take its toll. His portfolio had dropped 24.5 percent. But Kris just rebalanced his portfolio again, selling off some of his bond index to buy falling US and international stock indexes, bringing it back to the original allocation.

January 2010

Kris knew the stock markets took a beating during the previous year—everyone was talking about it. But because he sold off some bonds the previous year to buy stocks, he benefited from the low stock market levels. By January 2010, his account had increased 23.14 percent for the year thanks to the rebounding stock markets. Once again, Kris took 10 minutes in January to rebalance his account, selling some stock indexes to buy more of his bond index. When Kris was finished, he was back to his original allocation.

January 2011

By January 2011, Kris's account had gained another 11.6 percent over the previous 12 months. From January 1, 2006, until January 1, 2011, his account's profits had increased by 30.7 percent, despite going through the worst stock market decline (2008–2009) in many years. Rebalancing once again, he sold off some of his stock indexes to buy some more of his bond index.

January 2016

If Kris had continued this process over the next five years, his portfolio would have grown by 73.09 percent over the 10-year period. That's impressive, considering that the decade included the worst stock market crash since 1929.

Don't Forget the Enemy in the Mirror

Some investors might notice that Scott Burns' original Couch Potato portfolio (mentioned in Chapter 5) would have beaten

Table 6.2 $10,000 Invested: Global vs. Classic Couch Potatoes, 2006–2016

	Average Annual Return	End Value
Kris Olson's Global Couch Potato Portfolio (35% US stocks, 35% bonds, 30% International stocks)	5.64%	$17,309
Couch Potato (50% US stocks, 50% bonds)	6.09%	$18,148
Couch Potato (60% US stocks, 40% bonds	6.43%	$18,741
Couch Potato (70% US stocks, 30% bonds)	6.72%	$19,274

Source: portfoliovisualizer.com

Kris's Global Couch Potato portfolio over the 10-year period ending December 31, 2015.

Table 6.2 shows how the portfolios compared.

Scott Burns' Couch Potato portfolios won. That's because the original Couch Potato portfolios didn't contain international stocks. US stocks trounced international stocks for the decade ending December 31, 2015.

But that won't always happen. The stock market is cheeky. It lures investors toward a "better performing" asset class or geographic sector. It waits. And it waits. Then it conducts a bait and switch. One decade's better performing sector can become the next decade's loser.

Check out the five-year period ending January 2016 in Figure 6.4. US stocks crushed international stocks.

During the five-year period ending December 31, 2015, Vanguard's US Total Stock Market Index (VTSMX) gained 104 percent with dividends reinvested. Vanguard's International Stock Market Index (VGTSX) gained just 33 percent.

It's easy to give up on international stocks after seeing this performance. But investors shouldn't. Every sector has its day. From December 2000 until January 2006, (as seen in Figure 6.5) US stocks were losers. Vanguard's US Total Stock Market Index gained 10.2 percent. Vanguard's International Index gained 32.9 percent.

Trying to guess which geographic sector will outperform another is a fool's errand. Nobody can see the future. Results could be disastrous if investors try to guess. Whether investors choose one of Scott Burns' Couch Potato portfolios or whether they choose a Global Couch Potato Portfolio, they should stick

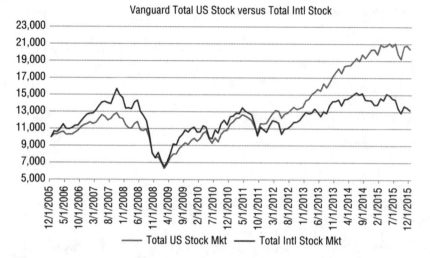

Figure 6.4   US Stocks Triumphed, 2011–2016

Source: © The Vanguard Group, Inc., used with permission

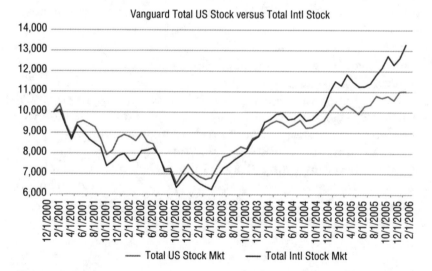

Figure 6.5   International Stocks Triumphed, January 2006–January 2011

Source: © The Vanguard Group, Inc., used with permission

to their strategy like barnacles to a boat. Over an investment lifetime, results should be similar if you rebalance once a year and ignore the media's sirens. The added diversification of an international stock market index can also reduce volatility.

Table 6.3   US Global Couch Potato Model Portfolios: Vanguard Index Funds

Fund Name	Fund Code	Conservative	Cautious	Balanced	Assertive	Aggressive
Vanguard's US Total Stock Market Index	VTSMX	15%	25%	30%	40%	50%
Vanguard's International Stock Market Index	VGTSX	15%	20%	30%	35%	50%
Vanguard Short-Term Bond Index Fund	VBISX	70%	55%	40%	25%	0%

Table 6.3 shows some model portfolios for investors with different risk tolerances. As investors grow older, many prefer balanced or cautious models, increasing their bond allocations to increase their portfolios' stability as they age. Note that I've included Vanguard's Short-Term Bond Fund instead of Vanguard's Total Bond Market Index. As I mentioned in Chapter 5, such a fund should beat inflation over any 3-year period, no matter what happens to interest rates or bond prices.

Investors with defined benefit pensions or trust funds (lucky devils) can afford higher-risk portfolios. Long-term, higher-risk allocations should produce higher returns.

Many investors, however, don't want to spend any time thinking about investing. They would prefer to have somebody manage their money for them. Fortunately, Americans can do this far more cheaply than anyone else in the world.

Read about how in the following chapter.

Indexing in Canada

TD e-Series Index Funds

In 2014, I wrote an article for *The Globe and Mail* titled "How Do TD's Mutual Funds Stack Up Against Its Index Funds?"[3] TD, like all of Canada's banks, loves to promote their actively managed funds.

I compared all of TD's actively managed funds with 10-year track records to the bank's e-Series index fund counterparts. I made apples-to-apples comparisons. For example, I looked at all of TD's actively managed Canadian stock market funds. I averaged their 10-year returns and compared them with TD's e-Series Canadian index fund. I did the same thing with all of TD's actively managed US and international stock market funds, comparing them with their index fund counterparts. The index funds won.

In fact, the indexes swept the actively managed funds in seven straight categories. They included Canadian, US, International, Japanese, and European stock funds. I also compared Canadian bond funds and balanced funds (using the bank's Investors Series fund because they don't have an e-Series equivalent).

On average, they beat their actively managed counterparts by 0.77 percent per year. Over an investment lifetime, such a compounding difference would buy a lot of beer and pretzels—as well as a Maserati.

An Aerospace Technician Uses TD's Best Kept Secret

Félix Rousseau is a 25-year-old corporal with the Royal Canadian Air Force. He works as an Aerospace Telecommunication and Information Systems Technician (ATIS Technician) in Comox, British Columbia.

He also figured out one of TD Bank's best kept secrets. Investors who open an account with TD Waterhouse can purchase the bank's e-Series Index funds. Such investors don't pay commissions to buy or sell. They can reinvest their dividends for free. These are the lowest cost index mutual funds in Canada.

Many investors pay lower fees if they purchase ETFs (exchange-traded index funds). But such investors can't always reinvest their dividends for free. They can't buy or sell without paying commissions. Nor can they set up direct automatic purchases each month. Félix can do all of these things with TD's e-Series indexes.

"My portfolio is relatively small for now," he says. "It's worth approximately $20,000. I would need to have about $50,000 before a portfolio of ETFs made economic sense."[4]

TD offers 11 e-Series index funds.[5] Investors require just four of them to build a low-cost diversified, global portfolio. They include the Canadian bond index (TDB 909); Canadian stock index (TDB 900); US stock index (TDB 902); and the International index (TDB911).

Investors might be tempted to look at which funds have performed best in the past. But don't. Last decade's winners can become next decade's laggards.

"I follow Dan Bortolotti's aggressive model portfolio," says Félix, referring to the portfolio models at the Canadian Couch Potato blog.

That means Félix has 10 percent of his portfolio in Canadian bonds, 30 percent in Canadian stocks, 30 percent in US stocks, and 30 percent in international stocks.

I listed Dan's portfolio allocation models in Table 6.4.[6] The Aggressive and Assertive portfolio models are best suited for younger investors, adventurous investors, or those who will be earning a guaranteed defined benefit pension when they retire.

The Balanced and Cautious portfolios are well-suited to investors who are in their mid-30s or older. The Cautious or Conservative allocations are well-suited for retirees. However, these are just rules of thumb. Consider your risk tolerance.

Table 6.4   Canadian Couch Potato Model Portfolios: TD e-Series Index Funds

Fund Name	Fund Code	Conservative	Cautious	Balanced	Assertive	Aggressive
TD Canadian Bond Fund-e	TDB 909	70%	55%	40%	25%	10%
TD Canadian Index Fund-e	TDB 900	10%	15%	20%	25%	30%
TD US Index Fund-e	TDB 902	10%	15%	20%	25%	30%
TD International Index Fund-e	TDB911	10%	15%	20%	25%	30%
Weighted Average Management Expense Ratio		.047%	0.45%	0.44%	0.42%	0.41%

Source: Canadian Couch Potato Blog

Also consider whether your portfolio will make up the bulk of your future retirement income or whether it will be icing on a guaranteed defined benefit pension cake. Investors with such pensions can afford to take higher risk, if they can psychologically handle their portfolios' higher volatility.

Just remember to rebalance your portfolio once a year. That means selling some of the indexes that have performed well and adding the proceeds to the indexes that haven't. Investors should maintain their original allocation—but slowly increase their bond allocation as they get older.

A Canadian Couch Potato Strips Down Costs

Dan Bortolotti is a Renaissance man. He has published books about blue whales, tigers, auroras, humanitarian aid, and baseball. But the 47-year-old father of two might be best known as the creator of the Canadian Couch Potato blog.

He launched it in 2010. It's now the best online source for Canadian index fund investors.

Dan began investing in his 20s. But like most Canadians, his money languished in actively managed mutual funds. "I didn't have much money at the time," he says, "so my mistakes didn't cost me much."

In 2008, he was writing for *MoneySense* magazine when his editor asked him to cover a project called the "7-Day Financial Makeover." The magazine had asked readers to write in and explain why they deserved a week-long financial boot camp. More than 200 readers applied.

The magazine sifted through the applicants, looking for financial train wrecks. They finally settled on three couples and one single person. "Our goal was to discover whether it's possible for people to change their financial personality," the magazine explained. "Can an impulse shopper become a bargain hunter? Can a couple who always argues about money live happily ever after?"

Dan's job was to follow one of the couples and write about their experience. But during one of the workshops on investing, he had a revelation. "The presenter talked about the difference between investing in high-cost funds versus low-cost

ETFs," says Dan. "I had read about the merits of the Couch Potato strategy in *MoneySense* for years, but I always thought it sounded too good to be true. That was the beginning of my real education. Something inside me clicked."

Dan began to read everything he could on the subject. In August 2008—just weeks before the beginning of the global financial crisis—he started his first ETF portfolio. Within six months, stock markets were down close to 50 percent. "It might have been the worst timing in history," he recalls, "but I was lucky I'd read as much as I did. Everything I had learned primed me to hang on. I knew that there was nothing wrong with the strategy."[7]

Dan started his blog to help other Canadians become DIY index investors. Then he took a step further. PWL Capital, a wealth management firm in Toronto, soon approached Dan about putting their skills together. In 2014, he became a licensed financial adviser. Now an associate portfolio manager and Certified Financial Planner at PWL, Dan and his colleagues build ETF portfolios for their clients. He continues to maintain the Canadian Couch Potato blog and write regularly for *MoneySense*.

ETFs make sense for investors with portfolios valued above $50,000. But they might not suit everybody with $50,000 or more. Unlike TD's e-Series index funds, brokerages charge commissions for investors to buy ETFs; investors aren't always able to reinvest dividends for free.

To purchase an ETF, an investor has to open a discount brokerage account. In June 2016, *MoneySense* magazine listed their top picks.[8] Four of their favorites were Scotia iTrade, Qtrade Investor, BMO InvestorLine, and Questrade. Many investors like the convenience of dealing with a brokerage that's aligned with their bank. Such brokerages include CIBC Investor's Edge, HSBC InvestDirect, National Bank Direct Brokerage, RBC Direct Investing, and TD Direct Investing.

Commission fees differ. But it's a competitive market and fees keep falling. Today's major online Canadian brokerages start at less than $10 per trade. Many of the brokerages charge a flat fee. RBC Direct Investing, for example, charges a flat $9.95 per trade. It's the same, whether somebody invests $1,000 or $10 million.

Expense ratio fees for ETFs have also dropped. When I wrote the first edition of this book in 2011, Canadian ETF expense ratios usually cost between 0.25 and 0.50 percent per year. Vanguard Canada shook things up in late 2011. They introduced a variety of lower cost ETFs. Since then, iShares and BMO have slashed their ETF's expense ratio fees as well.

Table 6.5 shows Dan Bortolotti's sample portfolios with Vanguard's ETFs.[9] Dozens of other ETF combinations could get the same job done. Don't sweat the small stuff. There's genius in simplicity. With just three ETFs per portfolio, investors have fewer moving parts. That makes rebalancing easier. Note that I've made just one change to Dan Bortolotti's portfolios. I've opted for a short-term bond market index. For an explanation on how such an ETF might be safer, see Chapter 5.

Vanguard's Canadian Short-Term Bond ETF (VSB) contains about 335 government and corporate bonds. Vanguard's FTSE Canada All Cap ETF (VCN) contains 216 Canadian stocks of various sizes (small caps, mid caps, and large caps). Vanguard's FTSE All World ex Canada ETF (VXC) is made up of about 8,100 stocks. Almost half of them are American stocks. Developed world international and emerging market stocks make up the remainder.

Table 6.5 Canadian Couch Potato Model Portfolios: Vanguard ETFs

Fund Name	Ticker Symbol	Conservative	Cautious	Balanced	Assertive	Aggressive
Vanguard Canadian Short-Term Bond ETF	VSB	70%	55%	40%	25%	10%
Vanguard FTSE Canada All Cap ETF	VCN	10%	15%	20%	25%	30%
Vanguard FTSE All World ex Canada ETF	VXC	20%	30%	40%	50%	60%
Weighted Average Management Expense Ratio		0.15%	0.16%	0.17%	0.18%	0.19%

Source: Canadian Couch Potato Blog

Whether you buy the e-Series index funds or build a port-folio of ETFs, you'll beat most professional investors—if you can harness your emotions.

That said, many Canadians don't want to spend even an hour each year thinking about investing. They would prefer to have somebody do it for them. In the following chapter, I list some low-cost firms that build and manage portfolios of index funds.

Indexing in Great Britain

England's national football team is about to play Germany at Wembley stadium. But a team of imposters shows up in their place. They all wear the uniform. On right wing, you can see your postman. Your former science teacher is the goalie. Your milkman plays midfield. Most people would have a pretty good laugh—before demanding that the real team take its place.

The United Kingdom's financial institutions play a simi-lar trick. But they aren't doing it for kicks. Many offer "index funds." But they're just high-cost imposters who wear the offi-cial kit. Richard Branson's Virgin Money was the first.

In his autobiography *Losing My Virginity,* Sir Richard says, "After Virgin entered the financial service industry, I can immodestly say it was never to be the same again. . . . We never employed fund managers . . . we discovered their best kept secret: they could never consistently beat the stock market index."[10]

Virgin created its own index tracker funds. But they aren't cheap. The company's FTSE tracker fund costs 1 percent per year.[11] Such costs are low, compared to actively managed mutual funds. But it's a stratospheric cost for a single index fund. In contrast, Vanguard UK's FTSE equity index, when it was first introduced, cost just 0.15 percent. It costs even less today.

Vanguard charges low fees because, unlike Virgin, its investors (everyone who buys its funds) actually own the com-pany. It's run much like a nonprofit firm. Tracking errors are also low because the company is an experienced index fund builder. If the stocks in the FTSE All Share Index rise by 10 percent, Vanguard's tracking index should earn roughly 9.85 percent, trailing the market by its 0.15 percent management fee. If it earned a result lower than 9.85 percent, in this case, the fund managers would be to blame. Any additional performance discrepancy would be called "tracking error."

Virgin Money's equivalent product would lag the market by at least its 1 percent annual fee. Any tracking errors committed would reduce profits further. Over time, high costs and tracking errors are compounding problems.

Virgin's FTSE All Share UK index earned 19.7 percent in 2013. Vanguard's FTSE UK Equity index earned 20.7 percent. They each track the same market. But Vanguard's index cost 0.85 percent less. As such, Vanguard's index should have beaten Virgin's index by 0.85 percent. But this wasn't the case. Vanguard outperformed Virgin by a full percentage point.

Virgin, living up to its name, lacks Vanguard's experience. Accurately tracking an index requires skill that Vanguard has honed over many years. Virgin has had a few years to practice. But they're still disappointing investors. And 2013 wasn't a one-off miss.

As seen in Table 6.6, between 2010 and 2015, Virgin's UK stock index underperformed Vanguard's by an average of 0.97 percent per year.

Such differences look small. But over an investment lifetime, paying more for the same product has costly compounding consequences. In 2016, Vanguard reported even lower costs for its FTSE UK Equity Index. Costs dropped from 0.15 percent to 0.08 percent per year.

Virgin isn't the only UK index fund provider with high expenses and poor tracking records. Kyle Caldwell, writing for *The Telegraph*, reported the UK stock market grew by 132 percent for the decade ending 2013. But the typical UK

Table 6.6   Virgin versus Vanguard, 2010–2016

Year	Virgin's FTSE All Share UK Index	Vanguard's FTSE UK Equity Index
2010	+13%	+14.4%
2011	−4.7%	−3.5%
2012	+11%	+12.2%
2013	+19.7%	+20.7%
2014	+0.2%	+1.1%
2015	+1%	+0.9%

Source: Morningstar UK

stock market index suffered zombie-like rigor mortis. Halifax's UK FTSE All Share Index tracker earned just 92.6 percent. It lagged the market by nearly 40 percent for the decade. Scottish Widows UK tracker earned just 94.8 percent. It underperformed the market by nearly 38 percent over 10 years.[12]

Paul Howarth won't trust his money to a poor index tracker. Nor does he want his money in actively managed funds. When he first started to invest he signed up with a Friends Provident Pension scheme. HSBC offered him the product. "I was advised to use the HSBC World Selection Funds," he says. "I didn't know about the many layers of fees involved. When I found out that I was paying more than 3.5 percent a year in fees, I jumped out."[13]

Paul opened a brokerage account and invested 30 percent of his money in an iShares global bond ETF (SAAA) with the remaining 70 percent in Vanguard's global stock ETF (VWRL). Vanguard and iShares both offer excellent index funds.

Once a year, Paul rebalances the portfolio. If global stocks rise, he sells some of his global stock index. He adds the proceeds to his bond market index to ensure that he gets back to his original allocation.

Originally from Manchester, Paul now lives in Dubai. He isn't sure where he wants to retire, so his portfolio represents full global representation without a home country bias.

Most UK-based investors, however, will pay their future bills in pounds. For that reason, it pays to have a home country bias. In Table 6.7, I've listed some model portfolios for British investors, based on different risk tolerances.

As investors age, many prefer balanced and cautious allocation models with higher bond market exposure. Such portfolios don't tend to perform as well, over long periods of time, but they are less volatile.

Those who expect a secondary source of retirement income (think sole heir to a millionaire's estate) might choose to invest in a higher risk portfolio, regardless of their age.

The financial website Monevator published the following blog post, "Compare The UK's Cheapest Brokers."[14] They continue to do a great job comparing and updating brokerage costs. It's an excellent source for UK-based investors who are looking for a brokerage.

Table 6.7   British Couch Potato Model Portfolios: Vanguard ETFs

Fund Name	Invests In	Fund Code	Conservative	Cautious	Balanced	Assertive	Aggressive
FTSE 100 UCITS ETF	100 of the largest UK companies	VUKE	10%	20%	25%	25%	30%
FTSE 250 UCITS ETF	243 mid-sized UK companies	VMID	5%	5%	10%	15%	30%
FTSE All World UCITS ETF	2,900 companies over 47 countries	VWRL	15%	20%	25%	35%	40%
UK Gilt UCITS ETF	39 UK government bonds	VGOV	70%	55%	40%	25%	0%

Source: Vanguard UK

Some investors, however, don't want to build their own portfolios. In the following chapter, I introduce some low-cost financial services companies that build portfolios of indexes for UK-based investors. They rebalance the holdings as well.

Indexing in Australia—Winning with an American Weapon

Andy Wang is a 37-year-old software developer. In 2016, he bought a home in Melbourne. He moved there from Adelaide in July of that year.

Many new investors start out with actively managed mutual funds. Andy's story is different. "I started to invest in the stock market in 2007," he says. "In the beginning I just bought stocks by recommendations from friends and relatives. But I soon realized that was crazy."[15]

Andy began to read some investment books. He liked Benjamin Graham's classic, *The Intelligent Investor.* Ben Graham taught at Columbia University. His best student was Warren Buffett, the man who many people consider to be the greatest investor of all time. Late in his life, Ben Graham also supported the index fund concept, much as Warren Buffett does today.

"I didn't really catch on to index fund investing," says Andy, "until I read some of John Bogle's books." Bogle, the founder of Vanguard, wrote a couple of classics. They include *Common Sense on Mutual Funds* and *The Little Book of Common Sense Investing*.

That's when something dawned on Andy. "I realized I didn't have the time and capability to do the fundamental analysis on individual stocks. And I didn't think I could beat the professional analysts who run actively managed mutual funds."

That's when Andy decided that he was better off with index funds. Today, he has a globally diversified portfolio of ETFs. He invests with the brokerage Nabtrade. "My portfolio is split between an Australian stock index, an International stock index, and an Australian bond index. I also invest $1,000 in my superannuation every month. All my super is also invested on index funds."

I've listed some model portfolios for Australians in Table 6.8. As investors age, many prefer balanced and cautious allocation models with higher bond market exposure. Such portfolios don't tend to perform as well over long periods of time, but they are less volatile.

Those who expect a secondary source of retirement income (guaranteed pension income or a multimillion dollar inheritance) might choose to invest in a higher risk portfolio, regardless of their age. Just remember, if you're banking on an inheritance from your old Aunt Matilda, she could end up

Table 6.8 Australian Couch Potato Model Portfolios: Vanguard ETFs

Fund Name	Invests In	Fund Code	Conservative	Cautious	Balanced	Assertive	Aggressive
Vanguard Australian Fixed Interest Index Fund	Australian Bonds	VAF	70%	55%	40%	25%	10%
Vanguard Australian Shares Index Fund	Australian Stocks	VAS	10%	15%	20%	25%	30%
Vanguard International Shares Index Fund	Global Stocks	VGS	20%	30%	40%	50%	60%

Source: Vanguard Australia

creeping around until she's older than 100. In a game of musical wills, she could also bequeath everything to her hairdresser if she starts to go gaga.

Not everyone, however, wants to build his own portfolio. In the following chapter, I introduce some low-cost financial services companies that build portfolios of indexes for Australian-based investors. They also rebalance the holdings.

Indexing in Singapore

Singaporeans looking to invest in low-cost indexes might Google their options online. But like hidden vipers in the jungles of the Lion City, there are snakes in the financial services industry. They wait to venomously erode your investment potential. Googling "Singapore Index Funds" will bring you to a company offering index funds that charge nearly 1 percent a year. That might seem insignificant. But paying one percent for an index fund can cost you hundreds of thousands of wasted dollars over an investment lifetime.

Singaporean index-fund retailer Fundsupermart flogs the Infinity Investment Series. It offers an S&P 500 Index that charges 0.90 percent per year. That includes Fundsupermart's platform charge.[16]

Let's assume that two Singaporean twin sisters decide to invest in a US index. One of them buys the S&P 500 Index Fund through Fundsupermart. The other chooses to go with Vanguard's low-cost S&P 500 ETF that charges just 0.08 percent annually. She could buy the ETF through any number of Singapore-based brokerages, including DBS Vickers, Standard Chartered, or Saxo Capital Markets.

Before fees, each of the sisters' funds would make the same return. That's because each fund tracks exactly the same market. Costs, when presented in tiny amounts—like 0.9 percent—look minimal. But they're not. Table 6.9 shows how seemingly small fees can kill investment profits. If the US S&P 500 index makes 5 percent a year for the next five years, an investor paying "just" 0.90 percent is giving away 18 percent of her profits, every year.

Table 6.9 Two Sisters Invest SGD$20,000

	Sister 1	Sister 2
$20,000 given to each sister to invest	Sister 1 invests in an S&P 500 index fund that costs 0.90% annually	Sister 2 invests in a Vanguard S&P 500 exchange-traded fund via DBS Vickers that costs 0.08% annually
Assume an 8% return for the S&P 500 index	Sister 1 makes 7.1% annually after expenses	Sister 2 makes 7.92% annually after expenses
How much will each sister have after 35 years?	Sister 1 will have $220,628	Sister 2 will have $288,136
After 40 years, assuming the same rate of return?	Sister 1 will have $310,891	Sister 2 will have $421,800
After 45 years, assuming the same rate of return?	Sister 1 will have $438,082	Sister 2 will have $617,471

What would happen if the S&P 500 averaged an 8 percent compound annual return? The sister paying 0.9 percent in annual fees would average 7.1 percent per year. Her twin, if she paid just 0.08 percent in fees, would earn 7.92 percent per year.

Over time, this makes a massive difference.

Small fee differences pack very big punches. In the above example, somebody paying 0.82 percent more in annual fees would have $179,389 less money after 45 years. Costs matter. Don't let the industry fool you into thinking differently.

Singapore Residents Embrace Their Indexing Journey

Seng Su Lin and Gordon Cyr met in 2001, while volunteering at the Special Olympics in Singapore. Gordon teaches at Singapore American School and Seng Su Lin (who goes by Su) teaches technical writing at Singapore Polytechnic and at the National University of Singapore. She has a PhD in psycholinguistics, the study of how humans acquire and use language.

The couple married in 2008, and Gordon (originally from Canada) looked over his investments with frustration. He explained his concerns:

"I used to teach in Kenya, and the school mandated that we invest our money with one of two companies. One of them was an offshore investment company called Zurich International Life Limited, headquartered on the Isle of Man. They invested in actively managed funds, but I started to feel cheated. Before opening the account, I clearly asked the representative if I could have control of how much or how little I was investing, and he said that I could. But after some time had passed, I wanted to stop contributing. The statements were really confusing. I couldn't see how much I had deposited over time and it was tough to see what my account was even worth."[17]

Feeling uncomfortable, Gordon thought it would be easy to stop making his monthly payments to the company. But the Zurich representative (who no longer works for the firm) said Gordon had signed a contract to deposit a certain amount each month—and that he had to stick to it. Frustrated, Gordon pulled his money from Zurich. The firm charged him a hefty penalty for doing so.

Gordon was keen to take control of his finances. He opened an account with DBS Vickers in Singapore to build a portfolio of low cost ETFs. But he doesn't know where he wants to retire.

Su's family is in Singapore. Gordon's family is in Canada. They own a piece of land in Hawaii. For that reason, Gordon thought it would be prudent to split his assets between Singaporean, Canadian, and other global stock and bond markets. Here's what their portfolio of exchange-traded funds looks like:

- 20 percent in the Singapore Bond index (Ticker Symbol A35)

- 20 percent in Singapore's Stock Market Index (Ticker Symbol ES3)

- 20 percent in Canada's Short-Term Bond Index (Ticker Symbol VSB)

- 20 percent in Canada's Stock Market Index (Ticker Symbol XIC)

- 20 percent in the World Stock Market Index (Ticker Symbol VXC)

The first two indexes above trade on the Singaporean Stock Market; the following three trade on the Canadian Stock Exchange. But you can purchase them all using an online Singaporean-based brokerage such as DBS Vickers or Saxo Capital Markets. Singaporeans shouldn't buy ETFs off the US market. By doing so, they might indirectly hand their heirs a hefty US estate tax bill when they die. Singapore's brokerage representatives won't tell you that. If you ask them about the US estate tax liability, they'll say, "We don't give tax advice." But if you die with more than $60,000 USD in assets, Uncle Sam will want his share.[18]

Some Singaporeans don't buy bonds. There's a reason for that. All citizens contribute to CPF (the Central Provident Fund). It's guaranteed, like a bond. Investors who choose to bypass bonds can rebalance their stock market ETFs once a year.

Gordon and Su rebalance their account with new purchases every month. For example, if the Singapore Bond Index hasn't done as well as the others, after a month it will represent less than 20 percent of their total investment. (Remember that they've allocated 20 percent of their account for each of the five indexes.) So when they add fresh money to their account, they would add to the Singapore Bond Index.

If the World Stock Index, the Canadian Stock Index, or the Singapore Stock Index decrease in value, they would add fresh money that month to the worst performing index. This ensures a couple of things:

- They're rebalancing their portfolio to increase its overall safety.

- They're buying the laggards. That could boost long-term returns.

If you are interested in following step by step instructions on how to buy exchange-traded index funds in Singapore, you can access my website at the following: andrewhallam .com/2010/10/singaporeans-investing-cheaply-with-exchange-traded-index-funds/.

Not everyone, however, wants to build their own portfolio of index funds. As of this writing, no low-cost financial services firm in Singapore will do it with small accounts.

Those with at least $500,000 (USD equivalent), however, could use Mark Ikels. He provides full-service financial planning. He uses low-cost index funds and ETFs. You can read a profile about Mark on my website.[19]

The Next Step

Once you learn how to build indexed accounts, you won't have to spend much time making investment decisions. It could take less than 1 hour a year.

Nobody knows how the stock and bond markets will perform over the next 5, 10, 20, or 30 years. But one thing is certain. If you build a diversified portfolio of index funds, you'll beat about 90 percent of professional investors.

There are only two risks standing in your way. Most financial advisers are your biggest risk. They'll try to convince you to buy actively managed funds. They'll use tactics that I outline in Chapter 8. To them, index funds are plagues. Most advisers will do what they can to keep you from buying them.

The second risk faces you in the mirror each morning. Harnessing your emotions is tougher than it sounds, especially when markets go haywire. That's why many investors need help. For them, the next chapter is a roadmap.

Notes

1. Juhani T. Llnnainmaa, "Do Limit Orders Alter Inferences about Investor Performance and Behavior?" *The Journal of Finance* (August 2010), citeseerx.ist.psu.edu/viewdoc/download?doi=10.1.1.680.8246&rep=rep1&type=pdf.
2. Personal interview with Kris Olsen, April 10, 2005, in Singapore.
3. Andrew Hallam, "How Do TD's Mutual Funds Stack Up Against Its Index Funds?" *Globe and Mail*, February 26,

2016, www.theglobeandmail.com/globe-investor/investment-ideas/strategy-lab/index-investing/how-do-tds-mutual-funds-stack-up-against-index-funds/article17126059/.

4. "Interview With Félix Rousseau," e-mail interview, July 1, 2016.

5. TD Canada Trust, e-Series Funds, www.tdcanadatrust.com/products-services/investing/mutual-funds/perfor Frame.jsp.

6. Canadian Couch Potato, Model Portfolios: TD e-Series Funds, canadiancouchpotato.com/wp-content/uploads/2016/01/CCP-Model-Portfolios-TD-e-Series-2015.pdf.

7. "Interview with Dan Bortolotti," e-mail interview, July 5, 2016.

8. MoneySense, "Canada's Best Online Brokers, June 2016," www.moneysense.ca/save/investing/canadas-best-online-brokers-2016.

9. Canadian Couch Potato, Model Portfolios: Vanguard ETFs, canadiancouchpotato.com/wp-content/uploads/2016/01/CCP-Model-Portfolios-Vanguard-2015.pdf.

10. Richard Branson, *Losing My Virginity: How I've Survived, Had Fun, and Made a Fortune Doing Business My Way* (New York: Times Business, 1998), 405.

11. Virgin Money, Unit Trusts, uk.virginmoney.com/virgin/unit-trusts/.

12. Kyle Caldwell, "The 500,000 Fund Investors Failed by Trackers," *The Telegraph*, www.telegraph.co.uk/finance/personalfinance/investing/10580063/The-500000-fund-investors-failed-by-trackers.html.

13. "Interview with Paul Howarth," e-mail interview, July 1, 2016.

14. "Compare UK's Cheapest Brokerages," Monevator, monevator.com/compare-uk-cheapest-online-brokers/.

15. "Interview with Andy Wang," e-mail interview, July 2, 2016.

16. Fundsupermart.com, www.fundsupermart.com/landing/welcome.jsp.

17. Personal interview with Gordon Cyr, October 18, 2010, in Singapore.

18. "Some Non Residents with U.S. Assets Must File Estate Tax Returns," IRS, www.irs.gov/individuals/international-taxpayers/some-nonresidents-with-u-s-assets-must-file-estate-tax-returns.

19. Mark Ikels-Singapore, May 8, 2016, https://andrewhallam .com/2015/04/marc-ikels-singapore/.

No, You Don't Have to Invest on Your Own

The world is Internet-savvy. Millions of people have learned that actively managed mutual funds pad Wall Street's pockets. Low-cost index funds, by comparison, give more to investors.

The public doesn't need an Occupy Wall Street protest. Instead, they can vote with their wallets. Many run to Vanguard. It's the world's biggest provider of index funds. It's also now bigger than any actively managed mutual fund company in the world.

Vanguard has a hippie-like backstory. John Bogle started the company in 1974. He set it up like a nonprofit firm. If you buy its index funds, you're an owner of the firm. No private investors own a piece of the company pie. Unlike most banks (and many mutual fund companies), no public shares trade on the stock market.

Instead, Vanguard was created for the people. It was capitalism born in a commune. Until recently, however, most people had to go solo if they wanted a portfolio of index funds. They waded through Vanguard's offerings of index funds without any guidance. Or they built their own portfolios with ETFs (hip little cousins of the traditional index fund).

These two options are still the cheapest way to go. They take less than an hour a year. You never have to follow stock market news or forecasts. Your results would also dust those of most professional investors.

But for some investors, that feels like running naked. Many prefer the clothing and the guidance of a financial advisory firm. Your grandparents couldn't have done this—without getting handcuffed and stuffed into actively managed mutual funds. Your parents couldn't have either. But times have changed.

Enter robo-advisers. No, they aren't run by robots. That's a media-created name that rings well with science fiction. I prefer to call them intelligent investment firms. Most are Internet-based. These firms have said, "People are getting smarter. Let's offer something better!"

Such firms are now present in the United States, Canada, Europe, Australia, and Asia. They build and manage portfolios of index funds, charging low fees to do so. Costs and services, however, vary. Some provide comprehensive financial planning (investments, estate planning, tax advice, etc.). Others just invest your money.

Traditional investment firms usually lie in bed with actively managed funds. These firms are like horse-drawn buggies. Intelligent investment firms (robo-advisers, if you must) are hybrids or Teslas. No matter how you slice it, they perform much better and they cost a lot less.

But why pay somebody, even a small amount, when you could invest on your own?

Are You Wired Like a Buddha?

Could you sit cross-legged on a stone . . . with a little smile on your face . . . in a five-hour rainstorm? If not, congratulations, you're normal. But investors who are capable of building and maintaining a portfolio of index funds might require something special. Don't feel misled. The process is simple. It takes less than one hour a year.

But it's easier said than done. Market rainstorms occur when nobody expects them. Stormy headlines will try to push you from that rock.

For years, I've been giving seminars to DIY investors. My lessons are simple. For Americans (as an example), I recommended a US stock index, an international stock index, and a US bond market index. Investors should add money every month. Ignore investment forecasts. Rebalance once a year to maintain a constant allocation.

In other words, if the portfolio were split equally in thirds between the three index funds at the beginning of the year, investors would need to make sure that it was adjusted, at year-end, so it was equally split in thirds 12 months later.

It's as simple as lying in a hammock. But most people get itchy butts. They add fresh money to the index that's "doing well." They often ignore the index that may be dropping in value. This damages long-term results.

It gets even worse if investors listen (and act on) financial pornography in the news. That's what I call financial forecasts. Such forecasts are almost always wrong. But they influence plenty of people.

Here's an example.

Vanguard's S&P 500 index averaged a compound annual return of 6.89 percent per year during the 10-year period ending March 31, 2016. That included the massive stock market crash of 2008–2009, when US stocks dropped nearly 40 percent. But the average investor in the S&P 500 did the funky chicken. The typical investor in the S&P 500 averaged a compound annual return of just 4.52 percent during that same time period.[1]

How Does the Average Index Investor Underperform the Index?

In Figure 7.1, you'll see a 13-year performance chart of the S&P 500. Note how the index rose, without much interruption, between 2003 and 2007. Each year, as the index rose higher, more investors piled in. They were happy. They were confident.

By 2008, stocks began to fall, as shown in Figure 7.1. News reports said that stocks would fall further. Buddhas didn't care. But many would-be meditators ditched their robes and sold. In 2011, after the index had a couple of good years, many investors on the sidelines started to buy once again.

This is like buying more rice when prices are high, and buying less (or none at all) when it's on sale. By doing so, people pay above average prices over time.

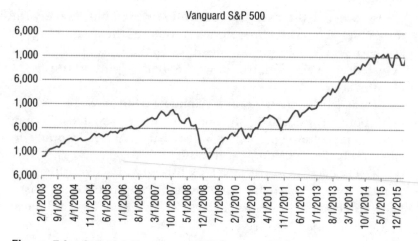

Figure 7.1 S&P 500, March 31, 2003–March 31, 2016
Source: © The Vanguard Group, Inc., used with permission

That tumultuous decade saw Vanguard's S&P 500 gain an average of 6.89 percent per year for the period ending March 31, 2016. But according to Morningstar, the typical investor in that fund averaged a compound return of just 4.52 percent per year. They preferred to buy on highs. They added less (or sold!) on lows.

The free online website Portfoliovisualizer.com shows how much a disciplined investor would have earned. Anyone adding a fixed monthly sum to the S&P 500 index between March 2003 and March 2016 would have averaged a compound annual return of 8.96 percent per year.

By purchasing a fixed amount every month, the investor would have bought more units when the fund prices were lower and fewer units when the fund prices were higher. The fund's posted return, during this time period, was 6.89 percent per year. But an investor who added regular sums each month would have paid a lower-than-average price for those fund units over time. That's how the investor would have averaged a compound annual return of 8.96 percent.

Building a portfolio of index funds on your own is simple. But if you can't sit on a rock (or in a hammock) and ignore the world's noise, consider hiring an intelligent investment firm. Like Buddhas, such firms would do the rock sitting for you. They would also rebalance your portfolio once a year.

Intelligent Investing for Americans

There's a growing number of intelligent investment firms now available to Americans. Such companies use low-cost index funds or ETFs. Best of all, they can also prevent investors from sabotaging their accounts. Are their extra fees worth it? Most of the time, yes.

Vanguard

My wife is a financial schizophrenic. We spend more than $5,000 a year on massages. She thinks nothing of it. But she would slap my hand if I picked up an extra basket of organic blueberries. She also draws the line on investment costs. She owns a Vanguard Target Retirement 2020 (VTWNX) fund, shown in Figure 7.2. Its total fees are just 0.14 percent per year.

Portfolio composition
Allocation to underlying funds as of 04/30/2016

Ranking by Percentage	Fund	Percentage
1	Vanguard Total Stock Market Index Fund Investor Shares	34.5%
2	Vanguard Total Bond Market II Index Fund Investor Shares†	28.4%
3	Vanguard Total International Stock Index Fund Investor Shares	23.5%
4	Vanguard Total International Bond Index Fund Investor Shares	12.2%
5	Vanguard Short-Term Inflation-Protected Securities Index Fund Investor Shares	1.4%
Total	—	100.0%

Figure 7.2   What's Under the Hood?: Vanguard Target Retirement 2020 Fund

Source: Vanguard Research Center, Vanguard.com

This product doesn't fall under the media's robo-advisory label. But it should. It's a low-cost, hassle-free way to have a complete portfolio of index funds that's wrapped into a single product. Her fund allocations are shown in Figure 7.2.

It's a balanced fund that contains a US stock index, two US bond indexes, an international stock index, and an international bond index. In other words, she has exposure to the world with just one fund. Vanguard automatically rebalances each fund's holdings once a year.

Studies show that nobody can predict, with any degree of accuracy, which country's stock market is going to do well in any given year. That's why smart investors don't speculate. Instead, as with investors in Vanguard's Target Retirement Funds, they own a bit of everything. They also maintain a fairly constant allocation without trying to forecast anything.

Data-crunching firm CXO Advisory proves that trying to forecast the stock market is like panning for gold with chopsticks. Between 2005 and 2012, the firm collected 6,584 forecasts by 68 experts. When predicting the direction of the stock market, the experts were right just 46.9 percent of the time.[2] Coin flippers would have beaten them.

Vanguard's Target Retirement Funds offer the cheapest all-in-one portfolios in the world. If you choose to invest in one, you don't need anything else. Once a year, Vanguard rebalances the portfolio's holdings. No, they don't shuffle the portfolio deck based on which of its index fund holdings are expected to soar in the year ahead. Speculation doesn't work. So Vanguard doesn't bother.

Instead, the firm rebalances the holdings once a year to reflect a constant allocation.

Each of Vanguard's Target Retirement funds has a slightly different name, with a year at the end of it. For example, investors who plan to retire in the year 2025 might choose Vanguard's Target Retirement 2025 fund. Those who hope to retire in 2035 might choose Vanguard's Target Retirement 2035 fund.

Every couple of years, each respective fund reduces its exposure to stocks, increasing its exposure to bonds. As people get closer to retirement, most people shouldn't have a stock-heavy portfolio. Stocks perform better than bonds over

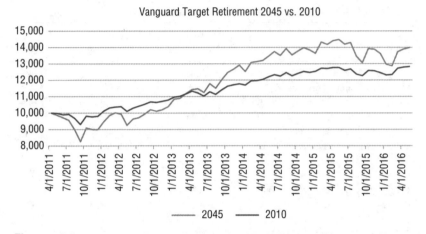

Figure 7.3 Vanguard Target Retirement 2010 Fund vs. Vanguard Target Retirement 2045 Fund: 5-year Performance Ending May 23, 2016
Source: © The Vanguard Group, Inc., used with permission

the long haul. But they are riskier over the short-term. Many retirees (and those getting close to retirement) prefer a portfolio that's more stable.

There are two examples in Figure 7.3.

Figure 7.3 tracks the performance of two such funds over the five-year period ending May 23, 2016. They include Vanguard's Target Retirement 2010 fund and Vanguard's Target Retirement 2045 fund.

Vanguard's Target Retirement 2045 fund was the better performer of the two. It gained a total of 42.65 percent over five years. By comparison, Vanguard's Target Retirement 2010 fund gained 29.55 percent.

But Vanguard's Target Retirement 2045 fund took on higher risk. It contains mostly stock market index funds, with far lower exposure to bond market indexes. Over time, stocks beat bonds. But bonds are more stable. Young investors, for example, can afford to take higher risk for the possibility of higher future returns. When stock markets fall, they have more time to recover.

Older investors usually prefer stability. After all, many are living on the proceeds of their retirement accounts. For this reason, most retirees would prefer a fund like Vanguard's Target Retirement 2010 fund. It's much more stable.

Table 7.1 Vanguard's Target Retirement Funds

Fund	Stock Allocation	Bond Allocation	Expense Ratio
Vanguard Target Retirement Income	30%	70%	0.14%
Vanguard Target Retirement 2010	34%	66%	0.14%
Vanguard Target Retirement 2015	50%	50%	0.14%
Vanguard Target Retirement 2020	60%	40%	0.14%
Vanguard Target Retirement 2025	65%	35%	0.15%
Vanguard Target Retirement 2030	75%	25%	0.15%
Vanguard Target Retirement 2035	80%	20%	0.15%
Vanguard Target Retirement 2040	90%	10%	0.16%
Vanguard Target Retirement 2045	90%	10%	0.16%
Vanguard Target Retirement 2050	90%	10%	0.16%
Vanguard Target Retirement 2060	90%	10%	0.16%

Source: Vanguard.com

As of this writing, Vanguard offers 11 Target Retirement Funds. I've listed them in Table 7.1. You can see their stock/bond allocations and their expense ratios.

I'm a huge fan of these funds. We own Vanguard's Target Retirement 2020 fund in my wife's account.

If a deranged mutual fund salesperson decided to toss me off a bridge, my wife wouldn't have to worry about her money. She would rather dine on dirt than manage it herself. Fortunately, Vanguard does it for her.

The average DIY investor could build a portfolio of individual index funds or ETFs at a slightly lower cost. But my wife's portfolio will beat most of them. Vanguard's Target Retirement funds keep investors calm. That might sound like a strange claim. But let me explain.

Most investors in these funds invest the same amount of money every month (dollar-cost averaging). Many do it through their employers' 401(k)s. Many never look at their portfolios or follow the markets. Not doing so gives them strong odds of earning good returns.

I looked at Vanguard's Target Retirement funds with 10-year track records. Morningstar reveals how each fund performed compared to how its average investor did.[3]

This 10-year period included the stock market crash of 2008–2009. This was when investors freaked. Between 2005 and 2015, Vanguard's S&P 500 Index averaged 8 percent per year. But the typical investor in the S&P 500 averaged just 6.37 percent per year during the same time period. Once again, fear, greed, and speculation pulled them by the gonads. They ceased to buy when they should have been buying. Sometimes they even sold.

Vanguard's Target Retirement funds had the opposite effect. Most of its investors kept adding money, every single month. This allowed them to buy more units when prices were low and fewer units when prices rose. As a result, they paid less than the average price.

That's how Vanguard's Target Retirement investors outperformed their indexes. At the end of April 2015, I used Morningstar.com to see how they did. Vanguard's Target Retirement 2035 fund averaged 7.04 percent for the 10 years ending April 30, 2015. But the typical investor in that same fund averaged a return of 8.65 percent per year. Remember, this included the market crash of 2008–2009.

Such was the case with all of Vanguard's Target Retirement funds. Their investors played cool. They weren't as worried about picking the wrong funds or rebalancing at the wrong time. As a result, their money outperformed the reported gains of their funds, as shown in Table 7.2.

Vanguard's Full-Service Financial Advisers

Despite owning Vanguard's Target Retirement Fund, my wife doesn't seek advice from Vanguard. She doesn't have a full-service adviser.

Table 7.2 Vanguard's Target Retirement Investors Outperformed Their Funds, April 30, 2005 to April 30, 2015

Fund	10-year Annual Fund Return	10-year Annual Investors' Return
Vanguard Target Retirement 2015	6.18%	6.64%
Vanguard Target Retirement 2025	6.58%	7.70%
Vanguard Target Retirement 2035	7.04%	8.65%
Vanguard Target Retirement 2045	7.39%	9.32%

Source: Morningstar.com; All Vanguard Target Retirement funds with 10-year track records

Full-service financial advisers deal with more than just investments. How much should you be saving? What kinds of investment accounts should you open to cover your children's college costs? How should you deal with estate planning? How could you legally reduce your tax bite? They help with everything.

Done right, it's a time-consuming process. That's why most of the better financial advisers won't take clients with accounts valued below $100,000.

Vanguard is changing that. Vanguard charges just 0.3 percent of a portfolio's value each year for full-service financial planning. That's just $300 on a $100,000 portfolio. A minimum of $50,000 is required for investors to qualify for this service. It's available to all American residents. My apologies to the intrepid expats who live overseas. Vanguard (as with many US-based firms) doesn't want you in their sandbox.

If you live in the United States, you might be tempted to race to your local Vanguard office. But you won't find one. To keep costs down, they don't have brick-and-mortar offices for retail investors. The new wave of low-cost firms is all online. Without multiple buildings to lease or buy, maintain, and power, such firms can save a lot of money. They pass the savings down to you.

I've listed a few intelligent investment firms below. Which is the best? That depends on what you're looking for. Some investors may want to start their journey with a financial advisory firm. But if they develop Buddha-like discipline, they might then choose to branch out on their own. Such investors might prefer Vanguard's advisory service or a boutique operation like RW Investment Strategies.

Is This the World's Strangest Financial Adviser?

RW Investment Strategies is run by Robert Wasilewski. If I had to vote for the world's strangest financial adviser, he would get my pick. Why? His goal is to ultimately fire himself. Most of the time he does.

He doesn't believe you need to be a Buddha to build and maintain a portfolio of index funds or ETFs. He thinks almost anyone can do it—with the right initial guidance. "I charge 0.4 percent to manage assets less than $1 million," says Wasilewski, "and 0.3 percent for assets above that. There's an additional $150 quarterly charge for accounts I manage. I offer three services: hourly consulting at $150 an hour, investment management, and investment management with the goal of the client taking over investment management after three months or six months."[4]

Of course, some of his clients want him to manage their money forever. "They're sometimes too busy to do it themselves," he says, "or they're math-o-phobic."

Investment Coaches Offer Guidance

PlanVision's Mark Zoril offers something similar. He guides investors to open low-cost brokerage accounts with a firm like Vanguard or Schwab. He then guides the investor in the portfolio's decision-making. PlanVision charges just $96 a year. As is the case with RW Investment Strategies, I hear great feedback from PlanVision's clients.[5]

Investment Firms That Do The Lifting

Other investors might prefer a firm like AssetBuilder. Its cofounder, Scott Burns, is the man who created and popularized the DIY strategy called the Couch Potato portfolio in 1991. Back-tested studies prior to 1991 revealed that a combination of stock and bond indexes, rebalanced once a year, would trounce most investment professionals.

After 1991, the Couch Potato strategy continued to embarrass professional advisers everywhere. Many investors wanted to try it. But they struggled. They feared investing without an adviser. So in 2006, Scott Burns and Kennon Grose created AssetBuilder. They built a series of couch-potato-like portfolios using a different kind of index, offered by the firm Dimensional Fund Advisors (DFA).

DFA's index funds can only be purchased through a specific type of advisory firm. The firm's advisers must attend a two-day educational conference, at their own cost, in Austin, Texas, or Santa Monica, California. Yet DFA, unlike most index fund companies, doesn't try to equal market returns. They aim to beat them by tilting their emphasis toward small-cap (small company stocks) and value companies (stocks that are cheap, relative to their business earnings).

Sonny Wadera, a Canadian financial adviser with Kelson Financial Services Firm explains it well.

"Think of water getting poured into an ice tray," he says. "The tray represents the entire market of stocks, but DFA tilts the tray slightly to one side, increasing the weightings of small-cap and value stocks."[6] Historically such stocks have outperformed the market.

Will they keep winning? Nobody knows for sure. But one thing is certain: DFA's index funds are cheaper than actively managed funds. That's why, like ordinary index funds, they'll trounce most actively managed funds over an investment lifetime.

Firms like Betterment, Rebalance IRA, SigFig, and Wealthfront (see Table 7.3) are a lot like AssetBuilder. Investors determine their risk profile with a company representative. Investors send their money. The company then builds and manages a portfolio of index funds or ETFs.

Intelligent Investing Firms for Canadians

Canadians are nice. Sure, there's a cross-section of folks who drop the F bomb and the gloves when they get knocked against the boards. But most Canadians are known for their politeness. They say please, thank you, and sorry a lot.

Kindness is a strength. But Canada's financial institutions take advantage. They charge Himalayan costs for their actively managed funds. Canada's banks also have their own brands of index funds.

I don't recommend that you buy the index funds offered by Canada's banks (with the exception of TD's e-Series indexes). But I bring them up to show you something about Canada's banking culture. I want to explain why you shouldn't walk into a Canadian bank and say, "Please build me a portfolio of your index funds."

Table 7.3 Intelligent Investment Firms That Build Portfolios of Index Funds

Firm	Minimum Account Size	Annual Account Charges*	Rebalance and Manage Investments	Full-Service Financial Planning Included	Can Expatriates Open Accounts?
AssetBuilder**	$50,000	0.24% to 0.45%	Yes	No	Yes (depending on country of residence)
Betterment	None	0.15% to 0.35%	Yes	No	No
PlanVision	$0	$96 a year	Yes	No	Yes
Rebalance IRA	None	0.50% Minimum $500 per year; $250 start-up fee	Yes	No	No
RW Investment Strategies	None	0.30% to 0.40%	Yes	No	Yes
SigFig	$2,000	0.25%	Yes	No	No
Vanguard	$50,000	0.30%	Yes	Yes	No
Wealthfront	$5,000	0.25%	Yes	No	No

*With account charge ranges, larger accounts are charged less, as a percentage of assets.

**Full Disclosure. I write for AssetBuilder.com.

First of all, most bank-sold index funds aren't cheap—as far as index funds go. True, they cost less than half of what the banks charge for their actively managed products. They also make the banks' active funds look silly. For the *Globe and Mail* I wrote a series of articles comparing the banks actively managed mutual funds to their index funds. In each case, overall, the indexes won.

But the smiling folks at the Canadian Imperial Bank of Commerce, the Royal Bank of Canada, or the Bank of Montreal aren't your buddies.

The banks make much more money when they sell actively managed funds. Millions of investors get the shaft.

In 2016, I joined a Facebook page for owners of a condominium complex in Victoria, British Columbia. I posted the following message:

> *I'm looking for four people who will each walk into a different Canadian bank. I'll pay you each $50. I would like you to book an appointment with a financial adviser and ask him or her if they could build you a portfolio of index funds.*

Four Generation Xers jumped at the offer. Within a week, I had received details of visits to the Canadian Imperial Bank of Commerce (CIBC), Royal Bank of Canada (RBC), Toronto Dominion Bank (TD), and the Bank of Montreal (BMO).

Some took a pencil and paper to write notes. Others recorded the conversations with their iPhones. None of the advisers wanted to build a low-cost portfolio with the bank's index funds. They offered actively managed funds instead. On average, the funds that they offered cost 2.2 percent per year—more than double the cost of the bank's index funds. The advisers' lack of knowledge and disclosure shocked Tim Godfrey.

Tim, an economics and finance graduate of Dalhousie University, was my first keen reporter. A few years previous, he had worked at the Australian Treasury. "I was advising the government on the regulation of financial advice," he said. "We were determining how investment fees should be disclosed to clients."

I had hit the jackpot. Without knowing it, I had recruited Sidney Crosby for a beer league game. "The adviser said that index funds are riskier than actively managed funds," said Tim. "That surprised me. After all, risk has nothing to do with whether a fund is active or passive [indexed]. Portfolio allocation is what determines risk."[7]

Tim is right. Take two portfolios. One is comprised of actively managed funds. It's split four ways between Canadian government bonds, Canadian stocks, US stocks, and international stocks. In other words, 25 percent of the portfolio is invested in Canadian government bonds and 75 percent is invested in global stocks.

Compare that to a portfolio of index funds. If it contains 40 percent in Canadian government bonds, with the remaining 60 percent invested in global stocks, such a portfolio would have a far lower risk profile than an actively managed portfolio with 25 percent in bonds.

Deborah Bricks, a 36-year-old events planner, was my second reporter who headed to the bank. She chose the Royal Bank of Canada (RBC). "I asked if she [the adviser] could build me a portfolio of index funds," Deborah says. "But she dismissed that idea pretty quickly."

Deborah already owned RBC's Select Balanced fund in her RRSP portfolio. It's an actively managed fund that charges 1.94 percent per year. The adviser suggested that she keep it.

"An index fund just holds a single market," said the adviser. "If you did buy an index fund, you would have to figure out which one to buy. Do you want a US index fund or a Canadian one? RBC's Select Balanced fund is more diversified. It's better because it's actively managed."[8]

Deborah spoke to an adviser who didn't have a clue. The adviser didn't seem to understand that she could build a diversified portfolio with the bank's index funds.

Marina McKercher is a 30-year-old dental hygienist who walked into the Canadian Imperial Bank of Commerce (CIBC). A great saver, she had $20,000 sitting in cash, ready to invest. The adviser immediately showed her CIBC's Balanced Portfolio fund and CIBC's Managed Income Portfolio fund. "He had data sheets on each of these two funds already printed out," she says. The management expense ratios for the funds were 2.25 percent and 1.8 percent per year, respectively.

The bank's index funds charged expense ratio fees that were less than half those amounts. Marina asked about the bank's index funds instead. "The higher fee balanced funds are worth the extra costs," said the adviser, "because the money is managed. The index funds would just sit there, not doing much of anything."[9]

Dan Bortolotti, an Associate Portfolio Manager with PWL Capital says, "I'm not surprised many advisers have no clue about how to properly build a portfolio of index funds or ETFs. The way advisers are educated and trained presumes that their job is to beat the market by analyzing stocks and picking winning funds. The idea that an adviser might add value in other ways is foreign to them."[10]

So far, there hasn't been a revolution. Nobody has stormed Canada's banks or mutual fund companies, armed with a hockey stick, demanding that they change.

That's good. There's no need to break noses. Evolution, instead of revolution, is a lot more Canadian. Canada's Intelligent Investment firms give a nod to Darwin.

Would You Like a Tasty Tangerine?

In 2008, online banking firm Tangerine (formerly ING Direct) offered something sweet to the Canadian public: diversified portfolios of index funds wrapped up into single products. They cost just 1.07 percent per year. That isn't cheap, by DIY standards. But it's a great deal for investors who want a diversified portfolio of indexes. Unlike DIY investors, those with Tangerine don't have to rebalance their portfolios. Tangerine does it for them.

That appeals to Katie Dixon. The 19-year-old from Kamloops, British Columbia, is far ahead of her time. "My high school offered the opportunity for some students to finish their graduation credits early," she says. "Instead of attending high school for my senior year, I finished my high school graduation credits one year early [by grade 11] and enrolled in a six-month Health Care Assistant program."

Katie graduated from the six-month program three months before most of her other friends finished their final year of high school. "The demand for care aides is high," she says. "So I got a great job right away." Katie will eventually study to become a nurse. Until then, she adds, "My work as a care aide pays a lot better than a typical summer job."

When Katie was 18, she started to track her daily expenses with an app on her iPhone. "Keeping track of what I spent helped me to free up some money," she says. That's when she decided to commit to investing.

"I opened a high-interest savings account with Tangerine. I added $150 a month. It comes automatically out of my savings account. When I turned 19, I was eligible to open a TFSA account. I switched the accumulated cash over to Tangerine's Equity Growth portfolio. Every month, I keep adding money to it."[11]

Like I said, she's way ahead of her time.

Tangerine is perfect for Canadians who are just starting out, want to invest small sums regularly, and would prefer to have a company build and rebalance a portfolio of index funds for them.

Katie's portfolio is geared for growth. It contains a Canadian stock index, a US stock index, and an international stock index. Once a year, Tangerine rebalances the fund's holdings.

Each of Tangerine's three other funds would work well for investors with different time horizons and tolerances for risk. You can see them in Table 7.4.

WealthBar

WealthBar offers five portfolio options for Canadian investors. They help clients determine their risk tolerance before they select a ready-made, diversified portfolio of ETFs. WealthBar does all the lifting. They offer full financial planning for those whose financial circumstances aren't too complicated. They also build and rebalance client portfolios. All investors need to do is add money to their accounts.

Table 7.4 Tangerine's Index Fund Portfolios

Fund	Best Suited For	Canadian Bonds	Canadian Stocks	US Stocks	International Stocks
Tangerine Balanced Income	Very conservative investors	70%	10%	10%	10%
Tangerine Balanced	Moderately conservative investors	40%	20%	20%	20%
Tangerine Balanced Growth	Investors looking for high growth with some stability	25%	25%	25%	25%
Tangerine Equity Growth	Young or aggressive investors	0%	50%	25%	25%

Source: Tangerine.ca.

The firm charges between 0.35 percent and 0.60 percent per year, depending on each account's size. That's WealthBar's take. Investors pay a further 0.20 percent (approximately) to the separate ETF provider. Investors with accounts valued below $150,000 pay total fees of about 0.80 percent per year. Investors with account sizes between $150,000 and $500,000 pay 0.60 percent in total fees. Those with more than $500,000 pay just 0.40 percent.

To get started, new clients create a login password at wealthbar.com. As soon as they do so, a message appears.

Hi Andrew, I'm David, a financial adviser at WealthBar. I'm here if you have any questions about investing with WealthBar.

I'm generally available to chat between 9AM-5PM PST M-F. You can schedule a call to discuss anything you like or contact me online through your WealthBar dashboard.

David, the financial adviser, isn't WealthBar's Siri. He's a real person. Neville Joanes is WealthBar's Portfolio Manager and Chief Compliance Officer. As he explains, "Everyone who logs in to WealthBar gets assigned a financial adviser."[12]

The advisers look at each client's long-term financial needs, based on their goals, savings rates, investment time horizons, insurance needs, as well as different tax-deferred account opportunities.

Investors can request a plan to be reviewed at any time, either online, or over the phone. Before doing so, investors fill in some easy-to-follow online questionnaires. They ask for information such as current savings rates, investment assets, types of accounts owned (if any), risk tolerances, and salary. Based on client-entered responses, they show a model of a suitable portfolio. Investors with questions can speak to an adviser.

WealthBar isn't the only low-cost Intelligent Investing firm in Canada. I've listed others in Table 7.5. Each will build and maintain a portfolio of index funds. In each case, the firm will also rebalance the holdings at least once a year. That's an important element that helps to reduce risk.

Some of the firms, however, adjust their portfolios based on market forecasts. That might sound sophisticated in a marketing brochure. But most market forecasts tend to be wrong. Statistically, firms that don't adjust a portfolio's position, based on forecasts, should perform better over an investment lifetime.

Intelligent Investing Firms for British Investors

Vanguard UK's Target Retirement Funds

In 2015, Vanguard UK introduced its Target Retirement Funds. These are complete portfolios of indexes, wrapped up into single funds. They represent diversified baskets of UK and global stock and bond index funds. In other words, if you buy one of these, it's all you really need.

Each fund has a designated date in the name. For example, investors who wish to retire in 2020 could buy Vanguard's Target Retirement 2020 fund. Those who wish to retire in 2050 could buy Vanguard's Target Retirement 2050 fund. There's no obligation to hold these funds for any given period of time. Unlike

Table 7.5 Intelligent Investment Firms in Canada Build Portfolios of Index Funds

Intelligent Investment Firm	Rebalances Index Holdings	Portfolios May Be Rebalanced Based on Market Forecasts*	Minimum Account Size	Annual Fees for a $5,000 Account**	Annual Fees for a $50,000 Account**	Annual Fees for a $200,000 Account**
BMO SmartFolio	Yes	Yes*	$5,000	$74 = 1.5%	$487 = 0.97%	$1,850 = 0.92%
NestWealth	Yes	No	None (but fees are ridiculously high on small accounts)	$347 = 6.9%	$415 = 0.83%	$1,360 = 0.68%
Questrade Portfolio IQ	Yes	Yes*	$2,000 (but fees are ridiculously high on small accounts)	$131 = 2.6%	$545 = 1.1%	$1,980 = 0.99%
WealthBar	Yes	No	$5,000	$12 = 0.25%***	$430 = 0.86%	$1,710 = 0.85%
WealthSimple	Yes	No	None	$12 = 0.25%***	$353 = 0.71%	$1,472 = 0.74%

*Be skeptical of market forecasts.

**Annual fees include costs charged by the investment firm, plus the expense ratio costs of the index funds (ETFs).

****WealthBar and WealthSimple don't charge fees for accounts valued below $5,000. Investors would just pay the expense ratios fees of the index funds (ETFs).

many UK-based fund companies, Vanguard doesn't charge penalties if investors choose to sell the fund after their initial purchase.

How Does Each Target Fund Differ?

Each target retirement fund has the same components. But the short-term risk and growth potentials differ. For example, in Table 7.6, you can see that investors who choose Vanguard's Target Retirement 2050 fund would have higher stock allocations than investors in Vanguard's Target Retirement 2020 fund. Younger investors can usually afford to take higher risks. When stocks fall, they have more time to wait for stocks to recover.

Conservative young investors, of course, could still buy Vanguard's Target Retirement 2020 fund. Adventurous older investors could do likewise with Vanguard's Target Retirement 2050 fund. Neither of the funds "expire" on any given date. Investors can remain invested long after the date in each respective fund's name.

There's another reason I like these funds. Vanguard rebalances the indexes in each of their target retirement funds once a year. Some investors might ask, "Why would I bother having Vanguard rebalance a portfolio of index funds for me? I could build and manage a portfolio of index funds on my own. It would also cost me less."

These Target Retirement funds cost 0.24 percent per year. A DIY portfolio of Vanguard's indexes or ETFs would cost slightly less.

But investors who build their own portfolios don't usually perform as well. Morningstar's studies report that DIY index fund investors usually underperform their funds because they often purchase high, sell low, and speculate on market news. Investors, who let Vanguard do the rebalancing, usually perform better (see Table 7.2 and the explanation that precedes it).

Table 7.6   Longer Time Horizons Warrant Higher Stock Allocations

Fund	% In Bonds	% In Stocks
Target Retirement 2020 Fund	41.3%	58.7%
Target Retirement 2050 Fund	19.9%	81.1%

Source: Vanguard UK, as of June 16, 2016

Table 7.7 Vanguard's (UK) Target Retirement Funds

Fund	Annual Expense Ratio
Target Retirement 2015 Fund	0.24%
Target Retirement 2020 Fund	0.24%
Target Retirement 2025 Fund	0.24%
Target Retirement 2030 Fund	0.24%
Target Retirement 2035 Fund	0.24%
Target Retirement 2040 Fund	0.24%
Target Retirement 2045 Fund	0.24%
Target Retirement 2050 Fund	0.24%

Source: Vanguard UK

Annual rebalancing reduces risk. It can also boost returns.

What's more, Vanguard increases each Target Retirement fund's bond allocation over time. As investors get closer to their retirement dates, the funds become more conservative.

I've listed Vanguard's Target Retirement funds in Table 7.7. Their annual expense ratios include all rebalancing. Vanguard also has a habit of reducing its fund expenses over time. By the time you read this, fees could be even lower.

What's the Only Problem with These Funds?

In the United States, Vanguard's Target Retirement funds require a minimum $3,000 initial investment. But if you want to buy one of these funds from Vanguard UK, you'll need a lot more money than that. The initial investment for a direct purchase through Vanguard is an eye-watering £100,000.

This doesn't mean that I've sent you down a rabbit hole. If you buy a Vanguard Retirement fund through a participating broker, you need far less money. Such intermediaries (or financial advisory firms) charge fees for you to buy these products. But it's still a lot smarter than buying actively managed funds.

Vanguard UK lists its participating brokers on its website. But be careful. Some of the firms charge a percentage of the investors' assets. Over time, this can be expensive. If a brokerage firm charges 0.45 percent and Vanguard's expense ratio is 0.24 percent, investors would pay 0.69 percent per year for a Vanguard Target Retirement Fund. On a £50,000 account, that would be £345 a year. On a £100,000 account, it would cost £690.

Instead, find a financial services company that charges a flat annual fee.

Not Interested in a Target Retirement Fund?

Many Intelligent Investment Firms are popping up in the UK. But few of them use index funds exclusively or offer services to retail investors. Nutmeg, however, is one firm that does. Its costs are high, compared to their Canadian and US counterparts. But Nutmeg offers one of the best values in Britain. As competition heats up, costs will likely lower.

Table 7.8 shows how much Nutmeg's investors would pay in fees to have a portfolio of index funds built and managed for them.

Intelligent Investing Firms for Australians

Ask an Australian on the street this question: What has performed better, Australian shares or Australian property? Nine out of ten will say that property prices have run circles around Aussie stocks.

Australian property values have certainly soared. But their stock market hasn't been too shabby, either.

According to Philip Soo, a Master's research student at Deakin University's School of Humanities and Social Sciences, Australian property prices rose 400 times faster than inflation between 1900 and 2012.[14] He sourced such data from the Australian Bureau of Statistics.

Table 7.8   Nutmeg's Annual Fees, Based on Account Sizes

Account Size	Annual Account Management Fee	Estimated Expense Ratio Charges for Index Funds	Total Annual Costs, Including Management and Fund Expense Ratios
Below £25,000	0.95%	0.19%	1.11%
£25,000 to £100,000	0.75%	0.19%	0.94%
£100,000 to £500,000	0.50%	0.19%	0.69%
£500,000+	0.30%	0.19%	0.49%

Source: Nutmeg.com[13]

Table 7.9   Vanguard Australia's Life Strategy Funds

Fund	Percentage in Stocks	Percentage in Bonds	This fund is best suited for . . .
Vanguard Life Strategy High Growth Fund	90.2%	9.8%	Aggressive and young investors
Vanguard Life Strategy Growth Fund	70.3%	29.7%	Moderately aggressive and young investors
Vanguard Balanced Index	50.2%	49.8%	Conservative investors
Vanguard Life Strategy Conservative Fund	30%	70%	Very conservative investors

Source: Vanguard Australia

Over the same 112 years, Australian shares have risen 2,208 times faster than inflation. Both asset classes have also done well over the five-year period ending May 31, 2016. According to GlobalPropertyGuide.com, the average house price change measured over eight capital cities saw an increase of about 28 percent.[15] Vanguard's Australian stock market index increased by 37 percent.

Australians who want a diversified portfolio of indexes could also choose Vanguard. Vanguard Australia offers five Life Strategy funds. They rebalance each of them once a year. The investment costs (as a percentage of the overall assets) decreases as each account grows.

Each of Vanguard's Life Strategy funds, which I've listed in Table 7.9, cost 0.9 percent per year for the first $50,000 invested; 0.6 percent for the next $50,000 and 0.35 percent for balances above $100,000.

Intelligent Investment Firms on the Rise

Several intelligent investment firms (robo-advisers) are set to challenge Vanguard. I've listed some below. Costs vary, as do their services. But over time, fees for all of these firms, including Vanguard's, could get reduced as competition ramps up.

Each of the firms listed in Table 7.10 builds and rebalances portfolios of exchange-traded index funds. Fees differ based on the amount that's invested. For example, Stockspot doesn't charge an annual fee for the first 12 months on accounts that

Table 7.10 Intelligent Investing Firms In Australia

Firm	Annual Fee	Additional Annual Percentage on Assets Fee	Estimated Total Annual Fees Including Fund Expense Ratio Costs
Stockspot	$77	0.528% to 0.924%	0.828% to 1.224%
Ignition Wealth	$198 to $396	0	0.3%
Proadviser	$75	0.79%	1.09%
Quietgrowth	$0	0.40% to 0.60%	0.70% to 0.90%
Vanguard's Life Strategy Funds	$0	0.35% to 0.9%	0.35% to 0.9%

are valued below $10,000. They charge 0.924 percent per year for accounts valued below $50,000. They charge 0.528 percent per year for accounts valued above $500,000.

Let me further explain the above table. Stockspot charges a $77 fee per year to every account holder. They then charge the client a percentage of the account's value each year. Depending on the account size, that ranges from 0.528 percent to 0.924 percent per year. But the fund companies charge small fees for their ETFs. Stockspot doesn't take this money. It would go to Vanguard, iShares, or the chosen ETF provider. When adding these estimated fund charges, investors would pay the annual $77 per year plus 0.828 percent to 1.224 percent of their account values each year, depending on their account size.

Ignition Wealth offers a great deal for investors with larger accounts. It charges a flat fee between $198 and $396 per year. That fee would eat aggressively into a small investment account valued below $10,000. But Ignition Wealth doesn't charge an annual fee based on the investment account size. It reminds me of what a friend once told me about his Jaguar sports car. "Anyone can keep up with me up to 60 miles per hour. But God help anyone who tries to keep up after that."

Intelligent Investment Firms in Singapore

In late 2016, a couple of robo-advisers were getting ready to launch in Singapore. One of them is called Smartly. They promise to build portfolios of low-cost ETFs.

This is a big, positive step. Singaporeans deserve a low-cost platform for a portfolio of index funds. But if such firms take shortcuts, somebody might get bit. Based on e-mail exchanges that I have had with these firms, they are planning to use some US-based ETFs.

For taxable reasons, that's a dangerous game to play. It's like saying, "We care about our investors. But let's toss their heirs in front of an MRT train." Such firms should build portfolios of ETFs that trade on the Singaporean, Canadian, British, or Australian stock market.

Here's why.

If a Singaporean dies owning US-based assets, the investor's heirs may have to pay a hefty US estate tax bill if their assets exceed the equivalent of $60,000 USD.

I can hear what you're thinking. "I'm not an American. I'm not even using a US brokerage." That might not matter. The IRS states that "Nonresident's stock holdings in American companies are subject to estate taxation even though the nonresident held the certificates abroad or registered the certificates in the name of a nominee."[16]

And the tax could be hefty, starting at 18 percent and rising to 40 percent for accounts exceeding $1 million.[17]

Table 7.11 lists three portfolios. Each has similar asset allocations that provide exposure to US stocks, international stocks, and international bonds. US estate taxes could slap the first portfolio once the investor dies. But the other two would be safe because the ETFs trade on the Canadian and UK stock exchanges.

Don't let a teething robo-adviser in Singapore threaten the money you could bequeath. If you do use such a firm, make sure they don't build you a portfolio with an ETF that trades on a US stock exchange.

Don't Ask about Another Lover

What would happen if a man asked his lover about the seductive woman who lives across the street? "Should I make the switch?" he might ask. If he asks such a question, he should record his stupidity and upload it onto YouTube.

Table 7.11   Singaporeans, Why Take The Extra Risk?

	Could Be Subject to US Estate Taxes	Would Not Be Subject to US Estate Taxes	Would Not Be Subject to US Estate Taxes
US Equity	Vanguard Total Stock Market ETF (VTI)	Vanguard US Total Market ETF (VUN)	Vanguard S&P 500 ETF (VUSA or VUSD)
International Equity	Vanguard FTSE Developed Markets ETF (VEA)	Vanguard FTSE Developed Markets ETF (VDU)	Vanguard FTSE Developed World ETF (VEVE or VDEV)
Fixed Income	iShares 1–3 Year International Treasury Bond ETF (ISHG)	Vanguard Global (ex US) Bond ETF (VBG)	iShares Global Government Bond UCITS ETF (IGLO)
Trading Exchange	US	Canadian	UK

He would get millions of hits if he got beaten to a pulp.

That won't happen if you ask your financial adviser about index funds. But the same rule applies. If the adviser invests using actively managed funds, she's not going to be happy.

She'll also be armed with a handful of arguments to keep you away from index funds. In the next chapter, I explain what she'll say. It's always best to peek inside a pilferer's playbook.

Notes

1. Morningstar.com
2. Guru Grades, CXO Advisory, www.cxoadvisory.com/gurus/.
3. Morningstar.com.
4. Interview with Robert Wasilewski via e-mail, April 1, 2014.
5. Interview with Mark Zoril via e-mail, December 5, 2015.
6. Interview with Sonny Wadera via e-mail, December 27, 2014.
7. Personal interview with Tim Godfrey, March 2, 2016, in Victoria, B.C.
8. Personal interview with Deborah Bricks, March 4, 2016, in Victoria, B.C.

9. Personal interview with Marina McKercher, March 8, 2016, in Victoria, B.C.

10. Interview with Dan Bortolotti via e-mail, June 30, 2016.

11. Interview with Katie Dixon via e-mail, June 15, 2016.

12. Personal interview with Neville Joanes, March 10, 2016, by telephone.

13. Nutmeg.com, www.nutmeg.com/our-fee.

14. "The History of Australian Property Values," MacroBusiness, February 13, 2013, www.macrobusiness.com.au/2013/02/the-history-of-australian-property-values/.

15. "Global Property Guide House Price Changes," Global Property Guide, www.globalpropertyguide.com/Pacific/Australia/price-change-10-years.

16. "Some Non Residents with U.S. Assets Must File Estate Tax Returns," IRS, www.irs.gov/individuals/international-taxpayers/some-nonresidents-with-u-s-assets-must-file-estate-tax-returns.

17. "2014 Unified Rate Schedule," Tax Policy Center, www.taxpolicycenter.org/sites/default/files/legacy/taxfacts/content/PDF/estate_rates.pdf.

RULE 8

Peek inside a Pilferer's Playbook

If you've read what I've written so far about indexed investing, I hope that you're planning to open your own indexed account. Or perhaps you'll choose an intelligent investment firm that can set it up for you.

Either way, if you currently have a financial adviser who's buying you actively managed mutual funds, you're probably thinking of making the split.

That's always easier said than done. I like to think that the majority of investors who have attended my seminars have decided to index their investments—to save costs and taxes— while building larger accounts than they would have done with baskets of less-efficient products. But not all have. I know many would-be indexers spoke to their financial advisers, fully intending to break free. But the advisers' sales pitches froze them in their tracks.

Many financial advisers have mental playbooks. They're designed to deter would-be index investors. The advisers initiate their strategies with remarkable success. Many of their clients are forced to keep climbing mountains with 100-pound backpacks.

How Will Most Financial Advisers Fight You?

Often, when a friend or family member wants to open an investment account, he or she asks me to come along.

Beforehand, I briefly talk to the new investor about the markets, how they work, and the merits of index investing. I tell the person that every single academic study done on mutual fund investing points to the same conclusion: to give yourself the best possible odds in the stock market, low-cost index funds are key.

Walking into a bank or financial services company, we're then settled into plush chairs across from a financial adviser. The adviser tries to sell us on his ability to pick winning mutual funds. When my friend brings up index funds, the salesperson has an arsenal of anti-index sales talk.

Here are some of the rebuttals the advisers will give you— desperate, of course, to keep money flowing into their pockets and the firm's. If you're prepared for what they'll say, you'll have a better chance of standing your ground. Don't forget. It's your money, not theirs.

> *Index funds are dangerous when stock markets fall. Active fund managers never keep all their eggs in the stock market in case it drops. A stock market index is linked 100 percent to the stock market's return.*

This is where a salesperson pushes a client's fear button— suggesting that active managers have the ability to quickly sell stock market assets before the markets drop, saving your mutual fund assets from falling too far during a crash. And then, when the markets are looking "safer" (or so the pitch goes), a mutual fund manager will then buy stocks again, allowing you to ride the wave of profits back as the stock market recovers.

It all sounds good in sales theory. But they can't time the market like that—and hidden fees still take their toll. Ask your adviser to tell you which calendar year in recent memory saw the biggest decline. He should say 2008. Ask him if most actively managed funds beat the total stock market index during 2008. If he says yes, then you've caught him talking out the side of his head. A Standard & Poor's study cited in *The Wall Street Journal* in 2009 detailed the truth: the vast majority of actively managed funds still lost to their counterpart stock market indexes during 2008—the worst market drop in recent memory.[1] Clearly, actively managed fund managers weren't able to dive out of the markets on time.

What's more, a single stock market index is just part of a portfolio. Don't let an adviser fool you with data comparing a single index fund with the actively managed products they're selling. As you read in Chapter 5, smart investors balance their portfolios with bond indexes as well.

You can't beat the market with an index fund, they'll say. An index fund will give you just an average return. Why saddle yourself with mediocrity when we have teams of people to select the best funds for you?

I've heard this from a number of advisers. And it makes me smile. If the average mutual fund had no costs associated with it—no 12B1 fee, no expense ratio, no taxable liability, no sales commissions or adviser trailer fees, and no operational costs—then the salesperson would be right. A total stock market index fund's return would be pretty close to "average." Long term, roughly half of the world's actively managed funds would beat the world stock market index, and roughly half of the world's funds would be beaten by the index. But for that to happen, you would have to live in the following fantasy world:

1. *Your adviser would have to work for free.* No trailer fees or sales commissions for him/her or the firm. The tooth fairy would pay his mortgage, food bills, vacations, and other worldly expenses.

2. *The fund company wouldn't make any money.* Companies such as Raymond James, T. Rowe Price, Fidelity, Putnam Investments, Goldman Sachs (and the rest of the "for-profit" wealth-management businesses) would be charitable foundations.

3. *The researchers would work for free.* Not only would the fund companies bless the world with their services, but their researchers would have to be altruistic, independently wealthy philanthropists giving their time and efforts to humanity.

4. The fund managers doing the buying and selling for the mutual funds would work for free. They would be so inspired by their parent companies that they would trade stocks and bonds for free while lesser-evolved mortals worked for salaries.

5. The fund companies could trade stocks for free. Large brokerage firms would take the financial hit for the trading done by mutual fund companies. Recognizing the fund companies' "value-added" mission, brokerage firms would pay every commission a fund company racked up from trading stocks.

6. Governments would waive your taxable obligations. Because the fund companies are such a blessing on the world, the world's governments would turn a blind eye to the taxable turnover established.

If the fantasy scenario above were correct, then yes, a total stock market index fund would generate very close to an average return.

But in the real world, advisers suggesting that a total stock market index gives an average return are proving to be well-dressed Pinocchios or post-Columbus sailors with a "Flat Earth" complex.

A tough salesperson, however, wouldn't stop there. Next, you might hear something like this:

I can show you plenty of mutual funds that have beaten the indexes. We'd only buy you the very best funds.

It's pretty easy to look in the rearview mirror at the last 15 winners of Golf's British Open Championship and say: "See, here are the champions who won the British Open over the past 15 years. These are people who can win. This knowledge qualifies me to pick the next 15 years' worth of champions—and we'll bet your money on my selections."

Studies prove that high-performing funds of the past rarely continue their outperforming ways.

Just look at the system used by Morningstar's mutual fund rating system. No one in the world has more mutual fund data than Morningstar. Certainly, your local financial adviser doesn't. But as detailed in Chapter 3, the funds given "top scores" by Morningstar for their superb, consistent performance usually go on to lose to the market indexes in the following years.

Even Morningstar recognizes the incongruity. John Rekenthaler, director of research, said in the fall 2000 edition of *In the Vanguard*: "To be fair, I don't think that you'd want to pay much attention to Morningstar's ratings either."[2]

So if Morningstar can't pick the top mutual funds of the future, what odds does your financial planner have—especially when trying to dazzle you with a fund's historical track record?

If you're the kind of person who enjoys winding people up, try this comeback the next time an adviser tries selling you (or one of your friends) on a bunch of funds that he claims have beaten the index over the past 15 years.

> *Hey, that's great. They all beat the index over the past 15 years. Now show me your personal investment account statements from 15 years ago. If you can show me that you owned all of these funds back then, I'll invest every penny I have with you.*

Okay—maybe that's a bit mean. You aren't likely to see any of those funds in his 15-year-old portfolio reports. You won't likely see them in any of his five-year-old portfolio reports either.

If the salesperson deserves an "A" for tenacity, you'll get this as the next response:

> *But I'm a professional. I can bounce your money around from fund to fund, taking advantage of global economic swings and hot fund manager streaks and easily beat a portfolio of diversified indexes.*

Just thinking about that kind of love gives me goose bumps. Many advisers will lead you to believe that they have their pulse on the economy—that they can foresee opportunities and pending disasters. Their sagacity, they will suggest, will enable you to beat a portfolio of indexes.

But in terms of financial acumen, brokers and financial advisers are at the bottom of the totem pole. At the top, you have pension fund managers, mutual fund managers, and hedge fund managers. Most financial advisers, as US personal finance commentator Suze Orman points out, are "just pin-striped suited salespeople."

Your financial planner could have just a two-week course under her belt. At best, a certified financial planner needs just one year of sales experience at a brokerage firm and fewer than six months of full-time academic training (on investment products, insurance, and financial planning) before receiving his or her certification. With some regular nightly reading, it wouldn't take long before you knew more about personal finance than most financial planners. They have to sell. They have to build trust. They have to make you feel good about yourself. These skills are the biggest part of their jobs.

When arbitration lawyer Daniel Solin was writing his book, *Does Your Broker Owe You Money?*, a broker told him:

> *Training for a new broker goes something like this: study and take the Series 7, 63, 65, and insurance exams. I spent three weeks learning to sell. If a broker wants to learn about (asset allocation and diversification) it has to be done on the broker's own time.*[3]

This might explain why it's often common to find investors of all ages without any bonds in their portfolios. Predominantly trained as salespeople, it's possible that many financial representatives aren't schooled in the practice of diversifying investment accounts with stocks and bonds.

Noted US finance writer William Bernstein echoes the gaps in most financial adviser training, suggesting in his superb 2002 book, *The Four Pillars of Investing*, that anyone who invests money should read the two classic texts:

1. A Random Walk Down Wall Street by Burton Malkiel

2. Common Sense on Mutual Funds by John Bogle

"After you're finished with these two books, you will know more about finance than 99 percent of all stockbrokers and most other finance professionals," he said.[4]

From what I've seen, he's right.

When my good friend Dave Alfawicki and I went into a bank in White Rock, British Columbia, in 2004, we met a young woman selling mutual funds. Dave wanted to set up an indexed account, and I went along for the ride. The adviser's knowledge gaps were extraordinary, so I asked the question: What kinds of certification do you have and how long did it take? She received her license to sell mutual funds through a course called Investment Funds in Canada (IFIC). It's supposed to take three weeks of full-time studying to complete the course, but she and her classmates finished it in just two intensive weeks.[5] Before the two-week course, she knew nothing about investing.

A year later, I went into another Canadian bank with my mom to help her open an investment account. We wanted the account to have roughly 50 percent in a stock index and 50 percent in a bond index. Of course, the adviser, as usual, tried to talk us out of it.

But once the adviser recognized that I knew more about investing than she did, she came clean. To paraphrase the discussion, she shocked us with this:

> First, we get a feel for the client. The bank suggests that if the client doesn't know much about investing, we should put them in a fund of funds, for example, a mutual fund that would have a series of funds within it. It tends to be a bit more expensive than regular mutual funds. This sales job only works with investors who really don't know what they're doing.
>
> If the investor seems a little smarter, we offer them, individually, our in-house brand of actively managed mutual funds. We don't make as much money with these, so we push for the other products first.
>
> Under no circumstances do we offer the bank's index funds to clients. If an investor requests them and we can't talk them out of the indexes, only then will we buy them for the client.

I appreciated her candor. By the end of the conversation, the adviser was asking me for book suggestions about indexed investing and she gratefully wrote down a number of titles. At least she was willing to take care of her own money.

Three years later, a different representative from the same bank phoned my mom. "Your account is too risky," he said. "Come on down to the bank so we can move some things around for you."

Thankfully, my mom was able to stand her ground. With 50 percent of her investment in bond indexes, the account wasn't risky at all—but it wasn't profitable for the bank.

If you notice a financial adviser has a university degree in finance, commerce, or business, hang tight for a moment. Find someone else with one of these degrees and ask this: During your studies at university, did you study mutual funds, index funds, or learn how to build a personal investment portfolio for wealth building or retirement? The answer will be no. So don't be fooled by an additional, irrelevant title.

Most brokers and advisers really are just salespeople, and well-paid salespeople at that. In the United States, the average broker makes nearly $150,000 a year—putting them in the top five percent of all US wage earners. They make more than the average lawyer, primary care doctor, or professor at an elite university.[6] And if they're recommending actively managed funds, they're a bit like vendors in the guise of nutritionists selling candy, booze, and cigarettes.

Why Your Financial Adviser Might Lie

Harvard economist Sendhil Mullainathan, Markus Noeth of the University of Hamburg, and Antoinette Schoar of the MIT Sloan School of Management published a study, *The Market For Financial Advice*.[7]

They hired actors to approach financial advisers with a fictitious $500,000 portfolio. In some cases, the portfolios were made with low-cost index funds. The researchers wanted to see what kind of advice the advisers would give. Over a five-month period, the actors made nearly 300 visits to financial advisers in the Boston area.

When shown a portfolio of index funds, most turned up their noses. Eighty-five percent said actively managed funds were better. As Upton Sinclair said long ago, "It is difficult to get a man to understand something when his salary depends on his not understanding it."[8]

But what makes them lie?

In 2006, Kathleen D. Vohs, Nicole L. Mead, and Miranda R. Goode published a study called The Psychological Consequences of Money.[9] It showed that money makes us selfish. Subjects played the board game Monopoly with an experimenter who posed as a subject. When the game was over, the board was put away. In some cases, a large stack of Monopoly money was left on the table. In other cases, a small stack or no money remained.

At this point, somebody walked into the room and dropped a box of pencils. It was a staged experiment to see if the subjects would help to pick them up. The subjects with a large sum of Monopoly money on the table picked up the fewest number of pencils.

During another test, an experimenter pretended to have a tough time with a problem. Those whose minds were imprinted by money beforehand weren't very helpful. It was the opposite for those who weren't primed by money.

According to Nobel Prize winner Daniel Kahneman in his book *Thinking, Fast and Slow*, "The psychologist who has done this research, Kathleen Vohs, has been laudably restrained in discussing the implications of her findings."[10]

Ask an adviser to build you a portfolio of index funds. The implications of the experiment will become obvious.

The Totem Pole View

Financial advisers and brokers are at the bottom of the totem pole of financial knowledge. At the top, you'll find hedge fund managers, mutual fund managers, and pension fund managers.

Generally earning the highest certification in money management—as chartered financial analysts—pension fund managers have the leeway to buy what they want. These are the folks managing huge sums of government and corporate retirement money. Arguably, they're the best of the best. If your local financial planner applied for the job of managing the pension for Pennsylvania's teachers or New Jersey's state-pension system, he or she would likely get laughed off the table.

Pension fund managers have their pulses on the stock markets and the economy. They can invest where they want. Typically, they don't have to focus on a particular geographic region or type of stock. The world is their oyster. If they want to jump into European stocks, they do it. If they think the new opportunities are in small stocks, they load up on those. If they feel the stock market is going to take a short-term beating, they might sell some of their stocks, buying more bonds or holding cash instead.

Your typical financial planner isn't as knowledgeable as the average pension fund manager. But most advisers will try to "sell" you on the idea that (like the pension fund manager) they have their pulse on the economy and that they can find you hot mutual funds to buy. They might try telling you that they know when the economy is going to self-destruct, which stock market is going to fly, and whether gold, silver, small stocks, large stocks, oil stocks, or retail stocks are going to do well this quarter, this year, or this decade.

But they are full of hot air.

Pension fund managers are more likely to know oodles more about making money in the markets than financial advisers or brokers.

Knowing that pension fund managers are like the gods of the industry, how do their results stack up against a diversified portfolio of index funds?

Most pension funds have their money in a 60/40 split: 60 percent stocks and 40 percent bonds. They also have advantages that retail investors don't have: large company pension funds pay significantly lower fees than retail investors like you or I would, and they don't have to pay taxes on incurred capital gains.

Considering the financial acumen of the average pension fund manager, coupled with the lower cost and tax benefits, you would assume that the average American pension fund would easily beat an indexed portfolio allocated similarly to most pension funds: 60 percent stocks and 40 percent bonds. But that isn't the case.

US consulting firm FutureMetrics studied the performance of 192 US major corporate pension plans between 1988 and 2005. Fewer than 30 percent of the pension funds outperformed a portfolio of 60 percent S&P 500 index and 40 percent intermediate corporate bond index.[11]

If most pension fund managers can't beat an indexed portfolio, what chance does your financial planner have?

The Best Odds to Win

If you told most financial advisers this, they would either begin talking in circles to confuse you or they would be battling with their ego.

If it's the latter, you might hear this: If it were so easy, why wouldn't every pension fund be indexed?

Pension fund managers are as optimistic as the rest of us. Many of them will try to beat portfolios comprised of a 60 percent stock index and a 40 percent bond index.

But they aren't stupid, and many pension funds maximize their returns by indexing.

According to US financial adviser Bill Schultheis, author of *The New Coffeehouse Investor*, the Washington state pension fund, for example, has 100 percent of its stock market assets in indexes, California has 86 percent indexed, New York has 75 percent indexed, and Connecticut has 84 percent of its stock market money in indexes.[12]

The vast majority of regular, everyday investors, however, buy actively managed mutual funds instead.[13] Unaware of the data, their financial advisers distort realities to keep their gravy trains flowing. It will cost most people more than half of their retirement portfolios—thanks to fees, taxes, and dumb "market timing" mistakes.

Sticking with index funds might be boring. But it beats winding up as shark bait, and it gives you the best odds of eventually growing rich through the stock and bond markets.

Why Did Fidelity's Employees Sue Fidelity?

Fidelity is one of the world's largest mutual fund companies. Most of their funds are actively managed. But they offer index funds, too. In 2012, I helped my friend Patti Smaldone build a portfolio with Fidelity's low-cost indexes. Three years later, a representative from Fidelity contacted Patti. "He said we should move the investments into some actively managed funds," says Patti. "He said they would perform better."

Ironically, Patti's portfolio had performed very well. But if you want an example of a conflict of interest, this one is a doozy.

Fidelity's employees prefer to invest in index funds. But the company's 401(k) fund options were full of actively managed funds. In 2013, Fidelity's employees put Fidelity to task for that. A group of Fidelity's employees sued Fidelity for trying to profit at its employees' expense.

At the time, company spokesperson Vincent Loporchio said, "We believe the lawsuit is totally without merit, and we intend to defend vigorously against it. Fidelity has a very generous benefits package that provides significant contributions to our employee's retirement planning."

But Fidelity lost that war. In August 2014, CNN reported that "Fidelity agreed to pay $12 million to settle the class-action suits, which alleged that the firm was profiting at the expense of its workers by offering high-cost fund options and charging excessive fees for a plan of its size."[14]

As for the Fidelity representative who contacted my friend Patti? I wonder how well he sleeps.

Is Government Action Required?

David Swensen, Yale University's endowment fund manager, suggests the US government needs to stop the mutual fund industry's exploitation of individual investors.[15] The United States has some of the lowest cost actively managed funds in the world. I wonder what he would think of Canada's, Great Britain's, Australia's, or Singapore's costs, all of which are higher.

You can't wait for government regulation. The best weapon against exploitation is education. You might not have learned this in high school. But you're learning it now.

Among those hearing the call to arms and taking action to educate others is Google's vice president, Jonathan Rosenberg.

In August 2004, Google shares became available on public stock exchanges and many Google employees (who already held Google shares privately) became overnight millionaires when the stock price soared.

The waves of cascading wealth on Google's employees attracted streams of financial planners from firms such as JPMorgan Chase, UBS, Morgan Stanley, and Presidio Financial Partners. Drawn like sharks to blood, they circled Google. They wanted to enter the company's headquarters so they could sell actively managed mutual funds to the newly rich employees.

Google's top brass put the financial planners on hold. Employees were then presented with a series of guest lecturers before the financial planners were allowed on company turf.

According to Mark Dowie who wrote about the story for *San Francisco* magazine in 2008, the first to arrive was Stanford University's William Sharpe, the 1990 Nobel laureate economist. He advised the staff to avoid actively managed mutual funds: "Don't try to beat the market. Put your money in some indexed mutual funds."[16]

A week later, Burton Malkiel arrived. The professor of economics at Princeton University urged the employees to build portfolios of index funds. He has been studying mutual fund investing since the early 1970s, and he vehemently believes it's not possible to choose actively managed funds that will beat a total stock market index over the long term. Don't believe anyone (a broker, adviser, friend, or magazine) who suggests otherwise.

Next, the staff was fortunate enough to hear John Bogle speak. A champion for the "little guy," John Bogle is the financial genius who founded the nonprofit investment group, Vanguard. His message was the same: the brokers and financial advisers swimming around Google's massive raft have a single purpose. They're a giant fleecing machine wanting to take your money through high fees—and you may not realize what is happening until it's too late.

When the sharks finally approached the raft, staff members at Google were armed to the teeth, easily fending off the well-dressed, well-spoken, charming advisers.[17]

I hope that you can do the same as the crew at Google. Always remember that for most financial advisers, index funds are pariahs. If you have an adviser today, and you're not invested in index funds, then you already know (based on their absence in your portfolio) that your adviser has a conflict of interest. In that case, asking your adviser how he feels about indexes is going to be a waste of time.

After one of my seminars on index funds, I often hear someone say: "I'm going to ask my adviser about index funds." That's like asking the owner of a McDonald's restaurant to sell you on Burger King. They won't want you stepping anywhere near the Whopper.

And they certainly won't want you paying attention to the leader of Harvard University's Endowment Fund, Jack Meyer. When interviewed by William C. Symonds in 2004 for *Bloomberg Businessweek*, he said:

> *The investment business is a giant scam. It deletes billions of dollars every year in transaction costs and fees . . . Most people think they can find fund managers who can outperform, but most people are wrong. You should simply hold index funds. No doubt about it.*[18]

Clearly, investing in index funds is a way to statistically ensure the highest odds of investment success. Doing so, however, means that you'll need to stand your ground. If you want to grow rich on an average salary, you can't afford to invest in the expensive products sold by most financial advisers.

Unfortunately, some investors think they can beat a portfolio of indexes with far more exotic methods. Such thinking is costly. The next chapter outlines such mistakes.

Notes

1. Sam Mamudi, "Indexing Wins Again," *The Wall Street Journal*, April 23, 2009.

2. An interview with Morningstar research director John Rekenthaler, *In the Vanguard* (Fall 2000), www.vanguard .com/pdf/itvautumn2000.pdf.

3. Daniel Solin, *The Smartest Investment Book You'll Ever Read: The Proven Way to Beat the "Pros" and Take Control of Your Financial Future* (New York: Penguin, 2006), 48.

4. William Bernstein, *The Four Pillars of Investing, Lessons for Building a Winning Portfolio* (New York: McGraw Hill, 2002), 224.

5. Investment Funds in Canada Course (IFIC), db2.centennialcollege .ca/ce/coursedetail.php?CourseCode=CCSC-103.

6. Daniel Solin, *The Smartest Investment Book You'll Ever Read: The Proven Way to Beat the "Pros" and Take Control of Your Financial Future* (New York: Penguin, 2006), 79.

7. Sendhil Mullainathan, Markus Noeth, and Antoinette Schoar, *The National Bureau of Economic Research*, March 2012, www.nber.org/papers/w17929.pdf.

8. Goodreads, Upton Sinclair quotes, www.goodreads.com/ author/quotes/23510.Upton_Sinclair.

9. Kathleen D. Vohs, Nicole L. Mead, and Miranda R. Goode, "The Psychological Consequences of Money," The American Association for the Advancement of Science, November 17, 2006, http://web.missouri.edu/~segerti/capstone/VohsMoney .pdf.

10. Daniel Kahneman, *Thinking, Fast and Slow* (New York: Farrar, Strauss and Giroux, 2011).

11. Larry Swedroe, *The Quest For Alpha* (Hoboken, NJ: John Wiley & Sons, 2011), 133–134.

12. Bill Schultheis, *The New Coffeehouse Investor, How to Build Wealth, Ignore Wall Street, and Get On with Your Life* (New York: Penguin, 2009), 51–52.

13. Paul Farrell, *The Lazy Person's Guide to Investing* (New York: Warner Business Books, 2004), xxii.

14. Melanie Hicken, "Fidelity Settles Lawsuits Over Its Own 401(k) Plan," August 18, 2014, http://money.cnn.com/2014/08/18/ retirement/fidelity-lawsuits/.

15. David F. Swensen, *Unconventional Success, a Fundamental Approach to Personal Investment* (New York: Free Press, 2005), 1.

16. Mark Dowie, "The Best Investment Advice You'll Never Get," *San Francisco Magazine*, December 2006, www.modernluxury .com/san-francisco.

17. Ibid.

18. William C. Symonds, "Husbanding That $27 Billion (extended)," December 27, 2004, www.bloomberg.com/news/articles/2004– 12–26/online-extra-husbanding-that-27-billion-extended.

RULE 9
Avoid Seduction

The trouble with taking charge of your own finances is the risk of falling for some kind of scam. Learning how to beat the vast majority of professional investors is easy: invest in index funds. But some people make the mistake of branching off to experiment with alternative investments.

Others wonder if they can find better index funds—those that promise to beat the market.

Achieving success with a new financial strategy can be one of the worst things to happen. If something works out over a one-, three- or five-year period, you'll be tempted to try it again, to take another risk. But it's important to control the seductive temptation of seemingly easy money. There's a world of hurt out there and rascals keen to separate you from your hard-earned savings. In this chapter, I'll examine some of the seductive strategies used by marketers who are out for a quick buck. With luck, you'll avoid them.

Confession Time

Any investor who doesn't have a story relating to a really dumb investment decision is probably a liar. So I'm going to roll up my sleeves and tell you about the dumbest investment decision I ever made. It might prevent you from making a similar, silly mistake.

The Dumbest Investment I Ever Made

In 1998, a friend of mine asked me if I would be interested in investing in a company called Insta-Cash Loans. "They pay 54 percent annually in interest," he whispered. "And I know a few guys who are already invested and collecting interest payments."

The high interest rate should have raised red flags. Around that time, I was reading about the danger of high-paying corporate bonds issued by companies such as WorldCom. They were yielding 8.3 percent. The gist of the warning was this: if a company is paying 8.3 percent interest on a bond in a climate where 4 percent is the norm, then there has to be a troublesome fire burning in the basement. Not long after WorldCom issued its bonds, the company declared bankruptcy. It was borrowing money from banks to pay its bond interest.[1]

The 54 percent annual return that my friend's investment prospect paid was a Mt. Everest of interest compared with Worldcom's speed bump. That's why it scared me.

"Look," I said, "Insta-Cash Loans isn't really paying you 54 percent interest. If you give the company $10,000, and the company pays out $5,400 at the end of the year in 'interest,' you've only received slightly more than half of your investment back. If that guy disappears into the Malaysian foothills with that $10,000, you get the shaft. You'd lose $4,600."

It seemed totally crazy. It's even crazier that I eventually changed my mind.

After the first year, my friend told me that he had received his 54 percent interest payment. "No you didn't," I insisted. "Your original money could still vaporize."

The following year, he received 54 percent in interest again, paid out regularly with 4.5 percent monthly deposits into his bank account.

Although I still thought it was a scam, my conviction was losing steam. He was now ahead of the game. He had received more money in interest than he had given the company in the first place.

He increased his investment to $80,000 in Insta-Cash Loans. It paid him $43,200 annually in "interest."

As a retiree, he was able to travel all over the world on these interest payments. He went to Argentina, Thailand, Laos, and Hawaii—all on the back of this fabulous investment.

After about five years, he convinced me to meet the head of this company, Daryl Klein (and yes, that's his real name). How was Insta-Cash Loans able to pay 54 percent in interest every year to each of its investors? I wanted to know how the business worked.

I drove to the company's headquarters in Nanaimo, British Columbia, with a friend who was also intrigued.

Pulling alongside the curb in front of Daryl's office, I was skeptical. Daryl was standing on the sidewalk in a creased shirt with his sleeves rolled up, a cigarette in hand.

We settled into Daryl's office and he explained the business. Initially, he had intended to open a pawn brokerage. But he changed his mind when he caught on to the far more lucrative business of loaning money and taking cars as collateral. As a result, Insta-Cash Loans was created.

In a narrative recreation, this is what he said:

I loan small amounts of short-term money to people who wouldn't ordinarily be able to get loans. For example, if a real estate agent sells a house and knows he has a big commission coming and he wants to buy a new stereo right away, he can come to me if his credit cards are maxed out and if he doesn't have the cash for the stereo.

"How does that work?" I wanted to know.

Well, if he owns a car outright, and he turns the ownership over to me, I'll loan him the money. The car is just collateral. He can keep driving it, but I own it. I charge him a high-interest rate, plus a pawn fee, and if he defaults on the loan, I can legally take the car. When he repays the loan, I give the car's ownership back.

"What if they just take off with the car?" I asked.

I have some retired ladies working for me who are fabulous at tracking down these cars. One guy drove straight across the country when he defaulted on the loan. One of these ladies found out that he was in Ontario (about a six-hour flight from Daryl's office in British Columbia) and before the guy even knew it, we had that car on the next train for British Columbia. In the end, we handed him the bill for the loan interest, plus the freight cost for his car.

It sounded like an efficient operation. But I wanted to know if the guy had a heart. "Hey Daryl," I asked, "Have you ever forgiven anyone who didn't pay up?"

Leaning back in his chair with a self-satisfied smile, Daryl told the story of a woman who borrowed money from him. She had used the family motor home as collateral. She defaulted on the loan, but she didn't think it was fair that Daryl should be able to keep the motor home. Her husband didn't know about the loan. He came into Daryl's office with a lawyer, but the contract was legally airtight; there was nothing the lawyer could do about it.

But, as Daryl explained, he took pity on the woman and gave the motor home ownership back to the couple.

It sounded like an amazing company.

However, nobody can guarantee you 54 percent on your money—ever. Bernie Madoff, the currently incarcerated Ponzi-scheming money manager, promised a minimum return of 10 percent annually and he sucked scores of intelligent people into his self-servicing vacuum cleaner—absconding with $65 billion in the process.[2] He claimed to be making money for his clients by investing their cash mostly in the stock market. But he was paying them "interest" with new investors' deposits. The account balances that his clients saw weren't real. When an investor wanted to withdraw money, Madoff took the proceeds from fresh money that other investors deposited.

When Madoff's floor caved in during the 2008 financial crisis, investors lost everything. His victims included actors Kevin Bacon and his wife Kyra Sedgwick, and director Steven Spielberg, among the many others who lost millions with Madoff.[3]

Yet the percentages paid by Madoff were chicken feed compared with the 54 percent caviar reaped by Daryl Klein's investors.

Daryl's story sounded solid, when we first met back in 2001. But still, I wasn't prepared to invest my money.

Meanwhile, my friend kept receiving his interest payments, which now exceeded $100,000.

By 2003, I had seen enough. My friend had been making money off this guy for years and my "spidey senses" were tickled more by greed than danger. I met with Daryl again, and I invested $7,000. Then I convinced an investment club that I was in to dip a toe in the water. So we did, investing $5,000. The monthly 4.5 percent interest checks were making us feel pretty smart. After a year, the investment club added another $20,000.

The easy money tempted some of my other friends, too. One of my friends borrowed $50,000 and plunked it down on Insta-Cash Loans. He began to receive $2,250 a month in interest from the company.

Another friend deposited more than $100,000 into the business; he was paid $54,000 in yearly interest. But Alice's Wonderland was more real than our fool's paradise.

As in the case of Bernie Madoff (who was caught after Daryl), the party eventually ended in 2006. The carnage was everywhere. We never found out whether Daryl intended for his business to be a Ponzi scheme from the beginning (he was clearly paying interest to investors from the deposits of other investors) or whether his business slowly unraveled after a well-intentioned but ineffective business plan went wrong.

Klein was eventually convicted of breaching the provincial securities act, preventing him from engaging in investor-relations activities until 2026.[4]

The fact that he was slapped on the wrist, however, was small consolation for his investors. A few had even remortgaged their homes to get in on the action.

Our investment club, after collecting interest for just a few months, lost the balance of our $25,000 investment. My $7,000 personal investment also evaporated. Many investors in the company lost everything. My friend, who borrowed $50,000 to invest, collected interest for 10 months (which he had to pay taxes on) before seeing his investment balance disappear when Insta-Cash Loans went bankrupt in 2006.

It's an important lesson for investors to learn. At some point in your life, someone is going to make you a lucrative promise. Give it a miss. In all likelihood, it's going to cause nothing but headaches.

Investment Newsletters and Their Track Records

In 1999, the same investment club mentioned earlier was trying to get an edge on its stock picking. We purchased an investment newsletter subscription called the *Gilder Technology Report*, published by a guy named George Gilder. He might still be in business. A quick online search in 2011 revealed a website boasting of his stock picks. It claims his picks have returned 155 percent during the past three years, and that if you buy now, you'll pay just $199 for the 12-month online subscription to his newsletter. By 2016, the website was unchanged. It said the exact same thing.[5]

Back in 1999, we were convinced that George Gilder held the keys to the kingdom of wealth. Unfortunately for us, he was the king of pain. Today, if George Gilder reported his long-term track record online (instead of trying to tempt investors with an unaudited three-year historical return) he would have a stampede of exiters. His stock picks have been abysmal for his followers.

We bought the George Gilder technology report in 1999, and we put real money down on his suggestions. I'm just hoping my investment club buddies don't read this book and learn that George Gilder could still be hawking promises of wealth. They'd probably want to send him down a river in a barrel.

Back in Chapter 4, I showed you a chart of technology companies and how far their share prices fell from 2000 to 2002.

In 2000, whose investment report recommended purchasing Nortel Networks, Lucent Technologies, JDS Uniphase, and Cisco Systems? You guessed it: George Gilder's.

Table 9.1 puts the reality in perspective. If you had a total of $40,000 invested in the above four "Gilder-touted" businesses in 2000, it would have dropped to $1,140 by 2002.

And how much would your investment have to gain to get back to $40,000?

In percentage terms, it would need to grow 3,400 percent.

Wow—wouldn't that be a headline for the *Gilder Technology Report* today?

Table 9.1   Prices of Technology Stocks Plummet (2000–2002)

	High Value in 2000	Low Value in 2002
Amazon.com	$10,000	$700
Cisco Systems	$10,000	$990
Corning Inc.	$10,000	$100
JDS Uniphase	$10,000	$50
Lucent Technologies	$10,000	$70
Nortel Networks	$10,000	$30
Priceline.com	$10,000	$60
Yahoo!	$10,000	$360

Source: Morningstar and Burton Malkiel's, *A Random Walk Guide to Investing*

"Since 2002, Our Stock Picks Have Made 3,400 Percent"

If that really happened, George Gilder might be advertising those numbers on his site.

Just for fun, let's assume that Gilder's original stock picks from 2000 did make 3,400 percent from 2002 to 2016. That might impress a lot of people. But it wouldn't impress me. After the losses that Gilder's followers experienced from 2000 to 2002, a gain of 3,400 percent would have his long-term subscribers barely breaking even on their original investment after a decade—and that's if you didn't include the ravages of inflation.

If there are any long-term subscribers, they're nowhere near their break-even point. Can you hear his followers scrambling in the Grand Canyon's lowest rings? I wonder if they're thirsty.

Where There Is a Buck to Be Taken

We already know that the odds of beating a diversified portfolio of index funds, after taxes and fees, are slim. But what about investment newsletters? They're about as common as people in a Tokyo subway. They selectively boast returns (like Gilder), creating mouthwatering temptations for inexperi-enced investors:

> *With our special strategy, we've made 300 percent over the past 12 months in the stock market, and now, for just $9.99 a month, we'll share this new wealth-build-ing formula with you!*

Think about it. If somebody really could compound money 10 times faster than Warren Buffett, wouldn't she be at the top of the Forbes 400 list? And if she did have the stock market in the palm of her hand, why would she want to spend so much time banging away at her computer keyboard so she could sell $9.99 subscriptions to you?

Let's look at the real numbers, shall we?

Most newsletters are like dragonflies. They look pretty, they buzz about, but sadly, they don't live very long. In a 12-year study from June 1980 to December 1992, professors John Graham at the University of Utah and Campbell Harvey at Duke University tracked more than 15,000 stock market news-letters. In their findings, 94 percent went out of business some-time between 1980 and 1992.[6]

If you have the Midas touch as a stock picker who spreads pearls of financial wisdom in a newsletter, you're probably not going to go out of business. If you can deliver on the promise of high annual returns, you'll build a newsletter empire. If no one, however, wants to read what you have to say (because your results are terrible) the newsletter follows the demise of the woolly mammoth.

There are several organizations that track the results of financial newsletter stock picks. *The Hulbert Financial Digest* is one of them. In its January 2001 edition, the US-based publi-cation revealed it had followed 160 newsletters that it had con-sidered solid. But of the 160 newsletters, only 10 of them had beaten the stock market indexes with their recommendations over the past decade. Based on that statistic, the odds of beat-ing the stock market indexes by following an investment news-letter are less than 7 percent.[7]

Put another way, how would this advertisement grab you?

You could invest with a total stock market index fund—or you could follow our newsletter picks. Our odds of failure (compared with the index) are 93 percent. Sign up now!

I don't think the *Hulbert Financial Digest* was created to be critical. But it's tough not to be. When investment newsletters fudge the truth, they can profit from new subscribers.

In 2013, Mark Hulbert wrote a story for *Barron's*. It was titled, "Newsletter Returns: Be Skeptical." Hulbert's firm has been tracking the performance of investment newsletters for years. When newsletters advertise, he says, they often lie.

As an example, Hulbert brought up one of Mark Skousen's investment newsletters. Skousen's newsletter claimed, "that for seven years running—through good markets and bad— my recommendations have racked up an annualized return of 145 percent."[8]

Hulbert responded to that claim. "My *Hulbert Financial Digest* performance monitoring service hasn't found Skousen's longest-lived newsletter to produce anywhere close to a 145 percent annualized return. . . . Over the last seven years, the time frame that the ad refers to, the HFD [*Hulbert Financial Digest*] calculates that the newsletter produced a 5.2 percent annualized return." A US index fund would have beaten it.

High-Yielding Bonds Called "Junk"

At some point, you might fight the temptation to buy a corporate bond that's paying a high percentage of interest. Ignore such investments. If a company is treading water or sinking, it's going to have a tough time borrowing money from banks, so it "advertises" a high interest rate to draw riskier investors. But here's the rub: if the business gets into financial trouble, it won't be able to pay that interest. What's worse, you could even lose your initial investment.

Bonds that pay high interest rates (because they have shaky financial backing) are called junk bonds.

I've found that being responsibly conservative is better than stretching over a ravine to pluck a pretty flower.

Fast-Growing Markets Can Make Bad Investments

A friend of mine once told me: "My adviser suggested that, because I'm young, I could afford to have all of my money invested in emerging market funds." His financial planner dreamed of the day when billions of previously poor people in China or India would worship their 500-inch, flat-screen televisions, watching *The Biggest Loser* while stuffing their faces with burgers, fries, and gallons of Coke. Eyes sparkle at the prospective burgeoning profits made by investing in fattening economic waistlines. But there are a few things to consider.

Historically, the stock market investment returns of fast-growing economies don't always beat the stock market growth of slow-growing economies. William Bernstein, using data from Morgan Stanley's capital index and the International Monetary Fund, reported in his book, *The Investor's Manifesto*, that fast-growing countries based on gross domestic product (GDP) growth produced lower historical returns than the stock markets in slower growing economies from 1988 to 2008.[9]

Table 9.2 shows that when we take the fastest growing economy (China's economy) and compare it with the slowest growing economy (the US) we see that investors in US stock indexes would have made plenty of money from 1993 to 2008. But if investors could have held a Chinese stock market index over the same 15-year period, they would not have made any profits despite China's GDP growth of 9.61 percent a year over that period.

Table 9.2   Growing Economies Don't Always Produce Great Stock Market Returns

Country	1988–2008, After Inflation Annualized GDP Growth (in Percentages)	Average Stock Growth (in Percentages)
United States	2.77	8.8
Indonesia	4.78	8.16
Singapore	6.67	7.44
Malaysia	6.52	6.48
Korea	5.59	4.87
Thailand	5.38	4.41
Taiwan	5.39	3.75
China	9.61	3.31 (as of 1993)

Source: The Investor's Manifesto by William Bernstein

China's GDP continued to soar from 2008 to 2016. But the country's stocks suffered. If $10,000 were invested in the iShares China Large-Cap ETF at the beginning of 2008, it would have been worth just $6,971 by October 10, 2016. By comparison, if $10,000 were invested at the same time in Vanguard's S&P 500 Index, it would have grown to $14,792 by October 10, 2016.[10]

Yale University's celebrated institutional investor, David Swensen, also warns endowment fund managers not to fall into the GDP growth trap. In his book written for institutional investors, *Pioneering Portfolio Management*, he suggests that from 1985 (the earliest date from which the World Bank's International Finance Corporation began measuring emerging market stock returns) to 2006, the developed countries' stock markets earned higher stock market returns for investors than emerging market stocks did.[11]

In Table 9.3, I updated those returns to January 1, 2016. Emerging markets pulled ahead of developed world markets, excluding the United States. But they aren't the runaway winners that many investors expect.

Emerging markets might be exciting—because they rise like rockets, crash like meteorites, then rise like rockets again. But if you don't need that kind of excitement, you might prefer a total international stock market index fund instead of adding a large emerging-market component.

Whether the emerging markets prove to be future winners is anyone's guess. They might. But it's best to remain diversified and keep such exposure low.

Table 9.3 Emerging Market Investors Don't Always Make More Money

Index	1985–2016	$100,000 Invested in Each Index Would Grow to . . .
US Index	11.3% annual gain	$2,744,193
Developed Stock Market Index (England, France, Canada, Australia)	8.9% annual gain	$1,401,378
Emerging Market Index (Brazil, China, Thailand, Malaysia)	9.2% annual gain	$1,529,888

Source: Pioneering Portfolio Management by David Swensen

Gold Isn't an Investment

Gold is a horrible long-term investment. But few people know that. Do you want proof? Try this on the streets.

Walk up to an educated person and ask them to imagine that one of their forefathers bought $1 worth of gold in 1801. Then ask what they think it would be worth in 2016.

Their eyes might widen at the thought of the great things they could buy today if they sold that gold. They might imagine buying a yacht or Gulfstream jet or their own island in the South China Sea.

Then break their bubble. Selling that gold wouldn't give them enough money to fill the gas tank of a minivan.

One dollar invested in gold in 1801 would only be worth about $54 by 2016.

How about $1 invested in the US stock market?

Now you can start thinking about your yacht.

One dollar invested in the US stock market in 1801 would be worth $16.24 million by 2016.[12]

Gold is for hoarders who expect to trade glittering bars for stale bread after a financial Armageddon. Or it's for people trying to "time" gold's movements by purchasing it on an upward bounce, with the hopes of selling before it drops. That's not investing. It's speculating. Gold has jumped up and down like an excited kid on a pogo stick for more than 200 years. But after inflation, it hasn't gained any long-term elevation.

I prefer the Tropical Beach approach:

1. Buy assets that have proven to run circles around gold (rebalanced stock and bond indexes would do).

2. Lay in a hammock on a tropical beach.

3. Soak in the sun and patiently enjoy the long-term profits.

What You Need to Know about Investment Magazines

If investment magazines were created to help you achieve wealth, you'd have the same cover story during every issue: Buy Index Funds Today.

But nobody would buy the magazines. It wouldn't be newsworthy. Plus, magazines don't make much money from subscriptions. They make most of their money from ads. Pick up a finance magazine and see who's advertising. The financial services industry, selling mutual funds and brokerage services, is the biggest source of advertisement revenue.

Advertisers pay the bills for financial magazines. That's why you see magazine covers suggesting "Hot Mutual Funds to Buy Now!"

In 2005, I wrote an article for *MoneySense* magazine titled, "How I Got Rich on a Middle Class Salary," and I mentioned the millionaire mechanic, Russ Perry (who I introduced in Chapter 1). I quoted Russ's opinion on buying new cars—that it wasn't a good idea, and that people should buy used cars instead.

Based on a conversation I had with Ian McGugan, the magazine's editor, I learned that one of America's largest automobile manufacturers called McGugan on the phone and threatened to pull its advertisements if it saw anything like that in *MoneySense* again. Financial magazines can't afford to educate because advertisers pay their bills.

I had the April 2009 issue of *SmartMoney* magazine on my desk as I wrote this book's first edition. The magazine was published one month earlier when the stock market was reeling from the financial crisis. Instead of shouting out: "Buy stocks now at a great discount!" the magazine was giving people what they wanted: A front cover showing a stack of $100 bills secured by a chain and padlock with the screaming headlines: "Protect Your Money!" "Five Strong Bond Funds," "Where to Put Your Cash," and "How to Buy Gold Now!"

Such headlines are silly when stocks are on sale. But if the general public is scared stiff of the stock market's drop, they'll want high doses of chicken soup for their knee-jerking souls. They'll want to know how to escape from the stock market, not embrace it. Giving the public what it pines for when they're scared might sell magazines. But you can't make money being fearful when others are fearful.

I don't mean to pick on *SmartMoney* magazine. I can only imagine the dilemma it faced when putting that issue together. Its writers are smart people. They know—especially for long-term investors—that buying into the stock market when it's on sale is a powerful wealth-building strategy. But a falling stock

Table 9.4 Percentages of Growth (April 2009–January 2016)

SmartMoney's Recommended Bond Funds

Osterweis Strategic Income Fund (OSTIX)	+60%
T. Rowe Price Tax-Free Income Fund (PATAX)	+45%
Janus High-Yield Fund (JHYAX)	+84%
Templeton Global Bond Fund (FBNRX)	+51%
Dodge & Cox Income Fund (DODIX)	+48%
SmartMoney's Recommended Fund Average Return	+58%
US Stock Market Index Return	+198%
International Stock Market Index Return	+86%
Global Stock Market Index Return	+131%

Source: Morningstar[13]

market, for most people, is scarier than a rectal examination. Touting bond funds and gold was an easier sell.

Let's have a look at the kind of money you would have made if you followed that April 2009 edition of *SmartMoney*.

It suggested placing your investment in the following bond funds: the Osterweis Strategic Income Fund, the T. Rowe Price Tax-Free Income Fund, the Janus High-Yield Fund, the Templeton Global Bond Fund, and the Dodge & Cox Income Fund.

Table 9.4 shows that with reinvesting the interest, *SmartMoney's* recommended bond funds would have returned an average of 58 percent from April 2009 to January 2016.

How about gold, which was also recommended by that edition of *SmartMoney*? It would have gained 13.8 percent during the same period.

So far, it looks like the magazine's recommendations weren't too bad, until you look at what they didn't headline. Stock prices were cheaper, relative to business earnings, than they had been in decades. The magazine headlines should have read: "Buy Stocks Now!"

Because they didn't, as demonstrated by Table 9.4, *SmartMoney* readers missed out on some huge gains. Stocks easily beat bonds and gold from April 2009 to January 2016.

The US stock market (as measured by Vanguard's US stock market index) increased 198 percent. Vanguard's international stock market index rose by 86 percent, and Vanguard's total world index rose by 131 percent during the same period.

The comparative results punctuate how tough predictions can be, while emphasizing that magazines cater to their advertisers and their reader's emotions.

Hedge Funds—The Rich Stealing from the Rich

Some wealthy people turn their noses up at index funds, figuring that if they pay more money for professional financial management, they'll reap higher rewards in the end. Take hedge funds, for example. As the investment vehicle for many wealthy, accredited investors (those deemed rich enough to afford taking large financial gambles), hedge funds capture headlines and tickle greed buttons around the world, despite their hefty fees.

But by now, it probably comes as no surprise that, statistically, investing with index funds is a better option. Hedge funds can be risky, and the downside of owning them outweighs the upside.

First the Upside

With no regulations to speak of (other than keeping middle-class wage earnings on the sidelines), hedge funds can bet against currencies or bet against the stock market. If the market falls, a hedge fund could potentially make plenty of money if the fund manager "shorts" the market by placing bets that the markets will fall and then collecting on these bets if the markets crash. With the gift of having accredited (supposedly sophisticated) investors only, hedge fund managers can choose to invest heavily in a few individual stocks—or any other investment product—while a regular mutual fund has regulatory guidelines with a maximum number of eggs they're allowed to put into any one basket. If a hedge fund manager's big bets pay off, investors reap the rewards.

Now for the Downside

The typical hedge fund charges 2 percent of the investors' assets annually as an expense ratio. That's one-third more expensive than the expense ratio of the average US mutual fund. Then the hedge fund's management takes 20 percent of their investors' profits as an additional fee. It's a license to print money off the backs of others.

Hedge funds *voluntarily* report their results, which is the first phase of mist over the industry.

When Princeton University's Burton Malkiel and Yale School of Management's Robert Ibbotson conducted an eight-year study of hedge funds from 1996 to 2004, they reported that fewer than 25 percent of funds lasted the full eight years.[14] Would you want to pick from a group of funds with a 75 percent mortality? I wouldn't.

When looking at reported average hedge fund returns, you only see the results of the surviving funds. Dead funds aren't factored into the averages. It's a bit like a coach entering 20 high school kids in a district championship cross-country race. Seventeen drop out before they finish. But your three remaining runners take the top three spots. You report, in the school newspaper, that your average runner finished second. Bizarre? Of course, but in the fantasy world of hedge fund data crunchers, it's still "accurate."

As a result of such twilight-zone reporting, Malkiel and Ibbotson found that the average returns reported in databases were overstated by 7.3 percent annually.

These results include survivorship bias (not counting those funds that don't finish the race) and something called "backfill bias." Imagine 1,000 little hedge funds that are just starting out. As soon as they "open shop" they start selling to accredited investors. But they aren't big enough or successful enough to add their performance figures to the hedge fund data crunchers—yet.

After 10 years, assume that 75 percent of them go out of business, which is in line with Malkiel and Ibbotson's findings. For them, the dream is gone. And it's really gone for the people who invested with them.

Of those (the 250) that remain, half have results of which they're proud, allowing them to grow and to boast of their successful track records. So out of 1,000 new hedge funds,

250 remain after 10 years, and 125 of them grow large enough (based on marketing and success) to report their 10-year historical gains to the data crunchers that compile hedge fund returns. The substandard or bankrupt funds don't get number crunched. Ignoring the weaker funds and highlighting only the strongest ones is called a "backfill bias."

Doing so ignores the mortality of the dead funds and it ignores the funds that weren't successfully able to grow large enough for database recognition. Malkiel and Ibbotson's study found that this bizarre selectiveness spuriously inflated hedge fund returns by 7.3 percent annually over the period of their study.[15]

According to hedgefundresearch.com, during the 13 years ending August 31, 2015, the average reported hedge fund averaged a compound annual return of less than 1 percent.[16]

But averages aren't chic. Let's look at the most popular hedge funds, based on size. They're large for a reason. Whispers of their greatness likely swept through country clubs like a billionaire's affair. That's when the rich poured in money—swelling the funds in size.

Your portfolio might not look like a Ferrari or a Porsche. But I'm guessing your Mazdas, Hondas, and Fords have left most of the 20 biggest hedge funds[17] gasping in their fumes, if you're investing with index funds.

Over the five-year period ending October 31, 2015, the 20 biggest hedge funds coughed and sputtered. They averaged a compound return of just 6.8 percent. That would have turned $10,000 into $13,894. The S&P 500, by comparison, roared on every cylinder. It averaged an annual compound return of 14.2 percent. The same $10,000 would have grown to $19,423.

As you can see in Table 9.5, just one of the 20 biggest hedge funds managed to keep pace.

Ok, I'll admit, my comparison isn't fair. Stocks soared over the five-year period ending October 31, 2015. Many hedge fund managers invest in different asset classes. So let's compare these faux Ferraris with something more diversified, like Vanguard's balanced index fund. It averaged a compound annual five-year return of 9.7 percent. Just three of the 20 biggest hedge funds beat this simple Chevy, which is composed of 60 percent stocks, 40 percent bonds.

Why do hedge funds lag? We know their fees are high.

Table 9.5 Index Funds Trounce the 20 Most Popular Hedge Funds Three-and Five-Year Returns Ending October 31, 2015

Hedge Fund	3-Year Total Return	5-Year Total Return
Bridgewater Pure Alpha Strat 18% Vol	17.6%	57.3%
Millennium International Ltd	41.3%	65.6%
Bridgewater Pure Alpha Strat 12% Vol	11.9%	35.6%
Winton Futures USD Cls B	27.1%	29.4%
Millennium USA LP Fund	42.6%	68.2%
Bridgewater All Weather 12% Strategy	2.3%	34.7%
Renaissance Inst Diversified Alpha Fund	36.0%	n.a.
The Genesis Emerging Mkts Invt Com B	−3.7%	−0.7%
Transtrend DTP−Enhanced Risk (USD)	12.4%	6.2%
EnTrust Capital Diversified Fund Ltd−C	11.3%	13.9%
Winton Futures GBP Cls D	28.2%	30.9%
Bay Resource Partners Offshore Fund Ltd	36.5%	42.8%
Baring Dyn Asset Alloc I GBP	15.9%	25.6%
MKP Opportunity Offshore Ltd	9.6%	25.7%
Pinnacle Natural Resources, L.P.	7.9%	17.6%
MKP Credit Offshore Ltd	18.9%	34.3%
The Genesis Emerging Mkts Invt Com A	−5.5%	−3.7%
Aristeia International Limited	7.3%	21.0 %
Babson Capital European Loan B EUR Acc	19.7%	n.a.
STS Partners Fund	77.4%	184%
Biggest 20 Hedge Fund Average	20.73%	38.7%
Vanguard S&P 500 Index	55.7%	94.4%
Vanguard Balanced Index	32%	58%

*Returns to October 31, 2015
Sources: Barron's; Morningstar

Many hedge fund managers also roll the dice. They borrow to invest.[18] When their bets crash and burn, they simply walk away. It's their passengers who perish. John Lanchester, writing for *The New Yorker*, reported that most hedge funds disappear after just five years. "Out of an estimated seventy-two hundred hedge funds in existence at the end of 2010, seven hundred and seventy-five failed or closed in 2011, as did eight hundred and seventy-three in 2012, and nine hundred and four in 2013."[19]

New hedge funds replace them. But the stats are clear. Every three years, one-third of hedge funds get rear-ended and explode just like a Pinto.

To make matters even worse, hedge funds are remarkably inefficient after taxes, based on the frequency of their trading. Plus, you never know which funds will survive and which funds will die a painful (and costly) death.

Hedge funds are like hedgehogs. Nice to look at from afar, but don't get close to their spines. Index funds are better.

Don't Buy a Currency-Hedged Stock Market ETF

There's a mantra that Wall Street would probably like to banish. *If it sounds too good to be true, it probably is.* Wall Street, after all, will sell what Wall Street can sell. Such is the case with currency-hedged index funds.

They sound exotic. But they're more common than a rusting third-world boat. In fact, when an ETF provider in Canada, Australia, or Europe first offers an international stock market ETF, they usually introduce a currency-hedged version first. They're also being sold to US investors. Currency-hedged ETFs aren't just rusting. They leak. That's why I haven't included currency-hedged ETFs in any of this book's model portfolios.

Here's what they're supposed to do. Assume you're an American who owns a European stock market index. If the stocks within the index gain 10 percent (measured in Euros) you would expect your index fund to earn something similar in US dollars. But reality could be different. If the Euro drops 10 percent, compared to the US dollar, Americans wouldn't profit. A currency-hedged ETF, on the other hand, would still make money for American investors. At least, that's the sales pitch.

Currency fluctuations, however, aren't always bad. If, for example, the US dollar falls against most foreign currencies, then investors could profit from a nonhedged international index, as the growing strength of foreign currencies against the dollar juice the returns of a foreign stock index in US dollars.

With a diversified portfolio of domestic and nonhedged international stock indexes, sometimes you'll win when currencies fluctuate. Sometimes you'll lose. If the international market drops 5 percent, but the US dollar drops 8 percent against international currencies, Americans gain money if they're invested in an international stock market ETF. On the flipside, if the international market drops 5 percent but the US dollar gains 8 percent against the index's foreign currencies, the same investors would lose about 13 percent.

Currency-hedged ETFs are made to help you sleep. They're made to limit fluctuations. But they have their own set of problems. First, their management fees are higher than with plain vanilla indexes. Second, they have higher hidden costs associated with the hedging itself. It's where the leaking boat comes in.

In a PWL Capital research paper, Raymond Kerzérho examined the returns of S&P 500 indexes hedged to the Canadian dollar between 2006 and 2009. Even though the funds were meant to track the index, they did much worse. They underperformed the S&P 500 by an average of 1.49 percent per year. Currencies were less volatile between 1980 and 2005. During that period, tracking errors caused by hedging would have cost 0.23 percentage points per year. Add the higher expense ratios of currency-hedged funds and they would have underperformed nonhedged funds by about 0.5 percent a year.[20]

The more cross-currency transactions that a fund makes, the higher its expenses—because even financial institutions pay fees to have money moved around. Consider the example of a currency exchange booth at an airport. Take a $10 bill and convert it to euros. Then take the euros they give you and ask them to return your $10. You'll get turned down. The spreads you pay between the "buy" and "sell" rates will ensure that you come away with less than $10.

Large financial institutions don't pay such high spreads. But they still pay them. And they reduce investors' returns.

Then there's the opportunity cost from the hedging itself. This gets a bit technical. But here's a Cliff Notes version. When hedging currencies, there's always a bit of money that gets left off the table. That money can't make money. Mr. Kerzérho provides an example of a theoretical S&P 500 fund hedged to the Canadian dollar. Assume that it has $100 million (US) in assets under management. At the beginning of the month, it would be long $100 million in the US S&P 500. At the same time, it would be short $100 million—in US dollars—in foreign contracts versus the Canadian dollar.

If the US index gained 3 percent for the month, then it would be long $103 million (because of the rise in the US market). Considering that $100 million was short as a currency hedge, it would leave $3 million exposed and unhedged. If the US dollar drops, the $3 million in unhedged dollars will depreciate.

Because most financial institutions adjust their hedging once per month, fluctuations in currencies ensure that part of the assets are always underhedged or overhedged. If, for example, the S&P 500 lost money over the course of a month, then the fund would become overhedged. Using the figures above, if the $100 million long position dropped 3 percent to $97 million, the fund would be overhedged by $3 million— exposing it to potential losses on currency movements.[21]

Ben Johnson (the research analyst, not the doped former sprinter) published results from a 20-year US study in Morningstar. He says nonhedged ETFs usually beat their currency-hedged counterparts. "By hedging foreign-currency exposure, investors can mitigate a source of risk—but at the expense of a potential source of return."[22]

Stay away from currency-hedged ETFs. Long term, they're leaking boats, compared to plain vanilla index funds.

Beware of the Smart Beta Promise

Marketers are smart. They've recognized that a growing number of investors are attracted to index funds. They smell opportunity. That's why many have created smart beta funds, also known as factor-based funds. Do you remember what I said about Wall Street? If it sounds too good to be true . . .

Smart beta firms use backtests. They claim that index funds weighted differently produce better returns. For example, take a plain vanilla index. Its stock weightings will emphasize the largest stocks. If Apple is the largest company in the S&P 500, then Apple's fortunes (good or bad) would have the greatest influence on the S&P 500. Smart beta indexes juggle the components differently. Sometimes, they build higher emphasis on stocks with momentum. Other times, they build an index that's equal weighted. In this case, larger stocks don't move the index fund's needle any more than smaller stocks do.

Backtests usually dazzle. They prove that such index fund strategies would have triumphed in the past. But the past isn't the future. Often, the newly emphasized stocks in these index funds become more expensive. This can hamper future returns.

Research Affiliates' Rob Arnott, Noah Beck, Vitali Kelesnik, and John West say that smart beta or factor-based funds could disappoint investors. They recently published "How Can 'Smart Beta' Go Horribly Wrong?"[23] In it, they show that much of the past decade's market-beating gains from such funds have come from rising valuations. Investors rushed into such funds because they had performed well. That raised the PE ratios of certain stocks to higher than normal levels.

Higher than normal valuation levels could bring poor returns in the future.

Smart beta funds are cheap, compared to actively managed funds. But they cost a lot more than most standard index funds. Strategies based on a cherry-picked past sell new Wall Street products. But they aren't necessarily better for investors.

Don't Jump Heavily into Small-Cap Stocks

Many people stack their portfolios with index funds that are heavily focused on small-cap stocks. And why not? Economists Eugene Fama and Kenneth French say that between July 1926 and February 2012, small-cap stocks cumulatively beat large stocks by 253 percent.[24] But not everyone agrees. That's why investors should temper their small-cap expectations.

In 1999, Tyler Shumway and Vincent Warther published a paper in the *Journal of Finance*, "The Delisting Bias in CRSPs NASDAQ Data and Its Implications for the Size Effect." They should have called it, "Size Doesn't Matter."[25]

They said small stocks often have shakier financial foundations. They have a tougher time weathering storms. That's why many get dumped (or delisted) from the stock market.

Shumway and Warther say that when we measure small-cap returns, we only see the storms' survivors.

Ted Aronson manages institutional money through AJO Partners. He runs two small-cap funds. But he doesn't believe in the small-cap premium. Interviewed in 1999 by Jason Zweig, Aronson said, "Small-caps don't outperform over time . . . Sure, the long-run numbers show small stocks returning roughly 1.2 percentage points more than large stocks . . . [But] the extra trading costs easily eat up the entire extra return—and then some!"[26]

The firm Research Affiliates is always looking for a performance edge. They created the Fundamental Index in hopes of beating traditional cap-weighted index funds. Their researchers Jason Hsu and Vitali Kalesnik dug deeply into the apparent small-cap premium to see if small stocks really outperform. Based on their research, it appears that they don't.

Following Fama and French's research method, they split stocks into two groups for a variety of different countries. The largest 90 percent were put in one group. The smallest 10 percent were put in the other. They examined performances from 1926 to 2014.

After adjusting for extra transaction costs and delisting bias, Research Affiliates' Vitali Kalesnik and Noah Beck say small stocks don't beat large stocks at all. "If the size premium were discovered today, rather than in the 1980s, it would be challenging to even publish a paper documenting that small stocks outperform large ones."[27]

That's why I like to keep things simple. Total stock market index funds include large-, small-, and medium-sized stocks. Those who do want a small-cap index should keep its exposure to a minimum.

When investing, seductive promises and get-rich-quicker schemes can be tempting. But they remind me of why I don't take experimental shortcuts when hiking. It's too easy to lose your way. I wonder if the famous French writer, Voltaire, would agree. In a translation from his 1764 *Dictionnaire Philosophique*, he wrote: "The best is the enemy of good."[28] Investors who aren't satisfied with a good plan—like simple index fund investing—may strive for something they hope will be "best." But that path doesn't pay.

Notes

1. Benjamin Graham (revised by Jason Zweig), *The Intelligent Investor* (New York: Harper Collins Publishers, 2003), 146.
2. Erin Arvedlun, *Madoff, The Man Who Stole $65 Billion* (London: Penguin, 2009), 6.
3. Ibid., 85.
4. "Daryl Joseph Klein and Kleincorp Management Doing Business as Insta-Cash Loans," The Manitoba Securities Commission, order no.5753: August 13, 2008, http://docs.mbsecurities.ca/ msc/oe/en/item/103467/index.do.
5. Gilder Technology Report, www.gildertech.com/.
6. Mel Lindauer, Michael LeBoeuf, and Taylor Larimore, *The Bogleheads Guide to Investing* (Hoboken, NJ: John Wiley & Sons, 2007), 158.
7. Ibid., 159.
8. Mark Hulbert, "Newsletter Returns: Be Skeptical," *Barron's*, October 3, 2013, www.barrons.com/articles/SB5000142405311 190332060457910952164286 0630.
9. William J. Bernstein, *The Investor's Manifesto: Preparing for Prosperity, Armageddon, and Everything in Between* (Hoboken, NJ: John Wiley & Sons, 2010).
10. Morningstar.com.
11. David Swensen, *Pioneering Portfolio Management, An Unconventional Approach to Institutional Investment* (New York: Free Press, 2009), 195.
12. Morningstar.com.
13. Calculated from 1801–2001 returns of US stocks and gold from Jeremy Siegel, *Stocks for the Long Run* (New York: McGraw Hill, 2002), then extrapolated further using gold's 2016 price.
14. David F. Swensen, *Pioneering Portfolio Management, An Unconventional Approach to Institutional Investment* (New York: Free Press, 2009), 195.
15. Ibid.
16. HFRX Indices Performance tables, www.hedgefundresearch .com/family-indices/hfrx.
17. "Hedge Funds Best-Worst Biggest," *Barron's*, www.barrons .com/public/page/9_0210-hedgefundbestworst.html.
18. "Hedge Funds, Borrowing and Betting," *Barron's*, June 10, 2004, www.economist.com/node/2752920.

19. John Lanchester, "Money Talks," *The New Yorker*, August 4, 2014, www.newyorker.com/magazine/2014/08/04/money-talks-6.

20. Raymond Kerzérho, "Currency-Hedged S&P 500 Funds: The Unsuspected Challenges," September 2010, www.pwlcapital .com/pwl/media/pwl-media/PDF-files/Articles/Currency-Hedged-S-P500-Funds_The-Unsuspected-Challenges_2010_10_21 .pdf?ext=.pdf.

21. Ibid.

22. Ben Johnson, "To Hedge or Not to Hedge," Morningstar, November 2, 2015, http://ibd.morningstar.com/article/article .asp?id=635705&CN=brf295, http://ibd.morningstar.com/ archive/archive.asp?inputs=days=14;frmtId=12,%20brf295.

23. Rob Arnott, Noah Beck, Vitali Kelesnik, and John West, "How Can Smart Beta Go Horribly Wrong?" Research Affiliates, February 2016, www.researchaffiliates.com/Our%20Ideas/ Insights/Fundamentals/Pages/442_How_Can_Smart_Beta_ Go_Horribly_Wrong.aspx?_cldee=aGV3ZXN0ZWFtQGhld2Vz Y29tbS5jb20%253d.

24. John Davenport and Fred Meissner, "Exploiting the Relative Performance of Small-Cap Stocks, *AAI Journal*, January 2014, www.aaii.com/journal/article/exploiting-the-relative-outperformance-of-small-cap-stocks.touch.

25. Tyler Shumway and Vincent Warther, "The Delisting Bias in CRSPs NASDAQ Data and Its Implications for the Size Effect." *Journal of Finance*, June 1, 1998, www-personal .umich.edu/~shumway/papers.dir/nasdbias.pdf.

26. Jason Zweig, "He's Not Picky, He'll Take Whatever Is Wounded," CNN Money, January 15, 1999, money.cnn.com/1999/01/15/ zweig_on_funds/zweig_on_funds/.

27. Vitali Kalesnik and Noah Beck, "Busting the Myth about Size," Research Affiliates, December 2014, www.researchaffiliates. com/Our%20Ideas/Insights/Fundamentals/Pages/284_Busting_ the_Myth_About_Size.aspx.

28. Goodreads quotes, Voltaire, www.goodreads.com/quotes/ 80000-the-best-is-the-enemy-of-good.

Conclusion

You probably know a few people who are financial train wrecks waiting to happen. You, however, have a choice. You can watch them crash, or you can teach them some rules that they should have learned in school.

With luck, many of the principles in this book will become part of a mandatory high school curriculum. People want to learn this. When I taught high school personal finance, it was one of my school's most popular electives. The school had class-size limitations and wasn't supposed to break those limits. But I couldn't, in good conscience, refuse any of the students who wanted to enroll.

Routinely, well-meaning counselors allowed my class sizes to swell beyond the maximum. I'm glad they did. One year, 40 percent of my American students opened index fund portfolios with Vanguard.

Those kids, and their parents, wanted to learn about money. They also wanted to teach. Many of my students recorded screencasts that they uploaded onto YouTube. They wanted to show how young investors could get started right away. I linked a few of them to this blog post at andrewhallam.com: andrewhallam .com/2013/04/high-school-students-open-investment-accounts/.

These students learned what we all should have learned in school:

1. Think and spend like a millionaire if you want to become rich.

2. Start investing early—after paying off credit card debt and any other high-interest loans.

3. Invest in low-cost index funds instead of actively managed funds. Nobody can consistently pick "winning" actively managed funds ahead of time.

4. Understand stock market history and psychology so you don't fall victim to the craziness that infects every investing generation (often more than once).

5. Learn to build a complete, balanced portfolio of stock and bond index funds that will beat most professional investors after fees.

6. Create an indexed account no matter where you live.

7. Find low-cost financial advisory firms that build portfolios of index funds.

8. Learn to fight an adviser's sales rhetoric.

9. Avoid investment schemes and scams that might tickle a greed button.

Live long, prosper, and please pass on what you learn.

Thank you!

Andrew

About the Author

Andrew Hallam was a high school personal finance and English teacher. He writes investment columns for *The Globe and Mail* and for *AssetBuilder*, a US-based investment firm. He was also a columnist for *Canadian Business* magazine. His work has appeared in a variety of publications, including *MoneySense* magazine, *Reader's Digest*, *Personal Money*, Malaysia's *Sun Daily*, and *L'actualité*.

Andrew and his wife, Pele, are Digital Nomads. They give public talks about money and investing around the world. They love to explore hidden (and not so hidden) corners of the globe—while avoiding cold winters whenever they can.

Index